*Internal Resistances*

# Internal Resistances
## The Poetry
## of Edward Dorn

*Edited by*

DONALD WESLING

UNIVERSITY OF CALIFORNIA PRESS

BERKELEY    LOS ANGELES    LONDON

University of California Press
Berkeley and Los Angeles, California

University of California Press, Ltd.
London, England

©1985 by
The Regents of
the University of California

Library of Congress
Cataloging in Publication Data

Main entry under title:

Internal resistances.

Includes bibliographical references and index.
1. Dorn, Edward—Criticism and interpretation—
Addresses, essays, lectures. I. Wesling, Donald.
PS3507.073277Z73 1985     811'.54     83–10534
ISBN 0–520–04993–4

Printed in the United States of America

1   2   3   4   5   6   7   8   9

# Contents

# Acknowledgments

The authors would like to thank Edward Dorn and his publishers for permission to reprint passages from his works:

Selections reprinted from *The Collected Poems, 1956–1974*, from *Interviews*, and from *Views*, ©1975 and 1980 by the Four Seasons Foundation, editor Donald Allen, San Francisco (formerly Bolinas), California.

Selections reprinted from *Slinger* and from *Hello, La Jolla*, ©1975 and 1980 by Wingbow Press, Berkeley, California.

Selections reprinted from *Recollections of Gran Apachería*, ©1974 by Turtle Island Foundation, editor Robert Callahan, Berkeley, California.

Selections reprinted from *Yellow Lola, Formerly Titled Japanese Neon (Hello, La Jolla, Book II)*, ©1981 by Cadmus Editions, editor Jeffrey Miller, Santa Barbara, California.

Selections reprinted from *By the Sound*, ©1971 by Frontier Press, editor Harvey Brown, Santa Rosa, California.

Selections reprinted from *The Shoshoneans: The People of the Basin Plateau*, ©1966 by William Morrow, Inc., New York.

Michael Davidson's essay appeared in *American Literature* 53 (1981):443–64. Robert von Hallberg's essay appeared in *boundary* 2 9 (Winter 1981):51–80; and some paragraphs appeared in *Contemporary Literature* 23 (Spring 1982):229–32. Our thanks to the original publishers for allowing us to reprint material which appeared first in their journals. Both essays have been revised and extended for publication here.

# Abbreviations
## and Note on the Texts

Abbreviations cited parenthetically in the text refer to the following works by Edward Dorn:

BS  *By the Sound* (Mount Vernon, Wash.: Frontier Press, 1971)

CP  *The Collected Poems, 1956–1974* (Bolinas, Calif.: Four Seasons Foundation, 1975)

HLJ  *Hello, La Jolla* (Berkeley: Wingbow Press, 1978)

I  *Interviews*, ed. Donald Allen (Bolinas, Calif.: Four Seasons Foundation, 1980)

RGA  *Recollections of Gran Apachería* (San Francisco: Turtle Island Foundation, 1974)

S  *Slinger* (Berkeley: Wingbow Press, 1975)

SB  *Some Business Recently Transacted in the White World* (West Newbury, Mass.: Frontier Press, 1971)

SH  *The Shoshoneans: The People of the Basin Plateau* (New York: William Morrow, 1966)

SL  "Strumming Language," in Anne Waldman and Marilyn Webb, eds., *Talking Poetics from Naropa Institute: Annals of the Jack Kerouac School of Disembodied Poetics*, vol. 1 (Boulder, Colo.: Shambala, 1975), 83–95

V  *Views*, ed. Donald Allen (San Francisco: Four Seasons
    Foundation, 1980)
YL  *Yellow Lola, Formerly Titled Japanese Neon (Hello, La
    Jolla, Book II)* (Santa Barbara, Calif.: Cadmus Editions,
    1981)

We have observed Dorn's occasionally idiosyncratic spelling
and typographic conventions throughout. All references to
*Slinger* are to the unpaginated Wingbow edition, which we
have paginated, beginning with page 1 on the first part title,
"Book I."

# Introduction

Edward Dorn was Visiting Professor at the University of California, San Diego, in the spring of 1976. On the evening of his first class, students entered the room and sat around the table where Dorn had assumed a chair at one end and had already begun to pile books and documents before him, each item emerging from a large leather bag. He remained silent, thumbing through various volumes, and the students became restless, gazing at one another and wondering why he did not speak. After a prolonged silence he grasped a roll of paper beside him and rose up from his chair. Leaning forward, he proceeded to unroll a map across a large expanse of the table. "This is our area," he said with a smile. The students stood up and gathered to see a map of the United States and Dorn's hand sweeping across the western expanse. This was not an ordinary road map or topographical map of America; it was a railroad map with corridors that ran throughout the country and took up large areas of the land mass. The corridors represented the land granted to the railroads as they were built, often for the sole purpose of gathering more land into their domains.

Of all the maps Dorn probably had in his possession and might have brought, he had consciously chosen the map that

The introduction was written by Donald Wesling with the help of substantial contributions by Paul Dresman, Michael Davidson, and Alan Golding.

began to reveal America in a way that united the nation's economic and sociocultural determinants. One could imagine an America where the dogs of the Apaches went howling for miles as they trailed the train that took their masters away (from Dorn's long poem *Recollections of Gran Apachería*, 1974), or where Daniel Drew crazily pronounced "spekulatin' " as he pleaded for a deal with Vanderbilt and double-crossed the other railroad barons of Wall Street (from the Drew memoir that Dorn introduced in the 1969 Frontier Press edition). There was the ornate private car of Robart, rolling west behind the steam of a nineteenth-century locomotive, headed for the aerospace of Vegas but then diverted south to Four Corners, that carried the Man of Power among his lackeys (from Dorn's *Slinger*, 1975). There were Pocatello and LeRoy McLucas and one more Union Pacific station standing beside the "shining double knife" projecting west across the basin plateau (an instance in Dorn's *Collected Poems*, 1975). There was a territory between here and formerly, a narrative that crossed and recrossed and doubled back and left the tracks to go inside the thoughts of the lives in this landscape, in a nation so given to a history of profit that the only way to comprehend it was through the bitter recognitions of irony—with the wry laughter only heard from someone (the character "I" in *Slinger*, whom Dorn kills off and later resurrects) who has understood America not geographically but profoundly, and, returning from the dead, says:

> Entrapment is this society's
> Sole activity, I whispered
> and Only laughter,
> can blow it to rags
> *But* there is no negative pure enough
> to entrap our Expectations
>                    (*S* 155)

Not that Edward Dorn is primarily a teacher, though he has taught; not that he is solely a political poet, though his work has been directly political at times. In fact, in the four books of *Slinger* Dorn mocks academic research and jargon, treating university towns as "natural centers of doubletalk," and he objects to didacticism even while practicing the mode—a paradox that is the focus of Robert von Hallberg's essay in this volume. And in fact, whenever he has spoken against international economic systems and wars, or against the American or English national character, or against agencies like the Bureau of Indian Affairs, or against injustices in everyday life, the voice has always been that of the self-mocking solitary whose only party is the party of *intelligence*. Education and politics are the active phases of entrapment, and they evoke from Dorn a literary guerrilla response that covers the range from stately declaration to the subtlest ironic thrusts.[1]

By selecting *Internal Resistances* as the title of this book, the metaphor that unifies and represents all the essays, we mean to convey what kind of writer Dorn is: nomadic and marginal in the circumstances of personality and publishing and yet central in his presumption to American culture.[2] The subject of the literary politics of a noncanonical poet is too immense to be pursued here; we only remark that Dorn has with integrity avoided all the routes to approbation in the literary establishment and that the establishment, however defined, has tried to behave as though he were not there.[3] Among the reasons that

1. In *Our Word* (London: Cape Goliard, 1968), Dorn collaborated with Gordon Brotherston to translate guerrilla poems from Latin America.

2. The situation is of course the same for all post-romantic poets of stature, but it is true in the special way we shall define in Dorn's case.

3. A 1980 review in *Poetry* (Chicago) treats Dorn as sufficiently defined by the theories of his Black Mountain College mentor Charles Olson, sees little of interest in Dorn's *Collected Poems*, and treats *Slinger* as a shaggy dog story (Paul Breslin, "Black Mountain College: A Critique of the Curriculum," *Poetry* 136 (July 1980): 219–39). When reviewers want to praise Dorn they usually single out one poem from 1956, "The Rick of Green Wood." Dorn's poems have been anthologized in most major anthologies since 1960, with hardly any overlap in the titles selected.

Dorn has not been taken up by the world that makes reputations, we would list these: his decision to publish with lesser-known houses outside New York City; his interest in politics and in the Far West; the declaratory nature of some of his writing. As students of his work, we are aware of other, even more pointed objections to claims for his stature: that apart from *Slinger* his work is relatively slight; that the tone of his shorter poems makes him merely the Clint Eastwood of American poetry; and that though Dorn's moral positions may well be right, they are righteously and simplistically expressed. Such issues eventually get raised about Dorn, and properly so. This first full-scale treatment of his achievement confronts these issues and provides a basis from which later accounts of his writings will be better able to explain his limitations and to show how they are inevitable—given his deliberate choice to remain an anti-establishment figure in an art that has been thrust to the margins of American society. By means of internal resistances against what is established, a writer on the margin may claim to understand the contradictions of a historical moment even while his work manifests and is deformed by those contradictions.

Arguably, the deformation is less, and the bias of intent and tone a more valuable part of the work, if a writer stays off the friable middle ground where big reputations are made. From this perspective, Edward Dorn's stance warrants attention in its response to the American polis and to the degenerate language of the public sphere. Norman Mailer has run for mayor of New York City; Gore Vidal has sought the Democratic primary nomination for a U.S. Senate seat from California. But what American writer besides Dorn has involved himself in the polity to the extent of publishing a newspaper? *Bean News*, and now the more coherent *Rolling Stock* (1981– ), are the pure products of the pronunciamento side of Dorn's mind, consciously quixotic kicks against the pricks, but withal offering a serious examination of issues too hot for poetry to deal with in the short run.

Despite the limitations of some of Dorn's pronunciamentos, our essays challenge the claim that little of Dorn's work besides *Slinger* has poetic merit. William J. Lockwood shows precisely how *Slinger* emerged from the context of shorter poems in *The North Atlantic Turbine* (1967), and Robert von Hallberg and others show that the shorter poems and *Slinger* exhibit similar qualities of mind. Yet the major unresolved issue for the study of Dorn and also for the study of modern poetry generally is that of a committed rhetoric. We hope in this book to move toward a resolution by showing the particular example of one temperament as it disposes of its materials and forms. The shape of Dorn's career, its articulation and enclosure within the triangular tensions of Wit, Song, and Pronunciamento (see Donald Wesling's essay), makes him the contemporary American poet whose example counts most. Where and why is he righteous? Can that charge be separated from the charge of his being simplistic? Against the latter charge we would set Paul Dresman's explanation of Dorn's morally nuanced relationship to the Shoshonean Willie Dorsey—and Michael Davidson's explanation of Dorn's rich scorn for Howard Hughes and for the idiom of technological jargon, even while Dorn takes these as subject and medium, respectively, during large tracts of *Slinger*. It is, in any event, useful to uncouple what is righteous from what is simplistic: nobody would now ask that Jonathan Swift give fair treatment all around. In fact, two of our chapters, those by Donald Wesling and Alan Golding, propose that we see Dorn as a Swiftian figure trapped in a modern democracy.

Yes, Dorn is righteous and occasionally simplistic. So were Ezra Pound, William Carlos Williams, and Gertrude Stein. So also were Bertolt Brecht, Antonin Artaud, the Russian Futurist and Zurich Dadaist proclamations—and Johnson, Swift, and Blake, to take some figures close to Dorn's heart. The question we find challenging is not whether Dorn is a bit narrow-minded, but whether his narrow-mindedness is interesting, whether it follows a contour and works its terms out. Dorn's simplicity is never simple: it is always framed by a series of code-breaking maneuvers. The ultralyricism of his early poems and the cryptic, epigrammatic quality of the later ones are both workings out of possible poetic moods and voices that are themselves historically inscribed. *Slinger* and some of the other long poems incorporate all these moods and voices, but only to temper what is lyric with what is narrative, or ironic, or argumentative.

It seems to us a mistake to demand of the noncanonical poet the consistency we rarely demand of the canonical ones. It is Dorn's idiosyncratic qualities that account for the energy and excitement of his work, especially when seen in contrast to other contemporary styles. Dorn does not work within the largely egocentric, expressivist, or personist modes of his predecessors on the avant-garde scene, nor does he accept the ultraformalism of avant-garde theorizers. Unlike the poets of the Iowa School, *Antaeus* magazine, or *The New Yorker*, he does not believe that one can so simply identify oneself with the landscape without encountering prior manipulations of the scene. The "self" is not some autonomous generator of emotions, opinions, feelings, or yearnings; like the landscape, it is subject to material and social forces beyond it. In this sense he is a historical poet like Olson or Pound, but one who is not content with the "great man" thesis, nor with the self-reliant position of an Emerson or Whitman. He is very much an original, a self-reflexive poet not satisfied with the dissolved fictive self of Wallace Stevens or John Ashbery, a lyric poet who cannot take for granted the solipsism of Robert Bly or Galway Kinnell, an ironic poet who nevertheless avoids falling into an empty metaphysical abyss. His originality lies in moving within the various moods and methods of postwar verse without ever losing sight of his own didactic, polemical purpose.

By including particular essays on all phases of Dorn's career, this book attempts to convince readers that he is a serious, complex, challenging poet who extends the terms of "postmodern" poetry well beyond its usually credited boundaries. In a sense he represents something post-postmodern in that he calls into question the ego-expressive base of much postwar poetry (whether Black Mountain, New York School, or Iowa workshop) and also the various methods of metaphysical deconstruction and linguistic defamiliarization in which the question of "value" is often held at a distance. Dorn is a profoundly moral poet in a time when some poets opt entirely for the subjective or for the infinite regressivity of semiotic systems. And Dorn is moral without being prescriptive. Rather, he understands how difficult it is to exist ethically in a society in which all systems are severely mediated. He provides a poetic methodology that, while rejecting absolute categories of genre, person, rhetoric, and point of view, understands how to make use of them, lovingly and ironically at the same time. We cannot think of any other writer working today in America who occupies this territory, who is so diverse and so challenging, and who is completely aware of the world beyond the poem, the world Olson said should continually inform the poem.

We have written this book, then, to insist on Dorn's vital presence as an American poet of stature and to make for readers paths of connection that lead to his independent highway. Now over fifty, Dorn has published his collected poems and a separate long poem of great intelligence and good humor. He is also author of an extended poem on the Apaches, an ethnographic study of the Shoshoneans, a novel, the mock-newspapers *Bean News* and *Rolling Stock*, many translations, and a book of stories and other prose. Groupings of his *Views* and *Interviews* have recently been issued. In the poetry alone, there is sufficient quantity, variety, technical range, finesse, and moral passion to justify our insistence. Readers of his works, or even of the many lively passages used as quotations in this volume, will find in Dorn an original way of looking at American experience, speedy in his perceptions, oblique in voice, above all comic in the generic senses of delight in the everyday and laughing anger at the falsely holy.

The poetry is our main matter, but personal and publishing circumstances do have a bearing here. The poet was born in 1929 into a poor farming family in Illinois, attended the University of Illinois briefly, and took his degree from Black Mountain College in North Carolina. Thereafter: the Pacific Northwest; Santa Fe; Pocatello; Colchester, England; Lawrence; Chicago; San Francisco; Riverside and La Jolla; Boulder— living frugally in sparsely furnished rented quarters, mostly supporting himself by teaching and occasional public readings. He is twice married, with children from both marriages. So much of fact do we care to present. Of rumor, it is said that there are Indians in the ancestry and that as a lecturer at the University of Essex in England Dorn spoke for a full hour on the greenness of money.

Dorn's publishers have included Jargon-Corinth, Fulcrum, Cape Goliard, Frontier Press, Black Sparrow, Turtle Island, Wingbow, Four Seasons, Cadmus. None of these is a major house, but for Dorn this has been an intentional choice from the start. The eighteen years' writing that went into *Collected Poems* was first divulged, Dorn says, "through persons . . . not with houses. I have stayed with that care because it is accurate and important. Important equally for those who have published me" (*CP* v). Those words, from the preface to his *Collected Poems*, a reader's best clue to the intent and method of his work, state his belief that even outside the mass-publishing system the poet may reach the audience that matters, the right people in the anonymous public. He goes on in that preface, crucially: "From near the beginning I have known my work to be theoretical in nature and poetic by virtue of its inherent tone. My true readers have known exactly what I have assumed. I am privileged to take this occasion to thank you for that exactitude, and to acknowledge the pleasure of such a relationship" (*CP* v). So the inner nature of a major poetry may be related to the circumstances of a small-press publication, and, not coincidentally as it is "theoretical in nature," it may be detached from the trivial detail of biography.

Wallace Stevens wrote of the force of poetry: "It is a violence from within that protects us from a violence without. It is the imagination pressing back against the pressure of reality."[4] Internal resistance: an idea of the poet's integrity, his power to understand the evil of external authority, to "blow it to rags" within the sphere of action of the poem. What Dorn's imagination presses back against, as a chosen "reality," is not aesthetic or, a word he hates, *epistemological*; it is a society divided by race, class in all its manifestations, and sex. Resistance to the social matrix makes his poetry sometimes abstract, discursive, declaratory—qualities Americans have not always appreciated in poetry. To the degree this writing is theoretical and repudiates what Charles Olson scorned as "the lyrical interference of the ego," it challenges its readership. Yet in its particular laconicism or in its tendency toward intimate or heroic song, the poetry is not difficult; it is the expression of what Lockwood's essay calls "the gnarled toughness of a working-class

4. Wallace Stevens, "The Noble Rider and the Sound of Words," from *The Necessary Angel* (London: Faber, 1960), p. 36.

stoicism." Really, a lyrical lightness is what Dorn likes most, what he does best (as in: "The banding of her slightsmiling lassitude"), but for him the lightness has to be earned, often, by working through certain necessary abstractions and explanations: resistances.

Why do the social materials presented by Dorn require the degree of abstraction he gives them? Unfortunately, everyday life can only be understood structurally and profoundly by a theory of everyday life. Existentialist Marxism has such a theory, albeit incompletely worked out, and Dorn converges on that position by his own routes. Dorn constructs his account based on what he has read and seen, a personal penetration behind the daily discourses that mystify the causes of, for example, why we love the music of Sousa, why the trains between London and Oxford are full of beautiful girls, why Western Europe puts down America, why Americans war with Indians and Vietnamese, why a father has no secret to tell his daughter about how to survive as a modern woman. *Slinger* is a full-scale treatment of the discourses of mystification, and its concerns and procedures may be seen in the simpler forms of Dorn's *Collected Poems.*

Donald Wesling treats the relation of the technical to the moral in Dorn's shorter poems, placing the songlike qualities of the work into relation with the declaratory qualities, showing how a poetry "theoretical in nature" can still be personal. Robert von Hallberg argues the thesis that a mind essentially skeptical can nonetheless display forms of political commitment and statement in poetry. Paul Dresman, from whose essay we take our general title, employs Dorn's many writings on Indians and race, and especially *Recollections of Gran Apachería,* to show the moral delicacy of a poetry that allows neither a romance of the Indians as noble savages nor a dismissal of them as plundering killers: "It is bright to recollect," writes Dorn, "that the

Apaches were noble / not in themselves / so much as in their Ideas" (*RGA* 1). Michael Davidson and William J. Lockwood perform book-by-book interpretations of Dorn's long narrative poem *Slinger*; they show how narrative may criticize narrative while performing it; how poetry that must use language may also be a hygiene for language. Alan Golding shows how the satiric bite in Dorn's more recent, propositional poetry often comes from affecting the same cultural ennui that is being attacked. Thus all the essays strive to validate the title-metaphor of this book by setting one Dornian direction against a counterpart, showing internal division and resistance and also the occasional failure of resolution. Except for the pieces by Wesling and Golding, the essays were not initially prepared for this volume but were written separately out of the process of understanding Dorn's poetry for ourselves and our students. Only after they were written and circulated did we realize that we had common interests. Then began the careful process of criticizing, improving, avoiding overlap, emphasizing the directions in argument that we had in common, and selecting a title that exhibits our shared understanding.

Three of the essays take up *Slinger*, and two of these three are full-length exegeses: *Slinger* bids fair to be Dorn's masterwork and one of the important long American poems of its moment, yet it is allusive and indirect. Must we wait thirty and more years for an understanding of the poem, as we have done with *The Waste Land*, the *Cantos*, and *Paterson*? We hope to have laid the foundation for future readings of this distinguished text.[5]

Though valuable commentaries on Dorn's work have al-

5. Extensive annotations to *Slinger* have been prepared by Dr. Stephen Fredman's graduate seminar class in the American long poem at Notre Dame, and these are due to be published with the same page-numbering method we have employed for the unpaginated *Slinger*: namely, from the first part title of the book itself, at "Book I."

ready appeared,[6] this is the first book to take his poetic achievement as its sole concern. By means of this book we hope to
further the process of establishing his place within the continuity of American poetry.

6. Other useful writings on Dorn are: Donald Davie, "The Black Mountain
Poets," in Martin Dodsworth, ed., *The Survival of Poetry* (London: Jonathan
Cape, 1970); the Edward Dorn-Tom Raworth number of *Vort*, Barry Alpert,
ed. (Silver Spring, Md., Fall 1972); Peter Ackroyd, "In Public," *The Spectator*
236 (London, 10 January 1976); Marjorie Perloff, untitled review of *Slinger*
and *The Collected Poems*, *New Republic* 174 (24 April 1976); Michael Davidson, "Archaeologist of Morning: Charles Olson, Edward Dorn and Historical
Method," *ELH* 47 (1980): 158–79; Sherman Paul, *The Lost America of Love:
Rereading Robert Creeley, Edward Dorn, and Robert Duncan* (Baton Rouge:
Louisiana State University Press, 1981); Kathryn Shevelow, "Ed Dorn's *Yellow
Lola*," *Chicago Review* 33 (Summer 1981): 101–4; Kathryn Shevelow, "Reading Edward Dorn's *Hello, La Jolla* and *Yellow Lola*," *Sagetrieb* 2, no. 1 (Spring
1983).

# 1

## "To fire we give everything": Dorn's Shorter Poems

### DONALD WESLING

> "We are bleached in Sound
> as it burns by what we desire"
> and we give our inwardness
> in some degree to all things
> but to fire we give everything.
>
> (Book IIII: "Prolegomenon," S 145)

As readers become acquainted with the work of Edward Dorn, they quickly learn that certain kinds of poetic pleasures are not going to be indulged.[1] Notably absent, and regretted because they sometimes make access more prompt, are (1) direct self-revelation from the poet; (2) straightforward narrative; (3) elaborate structures of metaphor to challenge the puzzle-solving impulse; (4) lines engraved on marble or gaily tripping or otherwise in traditional iambic pentameter. In their place are (1) persona and comedy, irony and sarcasm; (2) speculation and speculative politics; (3) a range of direct, unfigured dis-

---

1. After *Recollections of Gran Apachería* (1974) and *Slinger* (1975), Dorn gained a reputation primarily as a writer of long poems. This essay is an exposition of his shorter works as equal in importance to the long poems in the Dorn canon—and as more immediately accessible to the reader. The argument in brief: a major lyric sensibility gains its special signature by checking lyric expansiveness almost as soon as this has emerged—impulse to song and sound manqué; also impulse to declaratory pronouncement manqué.

course from song to argumentative wit to pronunciamento; (4)
free verse whose main attributes are speed of transition from
one thought to another and abstraction of diction. The mode
of address is laconic, often uncompromisingly stern in the midst
of love song and elegy. Dorn sometimes seems to merge into his
own fictional character, the *semidiós* Gunslinger, whose acts
are so magnificent that they can only be imaged as immaterial
thought and whose thoughts are so elegant that they must be
imaged as the curves of perfect acts:

> *Hey Slinger!*
> *Play some music.*
> *Right*, breathed the Gunslinger
> and he looped toward the juke then,
> in a trajectory of exquisite proportion
> a half dollar which dropped home
> as the .44 presented itself in the proximity
> of his hand and interrogated the machine
>                    (S 23)

There is in this poet an inability to stoop, a noble contempt for
Americans ("the mumbling horde") who fail to risk or examine
their lives, their language:

> The common duty of the poet
> in this era of massive dysfunction
> & generalized onslaught upon alertness
> is to maintain the plant
> to the end that the mumbling horde
> bestirs its prunéd tongue.
>                    (YL 63)

Contempt for the collective is so withering that it sometimes
seems strong enough to extend to Dorn's friends and readers,
but this is never the case.

To write this kind of poetry, Dorn requires a band of fellows.

These persons he salutes in his preface to *The Collected Poems, 1956–1974* (1975): "My true readers have known exactly what I have assumed. I am privileged to take this occasion to thank you for that exactitude, and to acknowledge the pleasure of such a relationship" (*CP* v). The writer separates himself and his readers from the horde rather like an Augustan satirist, whose effects depend on a privileged elite with inside knowledge that enables them to crack the codes of the writing, and, so doing, scorn the uninitiated. This analogy needs immediate qualification, however, because for Dorn there remains the chance that the horde might bestir itself, a chance that a giant public might turn into a great people: anyone might be, probably is, a true reader. The tone that pervades Edward Dorn's work is that of a Jonathan Swift trapped in a democracy. The writer understands that his saving remnant of fellows, his nomad elite of writers and readers and other outcasts, can have no direct influence in the corridors of action, power, and greed. Yet he keeps some trust that the collective can be redeemed, though not by poetry, which can only "maintain the plant."

Swift marshaled his ironies against the mob at the historical origin of modern mass culture; his ironies depended on an educated, urban, upper-class audience, small, concentrated in the centers of population and power, and therefore quick on the uptake. Swift's perspective was top-center, looking down. In an era when publishing and audiences are differently constituted, defined by the exigencies of dispersion on a massive scale, Dorn's perspective on his materials is from the level, looking out in a circular scan. Unlike Swift, Dorn affiliates with the *mobile vulgus*. He admires the great public to the extent that it has the potential of being shaped (though not by him!) into an American People. That potential was vast in the late Enlightenment moment when the country was founded, but it has radically diminished:

After all these pronouncements: What I already knew: not a damn
    thing
ever changes: the cogs that turn this machine are set
a thousand miles on plumb, beneath the range of the Himalayas.

(CP 77)

It is easy to show the violent flickering of Dorn's anger in the
pronouncements of *Collected Poems*, less easy to show how
this is one expression of his social and literary self-willed isolation, less easy still to show how nonetheless his writing in the
short poems is one valid record of the years from 1956 to 1974.
Why are some of these poems memorable beyond the moments
of their occasion? It is not only because of the incisiveness of
style, which comes frequently enough but plainly is not a major
criterion of success for Dorn himself. The poems are memorable because they acknowledge that the cogs turning the machine are deep in the flawed structure of American politics, and
in human nature itself. Here the analogy with an Augustan
humanist holds up particularly well, for while Dorn is never as
devastating as Swift he too travels the spectrum from political
satire (*Gulliver's Travels*, book 1) to tragic inquiry (book 4).

These poems are a record of Dorn's own life and movements
and thinking between 1956 and 1974. When he lives in the
Southwest and Northwest, he writes about the land and its
Indians, the impermanence of cowboy culture; when his daughter turns fourteen he writes about the coming of age of American women ("divided states do not create women, / Amelia
Earhart / was not carried off, she flew, like something familiarly / transvestite in us, a weirdly technical Icarus" [*CP* 95]);
living in England and Europe in the late 1960s he takes up
geopolitics, for the North Atlantic Turbine of his 1967 title is
none other than the greed that drives monopoly capitalism
across oceans. (In roughly the same time period covered by
*Collected Poems*, male poet B writes a poem about how the
bottom of a tortoise looks like a spaceship; female poet B writes

about catching a fish, and in another poem, a sestina, she writes about a child, a grandmother, an almanac, and a Marvel Stove; poet A writes about his erotic double; and poet S about getting back from the Frick Gallery.) Dorn has no interest in ecstatic states, as witness his recent private quarrel with Allen Ginsberg's Buddhism. Nor is he fascinated by interiority and the fleeting states of consciousness, or by domestic scene-setting. He has steadily defined his subject as the goings-on in the public sphere of the American West, in America more largely, and sometimes even in international trade, politics, and wars. From his outpost of solitude, he makes his public responses to events in the news. There are few poets like him in the extent of his scorn for personality and inwardness, or in his turn to public speech. The decision to turn toward the public sphere accounts for his interest in the writers and politics of the century before Romanticism arrived.

To say this as part of a chapter that tries to explain the unique content of his short poems is not, of course, to ignore those occasions in the poetry where personality notably distorts and limits public speech. That citizenly speech is attempted on this scale and with such eloquence is the primary fact. Yet Dorn also commands, as we shall see, a range of other subjects and tones of voice, and these are not unrelated to his public concerns.

A section from Dorn's extended poem "Idaho Out" has much that is characteristic of him. In a roadside diner he and his friends meet up with a woman who seems too beautiful for the anonymous space between Pocatello and Missoula:

> My desire is to be
> a classical poet
> my gods have been men . . .
> and women.
> I renew my demand
> that presidents and chairmen everywhere

> be moved to a quarantine outside the earth
> somewhere,
> as we travel northward. My
> peculiar route is across
> the lost trail pass past
> in the dark draws somewhere
> my north fork beauty's husband's
> dammed up small dribbling creek
>
> fetching a promising lake (she showed
> me the pictures) a too good to be true
> scheme she explained to me,
> to draw fishermen with hats on
> from everywhere
> they wanted to come from.
> One of the few ventures I've
> given my blessing . . . she
> would look nice rich.
>
> (CP 113)

There is humor of conscious overstatement in the first two
sentences, where the poet mocks his social ("I renew my demand") and poetic ("a classical poet") ambitions, and there is
the understated wry humor of economic comment in the last
sentence. In the lines about fantasy landforms,

> across
> the lost trail pass past
> in the dark draws somewhere
> my north fork beauty's husband's
> dammed up small dribbling creek,

density of syntax and clustering of sound values mark the turn
to a brief lyrical moment, as Dorn develops his argument in
and through a slightly wrenched, singing line. There will be
further and better examples of his fascination with the argumentative shades associated with sound, examples of the delicacy of his ear.

Most perplexing in this passage is the opening vaunt, with

its evident disparity between "My desire is to be / a classical poet" and the act of making into a goddess a brunette from northern Idaho. One explanation is that precisely by these means (ennobling or deifying one's contemporaries) the poet who is modern and American becomes classical for his countrymen. The great example is Whitman; another is William Carlos Williams, who announced *Paterson* as "a reply to Greek and Latin with the bare hands" and who, to tease a university questioner, said he got his language out of the mouths of Polish mothers; and yet another is Dorn's own polymath mentor, Charles Olson. But this is much too easy, because Dorn, through and beyond self-mockery, means what he says.

I have already hinted something about his version of the classical by comparing him with Swift. In fact Dorn has a scholarly interest in the English eighteenth century, and in recent interviews we find him discussing Augustan norms, Johnson's "Life of Savage," and American founding fathers; among the Romantic poets, he finds the most instructive the most Augustan, Byron (*V* 10–11, 18, 22–23; *I* 82–83, 112–16). Certain attributes of his own writing affiliate him with the Augustans he admires. These are, first, allusivity: the pressure on the poems of wide reading in history, philosophy, geography, anthropology, the sciences, popular culture, media of all sorts and levels. Next is his emphasis on the importance of consciousness, of judgment: as his preface to *Collected Poems* has it, "From near the beginning I have known my work to be theoretical in nature and poetic by virtue of its inherent tone" (*CP* v). Next is his emphasis on public statement in the genres of comedy, open letter, and pronouncement, in the mode of wit understood as hard thinking; and in the counterchallenges of the norms of different American jargons (e.g., "massive dysfunction" in the same short poem as "maintain the plant"). Last, there is in Dorn a certain abstractness of language and thought that is the local expression of a "work . . . theoretical

in nature"; in the diction there are quality words ending in
-*ness*, for example, and in the syntax there are frequent indirect formulations, as in "My desire is to be" rather than "I
want to be."

Dorn, as we have seen, is not afraid to use the first person in
his work; and except in *Slinger* where the evanescence of the *I*
is part of the fun, when he writes with *I* he means himself and
not, as with some writers, every other mentioned thing and
person in the poem. Nonetheless I believe his "desire . . . to
be / a classical poet," understood as the artistic manifesto of an
emerging writer, means nothing if not a determination to avoid
the intrusion of the merely personal, of the inauthentic language of gossip. Accordingly, Dorn is one of the least self-
revealing of poets, one of the least arrogant. As I think he
recognizes in the tone of his line, "I renew my demand," his
likely excesses will not be those of devouring everything with
the beak of the ego, rather those of an exuberant tendency to
public-spirited rant.

Since he believes in something he calls *the shared mind* (*I* 28,
67), Dorn doesn't present his consciousness in his writings as
something unique or remarkable. His *Interviews* (1980) show
him fully aware that the writing of poetry is an imaginative
activity, but he places there much importance on the receiving
of information from many sources. The image he uses for his
work with culture and language is that he will, perhaps in an
electronic sense, *pick up* what's significant from the continuous
swirl of public and private messages. Unite that with the theme
of travel that pervades his writing from the start and you have
one Dornian definition of the writer's function. The poet moves
across the American countryside and cityscape catching information from such sources as landforms, local dialect, Indians
and hoboes and other nomads, newspapers like *The Wall Street
Journal* ("Money anticipates movement by about a year"),
fashion shows, tanning salons, AM radio. But the *pickup* is not

like that of a tone arm or a receiver of radio waves. As Dorn says of AM radio in his dazzling and indispensable interview with Stephen Fredman, "I rarely find that content transfers from any given place. . . . I don't practice *finding*" (*I* 105). What is picked up as amoral, inert will be returned in a language, apparently, "bleached in Sound / as it burns by what we desire" (*S* 145). When he drives, Dorn says, radio is a "useful boon companion," but nothing like a supplier of poetic ideas. In radio's deployment of information, speed and content are alternatives, and if you can't have both, take speed:

I sparked between the two poles of Sonoma County and San Francisco quite a bit last winter [1976–77]. So I heard AM radio. It seemed to me very suited for the road. And I verified several dissatisfactions I had with FM: that it's slow, relatively stupid. The ideas that float across it have been too obviously reprocessed in certain chambers of the culture—like the counter-culture, the Third World, and so forth—and those ideas are reprocessed through FM in a way that tends to stultify. AM is slick, silly, superfast, superintelligent, in the sense that it treats ideas like shot from guns, like a kind of good breakfast cereal within which there's nothing.

(*I* 104–5)

Listening while traveling: a sum of two activities insufficient when taken by themselves because they lack the dimension of intensity.

Pursuing the driving metaphor in this interview, Dorn says that even in conversation he finds he is "always roadtesting the language for a particular form of speech" (*I* 106). In fact Dorn also means this literally. That driving and poetry are strictly compatible he has proven by including in *Hello, La Jolla* (1978) a whole section that he wrote while driving on California Route 101 with one hand tied to the wheel: "A rather open scrawl while one's eyes are fixed to the road is the only trick to be mastered" (*HLJ* 75). The same book has a poem denouncing the automobile air bag that ends:

> Driving is based on alertness
> whether that be loose or tight
> Those who let their attention wander
> must not be encouraged to survive
> by a bag full of air.
>
>                    (HLJ 22)

Consumer and governmental promotion of the air bag is, for Dorn, one instance of that "generalized onslaught on alertness" that we have already seen him condemn. But Dorn's poetics of attention is both theme and procedure much earlier than in *Hello, La Jolla.* Although Dorn's *Collected Poems* does not manifest this poetics of attention in such a specific, literal way, we must pay attention to attention in order to understand his achievement in the shorter poems.

■ 2 ■

"Now pay attention": deeply buried in that English idiom is a metaphor of exchange, of economics. We "pay" or give cognition, compensating something from without with something from within. Or we can attend to our own thoughts, tending them, as in a garden. Whether we are noticing outwardly or meditating inwardly, riveted or rapt, we consider our attention a focussing of the energy of thought, a payment of intensity. Attending to our task increases our efficiency and, if we are driving two tons of metal at the speed limit, our chances of salvation—always, of course, physical salvation. But in an era which impugns all spiritualities, the significance of attention must grow as traditional religion recedes, or seems to recede. "Take care" is the *adios* of a skeptical age.[2] Whatever one thinks of the anthropological value of Carlos Castaneda's

2. In one of the "Love Songs" Dorn takes apart this familiar blessing: "the clothed figures who beseech us / for Our lives to beware / destruction, *take care* is / the password to their stability" (CP 237).

books on Don Juan the Yaqui sorcerer, the vast popularity of those writings is due largely to their contribution to a concept of attention as a substitute religion. To some extent this holds true of other phenomena of the eighteen-year cultural moment of Dorn's *Collected Poems*: the rise of karate and yoga as practices involving meditation, cults of drugs and consciousness expansion, the new tribalism and orientalism in American poetry. For Dorn there is also the much more specific context of Black Mountain: Black Mountain as a college that once existed in North Carolina, and that Dorn attended; Black Mountain as a continuing school of American poetry. Charles Olson and Robert Creeley, Dorn's teachers, praise attention as a form of intensity wherever found; they can hardly finish a piece of writing without explicitly mentioning, or acting out, some form of moralized attention. This special concern is first in importance among the shared attributes that permit us to argue the existence of a Black Mountain School of writers, continuous from the fifties into the eighties.

Drawing on Dorn's poems and statements, I would bring out three leading features in his morality of attention:

1. *Attention is knowledge put to use.* Though Dorn has said he hates the word *epistemology*, his works show him everywhere concerned with the mind's mechanisms for receiving, focussing, and processing information. He is in favor of the widest *pickup*, with the most thorough sifting for what is precious, and thus we have his play with certain revealing binaries: the "inside real" and the "outsidereal" (outside real; S 111), information and exformation (I 45; CP 259–60). Thus too the frequent recurrence in his poems of the phrase "the world," a continuous reminder of outside materiality and circumstance. "We give our inwardness / in some degree to all things. . . ." For Dorn, quite a large measure of the information that comes from the world is the clutter of American popular culture, full

of lovable abominations; the mind's defense against being over-whelmed by the wave of triviality is attention in the specialized forms of the laconic, sarcasm, the razor of logic.

2. *Attention is a creative faculty, best defined by what it is not.* It is not description or taxonomy, those mechanisms of American expertise that are so fundamentally easy because inflexible, unselective, routine. To the theoretical intelligence realism must appear profoundly limited. Like Wordsworth at the end of *The Prelude*, Dorn writes as if "the mind of man" is "more beautiful than the earth / On which he dwells," and like Castaneda's sorcerer, Don Juan, he acts as if the world we all know is only a description.[3] Description is stupid and slow, like FM radio. Concentration of consciousness, moral penetration, use more of the brain more efficiently.

3. *Attention is intensity.* Real time and ordinary spatial per-ception are not nothing, but there is another dimension. Though it obviously needs space and time to subsist, intensity is for Dorn the dimension beyond space and time. Increasingly Dorn's work in the sixties isolates this dimension as he moves from *Geography* (1965) (physical space) to *The North Atlantic Turbine* (1967) (geopolitical space) to *Slinger* (1975) with its sustained deconstruction of the concepts of space and place. *Collected Poems* should be read as an examination of how we give our inwardness in some degree to all things—and of how we withhold it as much as possible from all forms of cliché and phoney presence. Dorn swerves from Olson to emphasize in-tensity over the manifold of American space, and he develops an interest in sequences of sounds as an adjunct to the Olsonian speciality of propulsive syntax. Emphasizing the ear over the eye as a source of information, his lyrics are instances of the

3. *The Prelude*, 1805 text, book 13, lines 446–48. In *Journey to Ixtlan* (New York: Pocket Books, 1974), p. ix, Carlos Castaneda says that Don Juan's "contention was that he was teaching me how to 'see' as opposed to merely 'looking,' and that 'stopping the world' was the first step to 'seeing.'"

way "sound . . . burns by what we desire." Attention is intensity is sense working by means of soundplay.

Before giving some examples, I would turn briefly to the question of Dorn's divergence from conventional lyric feeling. One might attribute some of the characteristics of music and attention just listed to Charles Wright or Robert Bly, or to the Richard Wilbur of this stanza:

> You, in a green dress, calling, and with brown hair,
> Who come by the field-path now, whose name I say
> Softly, forgive me love if also I call you
> Wind's word, apple-heart, haven of grasses.[4]

The contrasting lines from Dorn's *Love Songs* are:

> if you were my own time's possession
> I'd tell you to *fuck off*
> with such vivid penetration
> you'd never stop gasping
> and pleasure unflawed
> would light our lives
>
> (CP 239)

It is a matter of different decisions about what can and cannot be done with the short poem of love. Compared with this matter of perspective, the difference between metered and non-metered poetry is as nothing. Wilbur's lines recall the origin of the lyrical poem in music and the singing line, and they affiliate with Shakespeare and Donne by defining the voice through brevity, simplicity, purity, impersonality. The advantage of conventional lyric, according to Barbara Hardy's splendid essay, "comes from its undiluted attention to feeling and feeling alone, and its articulateness in clarifying that feeling. . . . The double voice of feeling can speak in a single form, as it must,

4. This is the second of two quatrains making up Richard Wilbur's "Apology," in *Poems, 1943–1956* (London: Faber and Faber, 1957), p. 119.

fusing reflection or even analysis with the stirring passion. . . . All we are certain of is the feeling, not the characters and conditions . . . and the absence of character and history is a positive strength and a symptom of the poet's concern, his truthfulness and his sense of proportion."[5] Unlike Wilbur's, Dorn's habits of attention, even in the lyric of love, are always forcing a reintroduction of context, making judgments, bringing irony to bear. If conventional lyric feeling thrives on exclusions, Dorn's impure "statemental" lyric mixes not only diction ("my own time's possession" versus "*fuck off*") but generic and moral contexts; Dorn is always *bringing things back in* to the lyric, including anger, politics. He abuses the innocence, the lilt, of received lyric feeling, plainly working with a quite different idea of what makes for concern, truthfulness and a sense of proportion.

As warrant for these claims, I would take instances from different moments in Dorn's handling of the shorter lyric, beginning with "The Rick of Green Wood" (1956). This is placed first in *Collected Poems*, and it is one of a handful of early pieces for which he gives bracketed dates of composition. Placement and date are worthy of remark, because this early text is absolutely of the first order of maturity and quality. It begins the book with the speaker already possessed of a wife, a daugh-

---

5. Barbara Hardy, "The Advantage of Lyric," in her book *The Advantage of Lyric: Essays on Feeling in Poetry* (Bloomington: Indiana University Press, 1977), pp. 2, 3, 13. C. Day Lewis is even more judgmental than Barbara Hardy when in *The Lyric Impulse* (Cambridge, Mass: Harvard University Press, 1965) he argues that the singing line of the lyric must "be unbroken. . . . I am inclined to think that our failure in the lyric today is largely a failure of nerve: we cannot commit ourselves absolutely to those simple feelings which are the essence of lyric poetry" (pp. 132–33). If Dorn is measured against the purity of the traditional lyric impulse, his mixed lyric may well appear awkward; refusing to subordinate "reflection" to "passion," he has contempt for simple feelings, wants to specify and prolong instants of feeling. This is yet another meaning of his own claim that his work is "theoretical in nature." The best way of stating the whole issue, to my mind, is that Dorn does not fail to write the lyric of simple feeling; he rather extends it from within by irony, internal criticism.

ter, and his own distinctive voice. The world in this poem is a place of exchanges: perceptual, vocal, monetary; it is pleasant enough—for now:

> In the woodyard were green and dry
> woods fanning out, behind
>                             a valley below
> a pleasure for the eye to go.
>
> Woodpile by the buzzsaw. I heard
> the woodsman down in the thicket. I don't
> want a rick of green wood, I told him
> I want cherry or alder or something strong
> and thin, or thick if dry, but I don't
> want the green wood, my wife would die
>
> Her back is slender
> and the wood I get must not
> bend her too much through the day.
>                             (CP 3)

Generally avoiding traditional end rhymes, this first half of the poem nonetheless (before and during the passage of represented direct discourse) manages a good deal of tone leading, keyed to a small set of repeated vowels and consonants in recurring words. "Green" and "dry," the choice the poem is built around, returns for the fifth time at the end where the speaker is still talking to the woodcutter—but also now attending to the way of the world, whose climate is about to turn:

> in the november
> air, in the world, that was getting colder
> as we stood there in the woodyard talking
> pleasantly, of the green wood and the dry.
>                             (CP 3–4)

In the poem, the speaker has a care for his wife's back and (in lines omitted here) for his daughter's singing; he is led from "pleasure for the eye" at the beginning through to the end's "talking / pleasantly," from the eye's evidence to a larger sense of the threat of climate, the context of our acts of attention. ("Rick" means a stack, but it also means a sprain, twist, wrench, or overstrain.) The speaker also attends to his own form of singing: this poem's amazingly (for free verse) intricate structure of sound recurrence is what principally conveys to the reader the pleasurable fragility of paying attention, of life and thought in and against "the world." The threat of the world is in this poem a mere suggestion, a hint of trouble; accordingly the poem's qualities of tension and contentiousness are minimal, and the signs of this may be heard everywhere, especially at the poem's beginning, in the poet's obvious pleasure at the dense play of American sounds.

A related early poem, in the last line of which Dorn found the title for his first book, is

### If It Should Ever Come

And we are all there together
time will wave as willows do
and adios will be truly, yes

  laughing at what is forgotten
and talking of what's new
admiring the roses you brought.
How sad.

You didn't know you were at the end
thought it was your bright pear
the earth, yes

another affair to have been kept
and gazed back on
when you had slept
to have been stored
as a squirrel will a nut, and half
forgotten,
there were so many, many
from the newly fallen.

(CP 38)

Sound recurrence influences the meaning here, too, in the special emphasis on "yes" and "many," and in the mid- and end-line rhymes, but here sound is subordinated to another feature, the metaphor of the newly fallen nuts. "How sad" that it is impossible to attend to every experience as if it were the only one, or the last. Elegy for one person, reminder for the rest, the poem shows humans to be enemies of time and prisoners of their habits of attention. The conquering counterforces of time, change, and death mock any presumption that we might claim the earth as our "bright pear," make "time . . . wave as willows do." Little likelihood of reunion after death; since that fancied reunion will never come, every one of our meaning-making acts of conscious attention becomes the more urgent. In this poem the writer attempts to see beyond the lapse of perfect attention in person and squirrel. His method is to contrast the imagined perfection with the single fatal instance, typical of the human lack of foreknowledge, of half-attention.

In another early poem Dorn imagines his way into the attentional habits of a wild creature, using the animal not as a metaphor like the squirrel but as the even purer value of unmediated experience. "The Deer's Eye The Hunter's Nose" moves among the writer's, the hunter's, and the deer's perspectives on a winter hunt:

> Idaho rocks drop
> inside an old mine where deers'
> eyes wind the light into
> yellow balls
> back of darkness—away
> down under the plaid hat hunter's tread
> who spreads a plaid tongue
> on his lip, guessing
> with his quick alcoholic glance—
> there is no scent
> in the nose of him

just snot
          and we in a shack
hear his shot, vowing
to return the fire
we have a howitzer
for such a siege—
but guess the horse runs, sparking eye
streaming nostrils, drops
gleaming froze turds
which, hitting the ground rattle
enormous grapeshot down the hill.
flash.
the deer eye opens in the mind
on the acoustics of the hunt—is it
the run of the horse is it
the blunt diarrhea of the gun
is it the rage of the horse.
                    (CP 38–39)

Sound, in "the acoustics of the hunt," is the theme of the poem.
The many recurring sounds support that theme, always to convey fury of condemnation against the hunter, as for example in

down under the plaid hat hunter's tread
who spreads a plaid tongue

Eye against nose: the deer's eye gives value, but the hunter's
nose has no sense or scent, "just snot." From the beginning the
theme of Americans as casual killers has fascinated Dorn, and
here as elsewhere his allegiance is with the victims.[6] Testing

6. All other essays in this book provide evidence for this point. An excellent
example of the theme, described in the next chapter, is the lyric "Death While
Journeying," about the murder of Meriwether Lewis at Grinder's Stand (CP
49); also see Dorn's introduction to Tom Clark's *A Short Guide to the High
Plains* (Santa Barbara, Calif.: Cadmus Editions, 1981), from which this concerning the New West: "No problems with abortion out here. They just stick
babies on a fence post and shootem. If you're walking across the street, they
just gun their 4 × 4s and run over you. If you're riding a bicycle they'll drop a
Coors bottle 6 inches ahead of your front wheel before they cut you into a
culvert. And that's to mention only the nice people."

what he already suspects, the speaker-listener imagines the
hunted animal's state of attention: "is it / . . . the horse is
it / . . . the gun / is it . . . the horse." The passage opens by
referring to "deers' / eyes," and it concludes with "the deer eye
opens in the mind" and the chance that the observer can "see"
the sounds of the hunt; in the same way "flash" is both sight
and sound. This doubling of senses, a synaesthesia of seeing
and hearing, is an instance of how rapt furious attention produces intensity; anger sharpens the faculties.[7]

In 1969 and 1970, Dorn published two small books of love
songs; these are now reprinted next to each other near the end
of *Collected Poems*. Taken together these forty-one short lyrics
contain a great deal of his very best personal writing. The first
set concerns strains in a new relationship between the speaker
and a younger woman, the contempt they meet from acquaint-
ances, and their return from England to America; the second
set deals with the coming of children to this couple and, so far
as I can determine from opaque poems toward the end, the

---

7. In an omitted line (line 11) from the poem's beginning, Dorn writes of
the "acaudate hunter." The hunter, to paraphrase, is a tailless animal, assimilated toward the predatory worst of the bestial just as the horse is assimilated
toward the human gun, turds hitting the ground like grapeshot. Poet and deer
share the function of attending, which is mental; hunter and horse share the
function of excreting ("snot" and "streaming nostrils"; "blunt diarrhea of the
gun" and "froze turds").
   A poem for comparison, on this subject of the likes and unlikes of human
and animal attention, is the third from the end of the book, "The Octopus
Thinks with Its Arms," about pattern-recognition and reproductive activity in
the octopus. The poem is partly a joke, partly a scholarly investigation of the
eye as the seat of memory. In his interview with Roy K. Okada, Dorn mentions
the source of the poem in "a book that's become very important to me," J. Z.
Young's *A Model of the Brain* (Oxford: Oxford University Press, 1964). There
Young, a professor of anatomy, takes octopus intelligence as the analogue for
human mechanisms of learning and form-discrimination. Dorn comments: "I
have the sense that we know totality all the time through our senses and what
part of that totality we can capture is the definition essentially of our sensate
capabilities" (*I* 46).

strife and union of sexes, and of groups of people. Though the term "attention" is used but once in each set, to refer to the woman "tended by my whole attention" (*CP* 240) and to the world as a battleground of unthinking pluralities ("their attention was attracted"; *CP* 256), all these poems are versions of a moralized attention. As it happens, three of the finest lyrics in the admirable first set all deal with speech and speech sounds. In the third poem, an American man speaks to an English woman:

> My speech is tinged
> my tongue has taken
> a foreigner into it
> Can you understand
> my uncertainties grow
> and underbrush and thicket
> of furious sensibility
> between us and wholly
> unlike the marvelously burning
> bush which lies at the entrance
> to your gated thighs
>
> My dear love, when I unsheathe
> a word of the wrong temper
> it is to test that steel
> across the plain between us
>                    (*CP* 237)

With imagery of thicket as against burning bush, he explains how intellectual understanding can lag behind sexual, asking her to allow for his uncertainties and attend to context not to a stray "word of the wrong temper." In the ninth poem, joy is reestablished and the lovers are "high" on each other, coffee, a fine morning, music from Otis Redding, and marijuana from Nick:

> EYE high gloria
>   a fine europ ean morn ing

> black coffee
> for Nick in the nick of time
> he gives me something for you
> and Otis Redd ing
> with his feet up watching
> infinity roll in and Nick
> his time ing
> and sudden lee the lid
> comes off
>            and we head straight for
> the thing we could be in
> cannabic warm
> and rime ing
>                       (CP 241)

For a poem of only fifty-eight words, this has all of three references to the perfection of ecstatic consciousness: "gloria," "infinity," and the utopian "thing we could be in." Intensity of this escape from the ordinary is carried, in large measure, by the arrangement of sounds: the six words that space their syllables, miming a slight loss of "timing" but not of sense; the pun on "Nick" and on "lid" in the drug dealer's meaning as well as the cliché; the rhymes and partial rhymes. In fact, the sounding of rhymes is here taken as the poetic equivalent, and the end product, of cannabic ecstasy. From "EYE" to "rime ing," the poem proceeds in the by-now-familiar attentional pattern from sight to the profounder intensity of sound. As attention is focussed by all these means, there is not loss of control but an increase of it.

Poem and people do not rhyme so well in the twenty-third lyric, where Dorn, after the colon, ironically appropriates conventional language to unmask conventional ethics:

> There is a vast smell of marriage
> not lightly said, some place
> some time ago I was there too.
> I've been everywhere.

> This afternoon I thought why not,
> why not get Jenny into something
> and we both fly off to meet,
> well, almost anyone. Away
> from the flat rancorous smell
> of their insinuation, which is
> just this: you've done the thing—
> you've presumed your body
> as well as your mind, *your mind*
> we like to watch go through its sideshow
> lifted up in the bright creative air
> but when you made other arrangements
> for your body, baby go away, that's it
> (CP 248)

The attention is mightily focussed by hatred—even in a love song! This poem's force is the Swiftian force of indirect declaration. A personal poem, yet one that uses the disguise, albeit transparent, of persona. Anger radiates from the stress and sound of angry imagined talk; enemies are portrayed through attention to their very turns of speech: "baby go away, that's it." These colloquial lines, in particular, call to mind Dorn's idea that his songs are not to be accompanied and sung; really they are "like language songs rather than music songs" (*I* 23–24). To repeat from Dorn's preface, his is a work "poetic by virtue of its inherent tone," not by virtue of musical techniques (meter, rhyme, metaphor) existing anterior to the poem's argument. Apparently, under certain conditions declaration can have a slight intended lyric glamor. The wide range of the statemental lyric, Dorn's staple of writing in the shorter poems up to 1974, must be our final concern.

■ 3 ■

Within his generation of American poets, Dorn is one of the most public in his themes. For someone who has always set the historical over the domestic, the "Love Songs" are something of an experimental detour. Argument, prayer, pronouncement, letter, explanation, chronicle are some of the declaratory genres he has marked in his titles for *Collected Poems*. Scorn, sarcasm, and hatred are not to him unusual emotions, though they are alien to many poets. And yet, although he has habitually spoken for and about persons thrust to the margins of society, Dorn is not a poet of causes. In fact, he is suspicious of anyone who *favors* anything; so his work becomes a test of the adequacy of any but the most subtle and rigorous definition of ideology. Irony, the writer's way of "provoking more than he is ever going to include," is for Dorn "a thing I've always admired, against the current of my time" (*V* 11, 12). *Statemental lyric* is the correct term for Dorn's shorter poems, if we remember that he never releases statement unguarded by irony. Thus the degree to which he is a self-critical critic is what must be studied: the degree to which the urge to statement, so powerful here, is held in check.

Let us show the range of moral and stylistic possibilities in *Collected Poems* by means of a diagram. A simple linear spectrum, a mapping of cline or graduality, will not display the system of counterforces as well as an equilateral triangle with Wit, Song, and Pronunciamento at the points. Wit comprises the local joke as well as the high-minded continuous argument on public themes; song, the most grounded in sound, comprises verbal impulses to celebration or to regret (in Dorn, song is never merely personal and is often part of a narrative design); pronunciamento comprises declaration, denunciation, the taking of certain stands against external authority.

The quintessential Dorn poem, which does not exist, would keep all the legs of the triangle equal, each pulling against the other, all three directions in perfect balance. Isolation of one angle from the other two narrows it, makes it less viable. The system is maintained by a kind of center, which we can call the

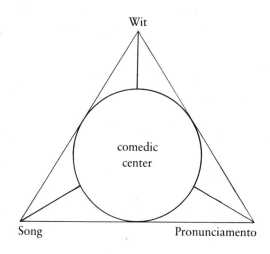

comedic center, represented here as a circle inscribed within the triangle and touching all three sides. The center's function is to pull all the points inward and keep them from undue isolation. This is the action, just described, of holding statement in check. Irony, figured in this comedic center, is here taken as the leading quality of style and character in these poems. One principle of the model, to be explored below, is the ability of any one point to move toward another point, either directly or through the mediation of the third point (e.g., Song to Pronunciamento directly, or alternately by way of the neutrality of Wit). The hypothesis that we must test is: the greater the integration of two or all three points, the more powerful the poem and the more characteristic of Edward Dorn.

It may be that our triangle should be isosceles, because the quality of wit in the poems seems closer to the comedic center than the other two directional points. There is in *Slinger* considerable wit in the sense of logical outrage, language play, and punning, but this sense of wit is not very apt for the shorter poems. The best definition for the *Collected Poems* is Dr. Johnson's from the "Life of Cowley": wit in the sense of the yoking of seemingly unrelated ideas by means of alarming suggestion and strenuous intellection. Epigram and local pastiche appear occasionally as examples of this type of wit, but more often the effect is more diffuse in poems of some length, which are lyrics extended in a flat arguing voice. We have already seen an instance from "Idaho Out" in the lines about "my north fork beauty." Perhaps the finest poem in the mode of wit is the longest, "Oxford": six parts in twenty-two pages of *Collected Poems*, a poem Dorn regards as one of his most successful. This from part 5:

> the
> Bodleian has as a copyright
> every book,
>                   Lincoln College
>           has high on the wall
>             in the first court
>           a small bust of John Wesley, fellow
> there is in Merton an Elizabethan
> stretch of building and beyond
> that, under a passage
> the treed lawn where only fellows
> and there is the garden where Hopkins
> as at Cambridge the tower
> where Byron's Bear near
>           the rooms of Coleridge
>       or Shelley's notebook in the
> case at the Bodleian, the Lock
> of His Hair, his glove, in a case.
> not two gloves as he must
> have had two hands to cover
> but that hip thing
> *one* glove you can do something
>                   with
> in terms of those and these brown spectacular
> times, two

> of course are a boring reminder
> we are the animals we are
> a lovely glove admittedly
> but not so lovely as Shelley.
> (CP 206–7)

Here is one American poet not overwhelmed by the prestige of the English poetic tradition. This replays in the mode of literary irony an earlier theme as a pronunciamento, in which Dorn says he does not "need to be reminded of anything / by Europe": "What they do in Freeborn County Minnesota is *more* my business" (CP 200). The long poem's passage from Wit (the whole of the marvelously funny part 1 on fornication and politics) to Song (the play on "Oolite" in part 2) to political-moral Pronunciamento (part 5, "socialism is shit turned only half way round") makes it a distillation of his most typical effects, though at the end pronunciamento gains control and some energy is lost.[8]

Excepting the forty-one poems in the two sets of "Love Songs," of the 106 items listed in the contents of *Collected Poems* seventeen are titled as songs. To my mind a number of others must be included in this category because of their heavier use of verbal equivalences, and because of their tone of open expansiveness. Among these is one of Dorn's earliest poems, "Vaquero":

> The cowboy stands beneath
> a brick-orange moon. The top
> of his oblong head is blue, the sheath
> of his hips
> is too.

8. Other first-order poems in the mode of wit are, in *Collected Poems*: "Hands Up" (CP 84); "Idaho Out" (CP 107); and "The First Note (from London)" (CP 180).

In the dark brown night
your delicate cowboy stands quite still.
His plain hands are crossed.
His wrists are embossed white.

In the background night is a house,
has a chimney top,
Yi Yi, the cowboy's eyes
are blue. The top of the sky
is too.

(CP 4)

This simplifies its color scheme to a comic-book vividness, its image and sound sequences to the most basic gestures; it is a stark instance of Dorn's own category of "language song." "Yi Yi" is very likely an allusion to the yippie-eye-ay ballads of cowboy life, an ironic reference to song just as the whole poem is an ironic version of the two-dimensional myth of the cowboy in American popular lore. From bare simplicities a tone is achieved of vague threat. Two other early poems, "Are They Dancing" and "The Air of June Sings," are songs in another and richer sense—elegies—the one beginning "There is a sad carnival up the valley," the other ending "Oh, the stones not yet cut." In sound, rhythm, and feeling, Dorn's song poems most display (while they also restrain) his wish for the bardic gesture.

Because devices of sound are somewhat chastened, submerged, the new reader will perhaps respond to the quickness of Dorn's mind sooner than to the delicacy of his ear. Yet "We are bleached in Sound / as it burns by what we desire" is nowhere more evident than in the poems of song. Here is the unpunctuated whole of "Song," where the sound of *r* gives or seems to give the note of sadness:

my wife is lovely
my children are fair
she puts color on her lips
in front of the mirror
there is stillness everywhere

my hand is on her shoulder
we are leaving the house
the sun is in her hair
and since october
it has grown darker
there is frost in the air
I am unwise
to think of her as there
　　those parts of her I adore
are here
the years have gone by
everywhere
now our house is near
alongside other houses
we laugh, sometimes,
sometimes we construct
a single blue tear
　　　　(CP 126–27)

It is essential to add that Dorn's lyrical flights are usually short, and usually thwarted in some way, even in *Collected Poems* where the impulse to sound and song is most frequent. Dorn apparently loves the singing line, but he cannot permit himself to indulge it.[9] The vexations of lyric expansiveness become one of the themes of *Slinger*, that long poem punctuated abruptly by coarse lute sounds of "STRUM" and "THWANG," and by consciously awful song lyrics like:

> *Oh a girl there was in the street*
> *the day we rode into La Cruz*
> *and the name of the name of her feet*
> *was the same as the name of the street*
> *and she stood and she stared like a moose*
> *and her hair was tangled and loose . . .*

> STRUM
> 　strum

　　　　　　　　(S 14)

9. It is reported that in 1980 Dorn began to study the Anglo-Saxon poets, and to learn to play the banjo.

The humorous final term of this checking of lyricism (how go further?) is Dorn's proudly announced habit of writing parts of *Hello, La Jolla* and all of *Yellow Lola* while driving, one hand tied to the wheel.[10]

In their preoccupation with inwardness, intensity, and sound, the song poems take short flights. The pronunciamento poems, which make their pronouncements out in the material world, tend by contrast to be weblike, meditative structures— showing an intensity of speculation, or of anger, one that is less coherent than the intensity of wit or song. In his preface, Dorn admits that "there are structures in this body to which I can no longer assign a use and whose functions are hidden" (*CP* v), a judgment that applies most, I should say, to three long pronunciamento poems: "The World Box-Score Cup of 1966" (*CP* 166), "A Theory of Truth" from *The North Atlantic Turbine* (*CP* 186), and "The Cosmology of Finding Your Place" (*CP* 233). Dorn's characteristic preference, we have said, is for irony: his great method is comic understatement in alternation with preposterous hyperbole, in order to provoke more than he includes. The pronunciamento poems sometimes pull away from this comedic center, yet even when they ramble they ramble with the energy of hatred and denunciation to interesting places. Often, in such cases, Dorn's analysis of American and world politics is arresting and original. But when Pronunciamento is drawn back toward the comedic center, it is also pulled into the influence of Wit and Song; under these conditions, it is briefer, more coherent, and commands even greater declaratory power.[11]

Very often the pronunciamento poems concern the neglected

10. Other first-order poems in the mode of song are, in *Collected Poems*: "Hemlocks" (*CP* 79); "Song: Europa" (*CP* 159); "Thesis" (*CP* 179); "Song: (Again, I am made the occurrence)" (*CP* 230); and "Easy's Best" (*CP* 261).

11. Examples of Dorn's political analysis: the denunciations of Churchill and Eisenhower in part 4 of "Oxford" (*CP* 200), and the study of the geopolitics of monopoly capitalism in "A Theory of Truth" (*CP* 186). All the other essays in this book are directly or indirectly studies of Dorn's political ideas.

or the oppressed, and while such statements are not the most socially analytical they are the most moving works within this category. "Like a Message on Sunday" is about a "forlorn plumber":

> Once World, he came
> to our house to fix the stove
>                and couldn't
>      oh, we were arrogant and talked
> about him in the next room, doesn't
> a man know what he is doing?
>
> Can't it be done right,
>                World of iron thorns.
> Now they sit by the meagre river
> by the water . . . stare
> into that plumber
> so that I can see a daughter in the water
> she thin and silent,
> he, wearing a baseball cap
>      in a celebrating town this summer season
> may they live on
>
> on, may their failure be kindly, and come
> in small unnoticeable pieces.
>                (CP 28–29)

A similar poem, which also ends with the high singing dignity of invocation, is "Mourning Letter, March 29, 1963":

> No hesitation
>                would stay me
> from weeping this morning
> for the miners of Hazard Kentucky.
>                The mine owners'
> extortionary skulls
> whose eyes are diamonds don't float
> down the rivers, as they should,
> of the flood

> The miners, cold
> starved, driven from work, in
> their homes float though and float
> on the ribbed ships of their frail
> bodies,
>
>      Oh, go letter,
> keep my own misery close to theirs
> associate me with no other honor.
>              (CP 147–48)

And the very last poem in the book is a pronunciamento poem, one which gives a brief history of the effects of capitalism on nature and mind. In the use of metaphor it moves toward wit; in the use of diction and syntax it moves toward lofty and angry song. Yet these motives serve but to concentrate Dorn's violence of statement in "The Stripping of the River":

> The continental tree supports the margins
> In return for involuntary atrophos
> Which can now be called the Shale Contract
> Not only are the obvious labors
> In metal and grain and fuel extracted
> But the spiritual genius is so apt
> To be cloven from this plain of our green heart
> And to migrate to the neutralized
> And individualizing conditions of the coasts
> That this center of our true richness
> Also goes there to aberrant rest
> Bought by the silver of sunrise
> And the gold of sunset.
>              (CP 267)

The final lines are strong parody of W. B. Yeats's fruity ending to "Song of Wandering Aengus": "The silver apples of the moon, / The golden apples of the sun." Dorn ends the poem and the book with *atrophos, cloven, neutralized, aberrant,* and *bought*, a careful sequence of curse words defined as such by means of the poem's argument. Since his opening "Rick of

Green Wood," with its hint of trouble, Dorn has traveled a considerable distance.[12]

*Hello, La Jolla* and *Yellow Lola* travel further yet, in their use of aphorism to check both song and pronunciamento. Dorn's more recent work is more streamlined for action. In this he comes closer to his name. *Dorn* in Old Provençal is a noun meaning "the width of the hand."[13] But this family name almost certainly comes from the German *Dorn*, meaning "thorn." Thorn and fist: emblems for one who provokes to alertness in perception, in language and sound, in social-historical understanding.

12. Other first-order works in the mode of pronouncement are, in *Collected Poems*: "The Argument Is" (*CP* 30); "Home on the Range, February, 1962" (*CP* 43); "Los Mineros" (*CP* 54); "The Land Below" (*CP* 57); and "The Sundering U. P. Tracks" (*CP* 231).

13. I rely on Émil Lévy, *Petit dictionnaire provençal-français* (Heidelberg: C. Winter, 1966).

# 2

## "*This Marvellous Accidentalism*"

### ROBERT VON HALLBERG

*Such a thing as humanity seems very relative, the final abjuring of any vision.*

("The Pronouncement," CP 76)

During the early 1950s Edward Dorn was one of that vanishing species at Black Mountain College, the student. More precisely, in academic taxonomy, he was a "transfer student" from the state college at Charleston, Illinois, near the tractor factory where he worked, and before that from the University of Illinois. In 1951 he went to Black Mountain to study painting—and to get a draft deferment. About five years and one leave of absence later, he took a degree from Black Mountain; by then he considered himself a poet. Robert Creeley, his outside examiner for the B.A., thought him a passable student, and Dorn left to settle in Skagit Valley, Washington. Within a couple of years the college had folded, and Charles Olson, former rector of Black Mountain, was lecturing about Alfred North Whitehead to a group of twenty in San Francisco.[1]

Olson's influence, though, was abiding. More than a decade later, in 1968, Dorn dedicated *Geography*, then his most ambitious book, to his former teacher—Dorn always "wears his

---

1. This biographical information is taken from Dorn's 1972 interview with Barry Alpert (*I* 7–14).

masters on his sleeve, the surest sign of a serious man."[2] He took from Olson a commitment to didactic, discursive poetry.[3] In 1973, looking back twenty years, Dorn reflected, "[Olson's] whole passion for a scope of knowledge that I hadn't dreamed of gave me a clue to what the extent of the mind might be. I'm speaking now more in the poetic sense, as enthusiast, really more than in the scholarly sense" (I 37). Poems like "The Kingfishers," "The Praises," and "In Cold Hell, in Thicket" show how Olson's mind, fueled by enthusiasm, can range over a wide terrain that encompasses nothing that might be construed as inherently poetic. Olson extended the bounds of what is considered poetry, by his use both of flatly discursive language and of scholarly subject matter. In 1961 Dorn spoke of this aspect of his teacher: "It seems to me that Olson is doing something I've never read before. . . . I don't think any previous work so attempts to tap the realities of a region in all its economic and political and human aspects" (I 2). In 1968 Dorn remarked to Olson, "[It] still gasses me that you can be the most *poetic* worker alive while saying something, nearly anything."[4] The extension of poetic subject matter counted heavily for Dorn, because he knew that poetry that takes personal experience, domestic and psychological, as its subject was out of his reach: Creeley could be his examiner but never his mentor (I 23–24).[5] Yet Olson's enthusiasm for his subjects was still more important, for ultimately the subject itself matters little: "What

2. Edward Dorn, "Report from the Front: The First Films of Don Lloyd," *Wild Dog* 2 (March 22, 1965): 3.

3. For a good definition and discussion of discursiveness in poetry, see Robert Pinsky, *The Situation of Poetry* (Princeton: Princeton University Press, 1976), pp. 134 ff.

4. Letter to Olson, 24 January 1968, in the University of Connecticut Library; subsequent references to this archive will be abbreviated as CtU.

5. In a letter to Olson, 1 December 1968, Dorn indicated his sense that Creeley is limited by a domestic subject matter: "I don't, also, find *The Finger* any indication, in itself, of an alteration of perception. It seems the same domestic inflexibility as ever" (CtU).

I *admire* about all of you is that Ability to start anywhere, Jesus, *that* must be *life*."[6] For Olson, this was more than an ability: convention demanded that he always seem to start in unfamiliar territory; his poems are meant to repeat what he called "the first American story," "exploration."[7] His discursive poems are made to seem exploratory, even when their arguments have been framed at the outset. Many of Dorn's poems too are exploratory in this discursive sense. "Idaho Out" is the best example, and others directly concern the theme. But for Dorn, this "first American story" is a tangle. The politics of exploration, he knew, were anything but clean; there is a further sense too in which exploration (in land or words) is at odds with what is commonly regarded as "human." And whatever else political poetry ought to be, for Dorn, it must be humane.

The clearest study of this problem is a poem Dorn wrote in 1958, "The Air of June Sings"—a bright elegy in a country graveyard. A few lines into the poem Dorn says,

And now, the light noise of the children at play on the inscribed stone
jars my ear and they whisper and laugh covering their mouths. "My
     Darling"
my daughter reads, some of the markers
reflect such lightness to her reading eyes, yea, as I rove
among these polished and lime blocks I am moved to tears and I hear
the depth in "Darling, we love thee," and as in "Safe in Heaven."
                                                              (*CP* 11)

Human sentiment is his subject: his daughter giggles with small embarrassment and Dorn is "moved to tears" before these stones that triangulate three generations. To the little girl the inscriptions speak an abstract language of conventions whose proprieties she does not yet fully comprehend. Dorn represents

6. Dorn to Olson, 14 December 1967 (CtU).
7. Charles Olson, *Call Me Ishmael* (San Francisco: City Lights, 1967), p. 11.

her interpretation through his diction: "the markers reflect such lightness to her reading eyes"; he becomes abstract just where she does, as the stones become texts for her. His own sense of the epitaphs is suggested by the solemnly archaic phrase that takes over the line, "yea, as I rove . . . ," and by the frank declaration of sentiment in the next lines: "I am moved to tears and I hear / the depth. . . ." Declarative diction is fitting, because what Dorn hears is the irreducible, inexplicable depth of common sentiment—to that, Olson's ear was never tuned. In the next lines he hypothesizes more fully articulated alternatives to these inscriptions—the "wisdom" of the dead:

> I am going off to heaven and I won't see you anymore. I am
> going back into the country and I won't be here anymore. I am
> going to die in 1937.
>
> (CP 11)

But these "explanations" of mortal separations are light in comparison to the declarative inscriptions, "My Darling," "Darling, we love thee," "Safe in Heaven"; they do not serve the needs of the living.

As these explanations speak from beyond the grave, as though retrospectively, so frontierism tries to transcend the mortal limits of the simply human:

> My eyes avoid
> the largest stone, larger than the common large, Goodpole Matthews,
> Pioneer, and that pioneer sticks in me like a wormed black cherry
> in my throat, No Date, nothing but that zeal, that trekking
> and Business, that presumption in a sacred place, where children
> are buried, and where peace, as it is in the fields and the country
> should reign. A wagon wheel is buried there.
>
> (CP 11)

That undated tombstone grossly violates the proprieties of the graveyard by its grasp beyond time and the common lot. Zeal for motion, the wagon wheel, did not fade away entirely in the nineteenth century:

> exhausted it still moves
> across "the precious uncluttered
> land" as its will takes it
> plastic boats behind.
>
> (CP 40)

Suburbs mark its wake, where "strange cowboys live / in ranch style houses" (CP 40). Dorn's response to frontier zealotry:

> Lead me away
> to the small quiet stones of the unpreposterous dead and leave
> me my tears for Darling we love thee, for Budded on earth and
>     blossomed
> in heaven, where the fieldbirds sing in the fence rows,
> and there is possibility, where there are not the loneliest of all.
>
> Oh, the stones not yet cut.
>
> (CP 11–12)

Sentimentality is a principle for Dorn, a disciplined unraveling of a tangled ideology; the dead have no need for sentimentality: they are "unpreposterous." The genre he chooses in which to oppose that preposterous hunger for new beginnings is one of the most hackneyed and debased of lyric forms: the graveyard elegy. "The swallows twittering from the straw-built shed" (1751); "the fieldbirds sing in the fence rows" (1958)—then to now, there are no new sentiments.[8] Inside the fenced enclosures "there is possibility" but not that timeless absolute of "No Date." The people whose inscriptions speak with such depth are tied to each other by simple, common sentiments and by the plainest of literary and funereal conventions; the pioneer is "the

---

8. The first line quoted is from Gray's "Elegy," *The Norton Anthology of English Literature*, ed. M. H. Abrams, et al., 3rd ed., vol. 1 (New York: Norton, 1974): 2377.

loneliest of all," for he is attracted by the landscapes that are
"refusing / population" (*CP* 40).

The solitary, though, has its attractions—even for Dorn.
The poem that celebrates pioneer loneliness most compellingly
is "Death While Journeying," which first appeared in the summer of 1960.

> At Grinder's Stand
> in his sleep
> on the Natchez Trace,
> in the Chickasaw country
> Meriwether Lewis
> had what money
> and incidently his life
> stole. And I never read what time of year
>
> it was, Fall? when the papaws
> 10  drop their yellow fruit,
> or Spring? and bear's grease.
> Enough now
> to write it down in celebration
> on first reading . . .
>
> At Grinder's Stand
> on the Natchez Trace
> in the Chickasaw country
> an exotic place
>                         to die
> 20  and it fit him.
>              (*CP* 49–50; ellipsis in original)

This is a poem about the ignoble end of a great beginner,
Meriwether Lewis, who died mysteriously at thirty-five, a few
years after his triumphant return from the Pacific Coast. From
1807 until his death Lewis was governor of the upper Louisiana
Territory. During the expedition to the Pacific he had grown
accustomed to the carte blanche Jefferson had permitted him.
But the Washington government was later unwilling to allow
him the same liberty in administering the Louisiana Territory;

several of his vouchers were not honored by the federal government. Severely disappointed by what he took to be a reprimand, Lewis set out alone in September 1809 for Washington, where he intended to straighten out these financial matters. (He also planned to visit his mother, who was not dying, at Ivy Creek in Virginia on his return route.)

Dorn honors his subject as much by the form of his poem as by explicit statement. The poem repeatedly asserts a beginning, but it cannot generate a principle of continuity. The first four lines are four prepositional clauses, each seeming to start the sentence from scratch. Once the syntax has produced a subject ("Meriwether Lewis") and a verb ("had"), it forestalls completion by convoluting the object: "what money / and incidently his life / stole." The sentence is syntactically complete, but in terms of semantics its conclusion is undisclosed, and the sense is aborted. Dorn then veers away from this subject with digressive conjectures about the time of year, as though he did not want the poem to continue along any one path. (The seasonal conjectures punctuate the poem [lines 9–11, 22–24, 38–41] with unsettling reminders of the poem's inability to get beyond its very beginning.) And those conjectures are similarly dismissed, unresolved, with a half-sentence of "conclusion" (lines 12–14). At this point (lines 15–17) the poem can begin again with its initial formula; the poem goes through five such beginnings (lines 1–4, 15–17, 33–34, 45–46, 58). The rhyme (lines 16–18) suggests that what interests Dorn is the exoticism not of the location but of the sound of those place names: "Grinder's Stand," "Natchez Trace," "Chickasaw country." The fourth strophe indicates that Dorn is truly engaged by a single personal quality:

> Going to see his dying mother
> or was it summer,
> the live oak waving
> in the clear air,

25  but imagine,
    trying to make a trip
    like that alone.
        (CP 50)

Motive (line 21), time (line 22), place (lines 23–24)—these
finally matter little. What is wondrous is Lewis's solitariness
(lines 25–27), which, the true heritage of the American frontier,
transcends all the mundane details.

              imagine
      along the Natchez Trace in loneliness
      to Grinder's Stand, and the ferret
      Grinder, eyeing you as you passed through
      the door. And an entire continent had flapped
      at your coattails.

50  But surrounding this death
      Boone had just returned to Femme Osage
      with sixty beaver skins "still strong
      in limb, unflinching in spirit"
      standing there with a gaunt eye
      watching the Astorians prepare their keel-boats,

      his old ear bent
      toward the Pacific tide.

      *But* at Grinder's Stand,
      which is south of Femme Osage
60  on the Trace, whom probably the Astorians
      had nearly forgotten, a man rode in
      to the final recognition
      and who would have been there
                   but money-eyed

      Grinder,

      while the Astorians prepared their keel-boats
      and Boone watched.
          (CP 50–51)

What Boone is made to watch here is the erosion of the
frontier heritage. Robert Grinder was the proprietor of Grind-

er's Stand, where Lewis died; he was said by his wife to be twenty miles away from home on October 11, 1809. About that, however, there is some doubt. Many years after Lewis's death, a friend of one of Grinder's servants stated that Grinder was present the night Lewis either killed himself or was killed by a robber. Lewis's watch and money (at least $200) were not with his body on the morning of the 12th; before long, Robert Grinder purchased more slaves and better property and moved away from the Natchez Trace. Dorn evidently takes the view, shared by others, that Grinder murdered Lewis for money. As an old man Daniel Boone trapped furs to pay his debts. Dorn makes the point that, more or less simultaneously with Lewis's death, John Jacob Astor chartered one of the first great trusts, the American Fur Company (1808), which established a post at Astoria, Oregon, near where Lewis and Clark had camped along the Columbia River. From Meriwether Lewis and Daniel Boone to Robert Grinder and John Jacob Astor, from lone explorers to weaseling capitalists—that is the decline of the West, as Dorn sees it.

A few months after "Death While Journeying" appeared, David Ignatow edited a special issue of *Chelsea* on political poetry that included "Los Mineros," one of Dorn's best political elegies.[9] During the two years since writing "The Air of June Sings," Dorn had learned to write cooler elegies addressed more to understanding than to sentiment. In "Los Mineros" he meditates on a mute group photo, as he had meditated two years earlier on the plain brevity of epitaphs:

> These men whom we will never know are ranged 14 in number
> in one of those pictures that are very long, you've seen them.
>
> And the wonder is five are smiling Mexicanos, the rest

9. The version in *Chelsea*, no. 8 (October 1960), pp. 66–68, includes about thirty lines omitted from the text of "Los Mineros" printed in *The Collected Poems*.

could be English or German, blown to New Mexico on another
winter's snow. Hard to imagine Spanish as miners, their
20  sense is good-naturedly above ground (and their cruelty).
In a silly way they know their pictures are being taken,

and know it isn't necessary honor standing in line with their
    hands hiding
in their pockets. I was looking to see if they are short
as Orwell says miners must be, but they aren't save two
25  little Mexican boys. What caught my eye at first was the way
they were so finely dressed in old double-breasted suit coats,
    ready for work.

Then I looked into their faces and the races separated.
The English or Germans wear a look which is mystic in its
    expectancy;

able men underground,
30  but the Spanish face carries no emergency
and one of the little boys, standing behind a post
looks right out of the picture faintly smiling: even today.

                                                    (CP 55)

The aspirations behind this casual style finally seem to be
pretensions (lines 28–30)—and for interesting reasons. Dorn
seems to address his reader directly, without the stylistic apparatus that might turn such an address into a formal occasion:
"you've seen them" (line 16); a common ground of experience
can be easily assumed. And he takes conspicuous advantage of
short-cutting colloquialisms, as though he were musing over
the photo while he jotted this poem down: "[It is] hard to
imagine . . ." (line 19); "they know their pictures are being
taken, / and know it isn't necessary [, but rather an] honor
standing in line . . ." (lines 21–22). That second ellipsis (with
its faulty parallelism) suggests that Dorn is simply talking while
he thinks. In 1964 Dorn praised LeRoi Jones's prose for its
plainness: "There are no devices of thought, happily."[10] That

10. "The Camp—LeRoi Jones' *Blues People*," in Edward Dorn, Michael
Rumaker, and Warren Tallman, *Prose 1* (San Francisco: Four Seasons, 1964),
p. 33.

year he wrote to Jones about his desire to talk openly to his readers: "I only mean that I consider the fight to tell other Men, just other Men, a little of what I know I've seen, in as straight a manner as possible, my only occupation. My only commitment. My only true duty. That's everything of course."[11] Yet a talking, didactic style is a complicated matter, for a too simply "straight" manner can be misleadingly casual: "It is that crucial talk that is so important, and indispensable, and phony. It's the only stuff there is to work with. The Western World hasn't yet come on to a language it can use to say something important, or, even, pertinent."[12] Casual talk is not the appropriate medium for what Dorn considers important subject matter; he will have no cracker-barrel contrivance. Instead, after invoking a colloquial manner, he displaces his diction from spoken usage, using ungainly terms, like "good-naturedly," which appear only in formal, written contexts. For Dorn is engaged here by a kind of cultural sociology that, though unprofessional, is directed toward an understanding commonly conveyed through formal discourse, not casual chat. His motive is close to that of the expository prose writer; like an essayist, he tests (lines 23–25) and posits (lines 28–30) general propositions. Yet the "laws" Dorn formulates are not intended to be definitive, as an essayist's customarily are. He wants to digress into his generalizations (lines 19–20). And his terms and categories— "above ground," "mystic," "expectancy," "emergency"—are suggestive and exploratory rather than determinate. He looks for the telling not the definitive detail (lines 25–26).

■ 2 ■

Between 1961 and 1965 Dorn's political poetry changed character; to show how distinct a change occurred I would like to

11. Dorn to LeRoi Jones, July 1964, in the Library of the University of California, Los Angeles.

12. Edward Dorn, "Dutchman & The Slave," *Wild Dog* 2 (28 October 1964): 6.

look at a poem probably written in 1959 but never published. In late April and early May 1959, Fidel Castro visited Washington; his two-week stay received wide coverage in American newspapers. While he was trying to convince Washington politicians and newsmen that his intentions were not to be feared, the *New York Times* ran this item: "A military court sentenced Dr. Olga Herrara Marcos today to death by firing squad. She is believed to be the first woman to be sentenced to death in the history of the republic."[13] Dr. Marcos was found guilty of informing officials of the Batista regime of the whereabouts of three rebels who were caught and executed in 1955. Her alleged motive: $200 and a better job.[14] On May 11, 1959, *Time* ran a particularly pathetic photo of her sitting, numbly terrified, in the courtroom.[15] The skeptical press estimated that she would be at least number 550 on the list of those executed for war crimes by the Castro government, but her sentence was reduced by a higher court to thirty years' imprisonment.[16]

Dorn evidently saw the *Time* photo and read newspaper accounts of her trial, for two years later he sent to LeRoi Jones "An Address for the First Woman to Face Death in Havana— Olga Herrara Marcos":

> (Mrs. Marcos went to havana
> all on a summer's night
> she was caught in a plot, which
> side,
> she forgot
> but her face was the picture
> of fright)
> . . . . .
> . . . face of the bullet
> smashing

13. *New York Times*, 30 April 1959, p. 12.
14. *Newsweek* 53 (11 May 1959): 62.
15. *Time* 73 (11 May 1959): 46.
16. Ibid., p. 46.

> against timber
> behind Mrs. Marcos
> whose practical crime was
> being on the wrong payroll, anybody's[17]

Dorn and Jones were close friends at the time. That year, 1961, Jones's Totem Press brought out Dorn's first collection of poems, *The Newly Fallen*. Dorn admired Jones's writing and, though from a distance, his political polemics as well: "Your social radicalism sounds very much to the point, as you'd know I'd feel, envious even, altho I know it is much more others' scene than mine. Keep slugging for whatever reason, and when you run out of reasons, the better."[18] It was natural for Dorn to send Jones this two-year-old poem, because Jones had not long before published an essay about his 1960 visit to Cuba.[19] Jones, however, disapproved of the poem; "counter-revolutionary" was his phrase. Jones pointed out that the title itself was misleading: "If you say of the woman in the poem 'The first' woman to die in Habana . . . you know it is strictly 'poetic.' Not at all true. Batista killed 20,000. . . . I think Castro means to do better. It is some small thing I want. Some goodness I have to see."[20]

Dorn was troubled enough by Jones's response to articulate an explanation of topical verse that is worth quoting at length.

Come on, back off. I'm not no fucking counter-anything. I'm as truly gassed as anyone, but much more embarrassed than others, at the poor prospect of fellow poets singing the praises of any thing so venal as a

17. The manuscript of this poem, which is undated, was apparently sent by Dorn to Jones in late September or early October 1961; it is now in the UCLA Library.

18. Dorn to Jones, 21 September 1961 (UCLA Library).

19. LeRoi Jones, "Cuba Libre," *Evergreen Review* 4 (November-December 1960): 139–59.

20. Jones to Dorn, October 1961, in the Lilly Library, Indiana University; the letter can be dated to the week following October 14 because of a reference to the death of Maya Deren.

State. I am afraid I am not very interested in the "argument" aspects of a statement like the Herrara poem. It wasn't written "against" anything, and . . . aesthetics . . . aside, you ought to know the very word Batista makes me puke. . . . I don't see the thing as "rational" at all, and perhaps you'd stick to the view that that's the trouble. Whatever the Cuban people are doing, God blesses them, and for however long they can make it. A statement in a poem such as I sent you is highly accidental, in the same way junk gathering sculpture is, and gratifying accidents are a really bigger part of the West than that aestheticism [?] you mention. If I had seen a picture of a Pre-Castro victim of the same system of organized horseshit, approximately the same thing wld have come out. This is one of the famous limitations of occasional writing. Its alignments are like the ligaments of a starved man, very clear.[21]

Dorn's response to the Herrara story was not political, he thought; his poem was an expression of sentiment, not ideology. He believed that he could easily write around the ideological encampments that are usually the governing forces, rhetorically and thematically, in political poetry; for him, ideological differences were "accidental" rather than essential. He could meditate on her photo as freely as he had meditated on gravestones in his earlier elegy.

The only point I ever had is that when a picture, namely of Mrs. Herrara Marcos, is printed, showing her puckered up babyface tears, brought forth by the lunatic braggart announcement of her death, it is a matter of *public shame*. *Sides*, are a bigassed drag. The biggest small-talk of all, like which one are you on? motherfucker. I think I know what kind of a stupid, scared, caught woman she was. But whatever she did, or what those who murdered her did, or their "reasons," my limited prospect of the thing is completely correct. And satisfying for everyone. Because there is no embarrassment in sympathy. Aside from the fact that "sympathizers" are always assholes.

Despite the title of this poem, Dorn had intended to write another elegy, not a polemic, not a discursive explanation of a political event. Jones seemed partly to have confused the genre of the Herrara poem, though he would not easily allow Dorn the propriety of an elegy on Dr. Marcos. He answered Dorn with backhanded apologies for the offense:

If my letter re your poem sounded crusadery and contentious I'm sorry. But I have gone deep, and gotten caught with images of the world, that exists, or that will be here even after WE go. I have not the exquisite objectivity of circumstance. Only we, on this earth, can talk of material existence as just another philosophical problem. . . . "Moral earnestness" (if there be such a thing) ought [to] be transformed into action. (You name it.) I know we can think that to write a poem, and be Aristotle's God is sufficient. But I can't sleep. And I do not believe in all this relative shit. There is a right and a wrong. A good and a bad. And it's up to me, you, all of the so called minds, to find out. It is only knowledge of things that will bring this "moral earnestness."[22]

Jones's apology was half-hearted, but Dorn's faith in Jones's defenses was not long-lasting anyway. For another year after this exchange, Dorn seemed to proceed with greater regard for particular situations than for the classes of events that anatomize ideologies. He has been highly praised for this sort of self-restraint. Donald Davie, in a discussion of Dorn's novel, *The Rites of Passage*, said,

What validates Dorn's lyric voice is, time and again, its humility, the instruction it looks for and gets from people and places and happenings. It reflects upon them, it moralizes on them; but the reflection and the moral are drawn not from some previously accumulated stock of wisdom, but (so the writing persuades us) immediately out of the shock of confronting each of them as it comes, unpredictably.[23]

In political terms a "stock of wisdom" is an ideology; occasional poetry, in Dorn's understanding, challenges ideological

22. Jones to Dorn, [14–21] October 1961 (Lilly Library).

23. Donald Davie, review of Edward Dorn, *The Rites of Passage*, in *Wivenhoe Park Review*, no. 1 (Winter 1965): 116.

certainties by pitting contingent events against the categories commonly used to hold political history in order. A more successful example of this technique than the Herrara "Address" is a poem Jones in fact wanted to publish in *Floating Bear*, "On the Debt My Mother Owed to Sears Roebuck" (1962).[24] After two strophes describing how his parents trudged their uneventful way on Sears's revolving track of debt, Dorn turns against his own conclusions:

> On the debt my mother owed to sears roebuck?
> I have nothing to say, it gave me clothes to
> wear to school,
> and my mother brooded
> in the rooms of the house, the kitchen, waiting
> for the men she knew, her husband, her son
> from work, from school, from the air of locusts
> and dust masking the hedges of fields she knew
> in her eye as a vague land where she lived,
> boundaries, whose tractors chugged pulling harrows
> pulling discs, pulling great yields from the earth
> pulse for the armies in two hemispheres, 1943
> and she was part of that *stay at home army* to keep
> things going, owing that debt.
>
> (CP 46–47)

It was easy enough in the first two strophes to suggest that Sears's promotion nibbled away at his mother's life the way mice nibbled at the corn in the crib, that Sears stripped his parents' dry, melancholy lives the way locusts stripped the rows of corn—too easy, too pat; the mind curls up to sleep in those metaphors. In this last strophe Dorn catches himself with the reminder that indirectly that debt helped him get to school, helped his family continue working their Illinois farm, even helped supply the allies in Europe and the Pacific, and helped strengthen the American economy. Dorn wants to redeem even

24. Jones to Dorn, undated (Lilly Library).

the tritest claims of the Sears catalogue ("clothes to wear to school") and the portentous propaganda of the war administration ("pulling great yields from the earth / pulse for the armies," "that *stay at home army*"). This reminder takes nothing away from the first two strophes, but these indirect consequences of the debt are also part of the story. Finally, he lets these two sides of the story sit together, neither trouncing the other; Dorn will not subordinate either side.

By 1965, however, it was more difficult to see signs in Dorn's work of that sort of humility, for a number of his most engaging poems were then Juvenalian diatribes. Jones seems finally to have made his point convincingly. Yet Davie's explanation of Dorn's method still holds, even for such opinionated poems as "The Problem of the Poem for My Daughter, Left Unsolved." The poem opens with a description of a surgical scar on Dorn's daughter's neck:

```
10      a thin line red with its own distinction
        some goiter
        of what she has been made to understand is civilization
        not the brand of the adventurous cutlass

        The misery is superficial now.
15      I have dwelt on that quality in other poems
        without attention to the obvious
        drain
              of social definition
        the oblivious process
        of a brutal economic calculus, where to
                                        place the dark hair
        save above moist eyes
                            (CP 93)
```

One of Dorn's points here is that as human misery has been lessened, made "superficial," so the explanation of why misery exists at all has been obscured. When suffering was profound, it was endured by classes; misery defined the social structure responsible for much suffering. Now suffering is superficial and cuts across what remains of the class structure. What has been lost is clarity and access to understanding. Dorn's method struggles against that loss. He skips back and forth in this poem between his daughter's misery, her literally "superficial" suffering of this scar on her neck, and the diffuse misery of Americans who are incapable of deep suffering, incapable of genuine culture (e.g., lines 13–14, 20–21); the poem might be entitled "On the Absence of True Culture."

Dorn's ease in moving from his daughter to Americans in general makes the poem seem wayward, but a serious point is implicitly registered by this method. The ways in which an individual owes his or her identity to the overall social structure ought to be at once too obvious and too all-embracing to mention; such links between the individual and the society should be taken for granted. For the purposes of this poem, his daughter is one of the American Women:

> the women are
> set loose to walk spiritless
> their marks are deep cuts on the neck, moist eyes, sagging nylons
> eyes painted to dry everything, loose figures of despair
> or hard flesh prolonged by injections and tucks into an isolated
> youngness
> a manufactured Galateability
> The end
> of applied genetics will be
> the elimination of freely disposed
> intellection, via the rule
> that a science is oriented toward
> Use, some predictable
> breed, is the end
> (Automation ends with a moral proposition, THE LESSON of
> one maximum factor of it
> will suggest all the correspondences . . .

(CP 96)

She is a member of a class identifiable by "an isolated young-ness" and "a manufactured Galateability."

Stiff phrasing is typical of Dorn's manner, in both his verse and prose; he characteristically insists on abstractness, especially where it might be resisted. For example, here is a descriptive paragraph from a short story, "A Narrative with Scattered Nouns," about a wiener roast:

> Plum Island became one of our favorite haunts. The lightness of its air, the fairness of its granulation and the extreme openness to the seas who run home there. The lightness of its air. That is the way it is aspected. There is not a great amount of driftwood. What driftwood there is scattered near the sea grass is of a compelling nature. Its surface is possessed of a mild satin glow, an encircling gestalt which seems independent of stock solar light. It is otherwise farctate.
>
> (*SB* 1–2)

Dorn regards description as "mind killing" (*SB* 6). He prefers to translate qualities into abstract substances: "lightness," "fairness," "openness." In this manner, he will go a long, clumsy way to sound formal, antiseptic ("aspected," "farctate"). Of course, the tongue is in his cheek; he is toying with the corruptions of academic prose, especially as they are, one might say, manifest in the pretensions of college freshmen whose desire to sound authoritatively intellectual exposes some of the shabbier conventions of academic discourse. Clarity and concision, the mass-dispensed antidotes for freshmen, are not held in Dorn's esteem; they are the muses of those who wish simply to "understand."

> Understanding, of course, is not the point. It is that you are not dancing with them, not chanting Tiwa with them. Which is much more important. Understanding is a device used to separate us.[25]

For Dorn, exploration and judgment are the proper goals of

25. Edward Dorn, "Beauty," in *The Moderns*, ed. LeRoi Jones (New York: Corinth, 1963), p. 66.

intellectual activity. Paradoxically, stony dogmatism is intended as a means of exploration. Courtesy, fair-mindedness, and comprehensiveness are some of the inhibiting virtues of intellectuals; those who are obviously coarse, rude, opinionated, and biased are not, by the academic code, on the human road to truth. Dorn claims that just these inhibitions keep intellectuals from a penetrating explanation of contemporary politics.

> There is always that compromising point beyond which you aren't allowed to go and beyond which there would lie the fullest explanation of a people [such as Native Americans] who have been so wholly maligned by crimes of omission. . . . If you are an artist you have to live with your art, which is on every level total.
>
> (SH 77)

That Black Mountain high seriousness about art suggests why, in *Slinger*, the Poet plays an Abso Lute. A poet can deliberately violate canons of fair-mindedness in order to push explanation beyond certain inhibiting barriers—that is his act of exploration. Stubborn opinionatedness and even name-calling are, in Dorn's work, the consequences not of crystallized conclusions but of the technology of fantasy.

> More and more people are writing political poetry, and it's not politics they're writing, at all, it's a fantasy of certain things. It doesn't name, the way poetry in the past has named actual names or substituted names that were well known, for actual names. It isn't that kind of thing that I think is possible today, because, frankly, politics is carried on by literal men—so it's a schoolboy's interest. . . . But the fantasy of politics, in terms of poetry, and the images and the ghosts of that kind of thing are very valuable in terms of the writing and getting of poetry further on a footing of meaning for a large mass of people. . . . For one thing, I don't know a thing about politics, and I think that gives me the greatest right in the world to be a zealot about it.
>
> (I 5–6)

Dorn's rough vulgarity is meant to be playful where others are serious, for play may generate possibilities that would otherwise remain locked behind the polite, conventional barriers to exploration. Rudeness is Dorn's version of literary frontierism: "The whole world of exploration where the object was not discovery but living in and playing with the great brutal elements of earth."[26] To stay within the bounds of polite discourse is stultifying: "The enclosure of the land / leads directly to / the enclosure of the mind."[27]

Dorn's discursiveness, his wandering in the pursuit of explanation, like Olson's, is an attempt to bring into poetry a frontier methodology. The poetry Dorn values displays "freely disposed / intellection"; it is not satisfied, despite its didactic ambition, "with a moral proposition, THE LESSON of / one maximum factor." Instead, his generalizations, his conclusions, seem to be happened upon, casual; they crop up in the midst of his poetry and prose.[28] Dorn once expressed admiration of Jones's ability to get "surplus verities" in his writing;[29] likewise Jones, after reading *Idaho Out*, wrote to Dorn, "That *discursiveness* I envy you so much for. . . ."[30] Despite their disagreements in 1961, in 1965 it was clear that these poets agreed that a writer deals in explanations—not reasonable but compelling ones.

That a poet's explanations might well be unreasonable is a proposition approved all too commonly now, with too little measure of what is given up with that assent. If it is proper, as I

26. In Jones, *The Moderns*, p. 56. As early as February 1961 Dorn knew that his writing was to take this rough turn: "It interests me . . . to make a political statement as hot as I can. . . . I think probably I'll also get over a fear of being vulgar and rough about it. I hope so, because I think that might be beautiful too, and it's time for it, it seems to me" (*I* 3–4).

27. Edward Dorn, "The Day Report," *Caterpillar*, no. 15/16 (April-June 1971): 186.

28. For one small example of how Dorn likes to come across general laws, see his description of Ramona's car in *By the Sound* (Mount Vernon, Wash.: Frontier Press, 1971), p. 18.

29. Dorn to Jones, 12 October 1961[?] (UCLA Library).

30. Jones to Dorn, undated (Lilly Library).

think it is, to ask of the very best political poets (Marvell would be a standard, but Robert Lowell would serve too) that they offer guidance on particular political issues, that they be of abiding help in the determination of political policy (that we ask of political poetry at least as much as we do of political prose), then the poetic program that Dorn outlines should lead to a lesser order of political poetry. Dorn is didactic the way satirists often are. He tries to be fresh, unpredictable, severe— not wise, or even right. He cannot be a faithful guide to the nation's political career, but a stunning maverick has his uses too. If we ask of political poetry only that it be surprising, opinionated, extreme, we would sell poetry short indeed, because along with such a notion goes the belief that prose, not poetry, bears the greatest intelligence and utility in regard to our collective public life. Yet satire is that one form of didactic writing that we go to mainly for vivacity. *The Dunciad*, not the *Essay on Man*, has that. Dorn's aspirations might best be measured, as Donald Wesling suggests, against the Augustan satiric tradition. Unlike Olson, he is more an ironist than an explainer; that, I think, means that he is by design a more modest poet.

■ 3 ■

By 1967, when the first *Gunslinger* passage appeared, Dorn had determined that the most compelling explanations were, as he had said six years earlier, "a fantasy of certain things." In the late sixties he moved from the audacious political "explanations" of poems like "The Problem of the Poem for My Daughter" and "Inauguration Poem #2" to the less didactic but still outrageous mode of explicit fantasy. Yet aside from such abstract continuity, when the first book of *Gunslinger* appeared in 1968 it was clear that Dorn's writing had taken a sharp turn. *Gunslinger* was unpredictable; it owed little to Dorn's earlier manner and nothing at all to the prevailing poetic styles of the late sixties. Dorn's major effort looked like a kind of stunning mutant.

Like so many of this century's long poems, *Slinger* (as the completed poem is called) is one more quest poem, but this quest has less to do with recovery than with genesis. Gunslinger's quest is literally genetic; he goes in search of mutations. His weapon is the dreaded .44:

> Look, into each chamber
> goes one bit of my repertoire
> of pure information,
> into each gesture, what
> you call in your innocence
> "the draw"
> goes Some Dark Combination
>                    (*S* 37)

He seems to be shy two chromosomes, but his mount carries that pair. Lil recollects her first encounter with Claude the talking horse:

> *he had the texan's hat on*
> *a stetson XX sorta cockwise*
> *on his head it was*
> *I tell you Slinger you would of*
> *split your levis and dropped your*
> *beads to seen it.*
>                    (*S* 13)

Claude's hat sits "cockwise" for a reason: he bears a mangled pair.[31] "I" inquires about the horse's name, "Claude Lévi-Strauss is that— / Yes, you guessed it / a homonym" (*S* 36). Actually, two homonyms are crossed with a pun: Clawed Lévi-Strauss→clawed jeans→clawed genes. Slinger's quest is to get

---

31. The fact that the Horse bears the "XX" pair helps explain why he is once (*S* 5) referred to as a mare; part of the mangling of his genes is that he carries the female chromosomes, whereas he ought to have the XY pair.

beyond the mangling of genes—of memory ("The Horse is a wringer for memory" [S 119])—that was accomplished in the past. He seeks a change predicated on nothing in the past—a mutation.

Doctor Jean Flamboyant (flamboyant gene, of course) presents himself as the all-promising mutant—"I can fix anything" (S 81)—but there is the depressing possibility that all mutations, all unpredictable changes have occurred in the past, that evolution is obsolete; this is why the "Anti-Darwinian" Mogollones pose so serious a threat (S 183), and why too Doctor Jean Flamboyant may be confined to "Beenville" (S 135–37). Slinger describes his dispute with Howard Hughes as a genetic duel between cattlemen (S 6–7), though more than steer are involved. Howard Hughes, Dorn has said, "is a rather pure metaphor of a kind of primitive, entrepreneurial capitalist take of what America is, which is still embedded in the political and social instincts of a lot of American activity. He's a great singular—in a strange way like a dinosaur, but nevertheless his lineage goes back to the seventies and eighties of the last century and I do see him as an extension of the earlier, nonelectronic, financial geniuses like Fisk and Gould" (I 51). As Robart, he represents the internalization of capitalism, "the psychological condition of the United States of America" (I 31). The race of poets is endangered by Robart (read *rob art*, a scrambled antithesis to "trobar" [S 61–62]), and even horses may not make it (S 64). The signs say that Western man's "Imprudential Behavior" (S 133) is catching up with him.

> The divisions of hunger
>    shut behind their Doors
> Pinned down by their Stars
> Kept going by their Rotors
> Waked up by their Alarms
> Attended by a Prose
>    which says how Dead they are

> Frozen by a Brine
>    which keeps them from Stinking
>    It looks to me Jack
>    like The Whole Set is Sinking
> And theyre still talkin œcology
>    Without even Blinking
>
> Ah Men, saith the Horse
>
> (*S* 121)

The media ("Stars"), industrial technology ("Rotors"), the scheduled bourgeois routine ("Alarms"), marked by "the inertia of National Lunch" (*S* 78), the compliant literature ("Prose"), and even underarm deodorant ("Brine") collaborate to enforce the distribution of income and resources ("divisions of hunger") that will bring the race to its garrulous end. Universe City "looks like a rundown movie lot / a population waiting around to become / White Extras" (*S* 70).

The solution envisioned, and finally achieved, is suggested by some apostrophic lines of the Poet's song, *Cool Liquid Comes*:

> oh people of the coming stage
> . . . . . . . . . . . . . . . . . . . .
> Oh temptation of survival
> oh lusterless hope
> of victory in opposites
>
> (*S* 51)

The "coming stage" is the approaching stagecoach bearing the poem's characters, but it also refers to the people of the future. Some small hope for the genetic survival of people rests on the possibility of a cosmic reversal of direction, a "victory in opposites." The prevailing program, Robart's design, is set to the principle of "Auto-destruction" (*S* 19). To turn a single individual around is easy enough to be managed at the beginning of Book II:

I is dead, the poet said.
. . . . . . . . . . . . . . . . . . . . . . .
Having plowed the ground
I has turned at the end of the row
a truly inherent *versus*
.daeha sa kcab emas eht si I ecnis
                    (*S* 56)

LSD, which the troupe takes at the opening of Book II (to the accompaniment of *Cool Liquid Comes* [*S* 50–51]), can alter human perception so as to bring to life all the objects of the world; that adjustment of "the perceptual index" is marked in the narrative by the filling of "I" 's body with Kool Everything's five-gallon batch of LSD:

What then, if we make I
a receptacle of what
Everything has,
our gain will be twofold,
we will have the thing
we wish to keep
as the container of the solution
we wish to hold
a gauge in other words
in the form of man.
                    (*S* 60–61)

The larger task is the reversal of the "cultural collective" (*S* 148), and that, Slinger says, is the Poet's job:

Turn the Great Cycle of the Enchanted Wallet
of Robart the Valfather of this race
turn the Cycle of Acquisition
inside the Cobalt Heads of these
otherwise lumpish listeners and make
their azured senses warm Make your norm
their own
                    (*S* 89)

Robart, or Howard Hughes, drives the cycle of acquisition through the heads of the citizenry; a mock Lenin, "riding backward" (S 148) in a sealed train to Las Vegas, he is ultimately turned around ("red-shifted"—deflected from this solar system) by his products, the Mogollones and the Single-Spacers, battling each other for supremacy in the mock-epic style of an STP television commercial. The cosmic reversal that resolves the genetic duel at the poem's conclusion (S 198) follows from a search for opposition. The Mogollones "got no vices / of course they got no virtues either" (S 183), and "the Single Spacers are Anythingarians / Ie, opposed to nothing" (S 184). (Like all the turning points in the poem, the resolution of this battle comes suddenly and inexplicably; there is aptly little causation behind the junctures of the narrative.) Robart's way is to eliminate contraries, to homogenize. His train gives out

> The scream of the Accomplished Present
> A conglomerate of Ends, The scream of Parallels
> All tied down with spikes These are the spines
> Of the cold citizens made to run wheels upon
>
> Parallels are just two things
> going to the same place that's a bore
> (S 97)

Against that steely cultural order, Dorn constructs a poem hungry for contradiction, especially on the level of style. The most obvious feature of this negative method is the pun, which generates signification out of not-meaning. The cleverest word play effectively seals the poem off as more a language game than a narrative. For instance, this is a quick, casual exchange between "I" and Claude the talking horse:

> Are you trying
> to "describe" me, boy?
> No, no, I hastened to add.
> And by the way boy

> if there's any addin
> to do around here
> *I'll* do it, that's my stick
> comprende?
>
> (*S* 25)

Aside from the wonderful joke on "add," these lines succeed in subordinating the plot to the narration, the action to the language. Normally, the language of narration is subsequent to the events of the plot—first the events, then the telling of them. Yet in this poem the characters themselves are pronouns ("I") and puns (Claude Lévi-Strauss and Jean Flamboyant), and they respond to the narrator's language ("I hastened to add") as readily as to the actions of other characters; neither the plot nor the characters claim priority over the language of narration. For the poem is really seeking the unsystematic possibilities for meaning that inhere in language: "I'm trying to grasp what the words *can* mean" (*I* 47). Narrative poems are customarily committed to an action, often a realistic one; their language is meant to seem referential. In such poems, what the language *does* mean is confined in part by criteria of plausibility and consistency of character. All realistic possibility, in *Slinger*'s world, is controlled by Robart, and consistency is part of his technology. Dorn is looking for the unpredictable possibilities in language—the mutant puns; hence referentiality is a constraint that "I"—the "referee" (*S* 23)—must get rid of (*S* 32). As a system of connections and homologous structures, language is the métier of the poem; once Robart's death grip on political activity was firm, language became the only promising arena. "*The* Art of poetry will choose to be born by the agent of the greatest syntactical density in the language, which we naturally call the world. And there is no other responsible definition of *the world*" (*V* 121). Alternative conceptions of the world do not respond to desire, to the human sense of possibility, which keeps even Robart's city, Las Vegas, going night and day.

Dorn makes the language of this poem turn in on itself, rejecting obligations to ordinary signification. On its verbal surface, the poem is a web-like system of interconnections. Sometimes one phrase will clown about an earlier formulation, the way "I"'s description of the horse as "lathered . . . with abstract fatigue" (S 8) casts an arched eye back on Gunslinger's remark that his "mare lathers with tedium" (S 5). The point is not just that statements hook up to each other but rather that their connections are made on some verbal ground—here, that abstracting figure, personification. The words have lives of their own; they can squirm free of a speaker's grip without warning. Metaphors refuse to stand still; they slyly, unpredictably insinuate themselves from the figurative to the literal level. Lil, impressed by the Horse's large joints, refers to them in passing as telescopes (S 23); a few pages later the narrator seems not to have noticed that she was speaking only figuratively:

> Umm, considered the Gunslinger
> taking the telescope
> from the Turned On Horse.
>
> (S 29)

Not that the narrator is obtuse; literalizing is a convention of the poem, part of the *Slinger* manner. That convention prevails nicely over puns. Gunslinger refers to his adversary, a "plain, unassorted white citizen," as "this Stockholder" (S 27), which is literally correct because the citizen is holding the stock of a gun. Lil then identifies the citizen as an "investor" (S 28). The words of the poem play havoc with the conventions of narrative, character, plot; those greedy signs steal the whole show. Kool Everything responds even to the narrator's dead metaphors:

> Would you like a light
> I see yor roach has gone out
> continued the Doctor Catching his breath

> Slinger, did you flash how
> the PHD caught his breath,
> never saw anybody do it with their *hand*
>
> Yes agreed the Slinger, Brilliantly fast
> (*S* 81)

High praise from a gunslinger.

Dorn wants possibility, "what the words can mean," to urge the poem on. Dead metaphors spring, one might say, to life, and hidden ones reveal themselves in the poem. Once the horses pulling the coach have been referred to as "driverless" (*S* 67), calling them "autocephalous" (*S* 161) seems to come naturally. The middle step in this literalizing process, the colloquial phrase that a driverless horse "has its own head," hardly needs to be stipulated; part of the fun of the poem is that such middle steps are typically elided. This process of literalization, kept going by puns and metaphors—live, dead, and merely implied—gathers enough momentum to absorb even what appear to be typographical errors. "An Idle Visitation" (1967), the short poem that gave birth to *Gunslinger*, now, revised, stands as the opening of the book. In this poem and in the first edition of Book I, Howard Hughes rents the second floor of "a hotel" in Boston; in *Slinger*, however, his domain is "ahotel" (*S* 6). It seems that a copyist's error appealed to Dorn's imagination: in *The Cycle* (1971) Robart occupies "the blank hotel"—an apt abode for this phantom.

The systemic properties of language may assert themselves at any point, turning the narrative from action to grammar. Discussion of the object of Doctor Jean Flamboyant's dissertation, *The Tensile Strength of Last Winters Icicles*, slips easily into a grammarian's colloquy on the third-person pronoun "it," which does not change form when it is shifted from the nominative to the accusative or dative case (*S* 82). The best example of this grammatical bent comes in the last book:

Uh, I'm not sure I get your question Lil
the Horse exhaled, but
are you speaking of the need for horsepower?

*Yes, I suppose I am, In Horses!*

How would you like poco coito, Lil?
Claude asked suddenly

*My virtue is not presently on the market, fella*
Lil glared, *which is bad timing of course*
*because I might be amused*
*to make it with a horse.*

Make *It*, Claude frownd
*It* aint nothin but a neuter pronoun.

(*S* 170)

The Horse turns the talk from flesh to grammar here, because
he has taken offense, as though Lil had called a stud a gelding.
One of Elizabeth Sewell's remarks about nonsense literature
provides a nice hold on the conventions of *Slinger*: "In Nonsense all the world is paper and all the seas are ink."[32] Dorn
often acknowledges his lineage from Lewis Carroll. The Gunslinger wears a Queen of Hearts on his gauntlet (*S* 4), and his
only song is a nonsense verse that specifically recalls a remark
by Alice.[33] "I," the naïf, is capable of sounding as confused and
apologetic as Alice ("No . . . I mean I've never / seen his wife"
[*S* 35]), and there are particular passages in Carroll that could
have been models for this poem:

"What do you mean by that?" said the Caterpillar, sternly. "Explain
yourself!"

32. Elizabeth Sewell, *The Field of Nonsense* (London: Chatto and Windus,
1952), p. 17.
33. Gunslinger's phrase "the name of the name of her feet" (*S* 14) alludes
to Alice's fantasy of sending presents to her feet—"Alice's Right Foot, esq.";
Lewis Carroll, *Alice's Adventures in Wonderland*, in *The Annotated Alice*, ed.
Martin Gardner (New York: Clarkson N. Potter, 1960), p. 36.

"I can't explain *myself*, I'm afraid, Sir," said Alice, "because I'm not myself, you see."

"I don't see," said the Caterpillar.[34]

Carroll would have been a useful model because he too was after conversions, "REVERSE SENSE," as "I" puts it (*S* 140); in the world of language, though not of men, the poet has the leverage to turn things upside down. From his new domain, as Secretary to Parmenides, "I" sees the poem as an "ABSOLUTE LINGUATILT" (*S* 141). The words of the poem tilt in several directions: toward the scientists with offerings like "azimuthal" (*S* 58), "presyntactic metalinguistic urgency" (*S* 73), "organic radicals" (*S* 90), "epactos" (*S* 110), and "monotremata" (*S* 184); toward the hallowed past with such archaic formulations as "where will you now" (*S* 6) and "What meanst thou?" (*S* 171); and those tilts become formal bows with such contrivances as "a bed / will be my desire" (*S* 5). Yet the most severe inclination of Dorn's manner is colloquial. "I"'s night letter notes that "COLLOQUIAL LOCKS HOLD AGAINST ANY METHOD APPLIED OUTSIDE TIME . . ." (*S* 141); Robart's mentality depends on the illusion that the present cultural order is timeless (one of his slogans—a nicely reversible one—is "EMIT NO TIME" [*S* 104]). *Slinger* is a hodgepodge of allusions: to Shakespeare and Keats, for example, but also to Grateful Dead song lyrics and Kay Kaiser's Musical Question. Almost any source may supply a phrase, any idiom may serve for a line or two. The *Slinger* manner is as absorbent as it is distinctive. Dorn has always been a mannered writer; the *Slinger* manner, however, is so peculiar a way of talking that Dorn can encompass competing idioms without endangering the coherence of his voice. In fact, the coherence of the poem rests more on that manner than on the plot or thematic structure.

34. Ibid., p. 67.

Although the conventions of *Slinger* are taken over largely from nonsense literature (and Dorn's manner is above all jokey)[35] the ultimate seriousness of *Slinger* should not be in question; Lewis Carroll is one acknowledged master, but Parmenides is another. From the poet-philosopher Dorn takes details such as the topos of the driverless horses, yet he also pursues Parmenides' ontological claim "that it *is* and cannot not-be."[36] In *Slinger* the dimensions of being, of what is, are plotted around a series of antitheses: language versus being, meaning versus being, thinking versus being. Discourse *about* that which exists, like description, is deadly: "We'd all rather *be* there / than talk about it" (*S* 24). Language clumsily gropes after being, and meaning mongers woodenly try to tug loose a lesson from being:

> What does the foregoing mean?
> I asked. Mean?
> My Gunslinger laughed
> *Mean*?
> Questioner, you got some strange
> obsessions, you want to know
> what something *means* after you've
> seen it, after you've *been* there
> or were you *out* during
> That time? No.
> And you want some *reason*.
> How fast are you
> by the way?
>
> (*S* 28–29)

Dorn wants the poem to occupy "*the Very beginning of logic*" (*S* 23). Before logic, before language, is a field of experience

---

35. This is Donald Davie's point in "Ed Dorn and the Treasures of Comedy," *Vort*, no. 1 (1972), 24–35.

36. G. S. Kirk and J. E. Raven, *The Presocratic Philosophers: A Critical History with a Selection of Texts* (Cambridge: Cambridge University Press, 1966), p. 269.

fresh enough to generate mutant psyches. "Oh, yea, man I *never thot* I'd see this place. / Then you'll have the privilege of seeing it / without having thot it, prompted the Slinger" (*S* 65). That is the proper structure of mental activity: first perception, then conception; the more common, reverse procedure—"*askin so many questions / his eyes had already answered*" (*S* 57)—is simply preposterous, because it presumes that sense experience is directed toward knowable ends.

Gunslinger sets himself against the teleological motive of experience, and he claims the sanction of Olson's Maximus:

> When the act is
> so self contained
> and so dazzling in itself
> the target then
> can disappear
> in the heated tension
> which is an area between here
> and formerly
> In some parts of the western world
> men have mistakenly
> called that phenomenology—
> (*S* 30–31)

Such worthy acts come to transcend the ends they were intended to serve, and the "conglomerate of Ends" (*S* 97) ordinarily envisaged is just what Gunslinger and his companions plan to avoid.[37] Gunslinger means to challenge readers to "inhabit themselves" and "occupie their instant" (*S* 93); put simply, the test is whether one is satisfied to be oneself, without straining after distant goals.

> There is your domain.
> Is it the domicile it looks to be

37. Dorn is alluding to Olson's discussion of "self-acts": "these things / which don't carry their end any further than / their reality in / themselves"; Charles Olson, *The Maximus Poems* (New York: Jargon/Corinth, 1960), p. 42.

or simply a retinal block
of seats in,
he will flip the phrase
the theater of impatience.

    If it is where you are,
the footstep in the flat above
in a foreign land
or any shimmer the city
sends you
the prompt sounds
of a metropolitan nearness
he will unroll the map of locations.

        (S 3–4)

The choice is between two sorts of consciousness: one, "the theater of impatience," is a phantom consciousness tuned to the "perceptual index" of television; this is Robart's mentality, and his lack of being is indicated by the fact that "He aint never bin seen!" (S 93). The alternative is to make of one's consciousness a "domain" or "domicile" where one can truly be present. Gunslinger's "map of locations," his quest, can be of use only to those who seek such presence. The wittiest expression of Dorn's skepticism about motives and ends is the "*Literate Projector,* / which, when a 35 mm strip is put thru it / turns it into a Script / *Instantaneously!* / and projects that—the finished script / onto the white virgin screen" (S 76). This parodic contraption disassembles the apparatus of causation:

Yea,
it will Invent a whole new literachure
which was Already There
a lot of big novels will get restored
in fact Everything, uh, I mean
*all of it* can be run the other way—
some of the technikalities
havent been worked out for documentaries
but let's face it,

you could rerun I mean all of it
¡atención!—Shoot a volcano, project it
and See the Idea behind it
sit down at the geologic conference
and hear the reasons Why
skip the rumble, move into the inference.
Eventually you could work your way back
to where it's still really dark
all the way back of the Brain?!

(S 76–77)

In the dark area, prior to all intentions, mental mutants lurk.
Dorn hopes that *Slinger*'s puns, paradoxes, palindromes, and
gags lead there, for that way lies beyond description.

■ 4 ■

Dorn now has behind him one of the most remarkable long
poems of the last thirty years. For a poet who is not yet ready to
stop writing, that can be a difficult position: witness how few
long poems are brought to conclusion by middle-aged writers.
Perhaps Dorn is uncomfortable, yet among his contemporaries,
no one is more adept at beginnings. His eye for contingent
events is too sharp ever to allow him the resting-spot of a
comprehensive achieved vision. That attention to circumstance
makes him a hard poet to second-guess—which is an odd thing
to say of one whose principal concerns are political. Political
poets, we tend to think, are programmatic, predictable—*if* they
are sincere; a political poet who publicly changes his mind
(Dryden, say) is suspect. Dorn has not shifted allegiances; allegiances have never been his concern. His political poetry either
focuses elegiacally on individuals, such as Dr. Herrara, Cleve-
land Thompson, Bigbear, and Reeta Poonee, or improvises
general propositions to account for the behavior of social
groups. His topics are either poignantly human or impersonal

and abstract; the middle ground of political parties and factions, or of consistent application of policy, lies barren for him.[38]

> what is unmistakable is
> that DeGaulle,
> Ho Chi Minn, Chou en-Lai,
> LeRoi Jones, Dean Rusk
> are all doing the same bit:
> pressing
> and they are
> all correct—it is their thing
> against anybody else's
> (there is no longer
> any *cause*, the fastest
> with the mostest is the rule
> (*CP* 209–10)

Dorn's analytical cool can generate new groupings, but they are not directly political. There is nothing unusual about recent poets rising above ordinary political categories; rather rarely do they commit their writing to a politically working "side." This aloofness implies a generation's residual doubt about political poetry, as though to take sides (as Dryden did) were inappropriate, as though poetry can accommodate politics only on the level of abstraction above particular factions. However voguish political poetry has been in the last fifteen years (Dorn has been at it longer, of course), it has typically been a spectator art; Lowell's *History* is the grandest work of this political watching. Even Dorn, whose poetry is more intelligently political and more sensitive to wide complicity than that of almost any of his American contemporaries, has not written as a political participant, as a citizen. This general limitation

38. For a good discussion of Dorn as a political poet, see Donald Wesling, "A Bibliography on Edward Dorn for America," *Parnassus* 5 (Spring-Summer 1977): 142–60.

may well descend from the Victorian sense—certainly not
shared by Dorn—that the "worlds" of poetry and of politics
are essentially at odds. Dorn's didacticism, however, invokes
older sanctions that might seem capable of encouraging a more
human engagement of contemporary politics. Yet the danger of
taking Dorn too strictly as a didactic political poet should be
clear from my epigraph.

Dorn seems now less than ever a poet of ideas. Since *Slinger*
he has published two insistently small books, *Hello, La Jolla*
(1978) and *Yellow Lola* (1980). He is using epigrams to break
his narrative habits, but he remains committed to an acerbic,
brittle manner:

> A Pontificatory use of the art
> is both interesting & a lot of fun
> the pope's got a really good role
> (*YL* 31)

These books of sententiae are didactic for the fun of it, sarcastic
and cutting, it seems, out of conviction that the pleasure of
severe judgment is part of what poetry now needs. A poet, like
the pontiff, can exercise the authority that comes of judgment
almost at will, for his constituency is so vague as an institution
that it imposes no unnegotiable limits. Dorn roams like a tour-
ist through American mass culture, with allegiance to nothing
local, an eye for the strange, and the desire to get at the thinking
or feeling behind the strangeness commonly taken as normal.
Often he comes up with just a quick gag:

> 1 Billion Chinese are telling me
> the gang of 4 are wrong
> Doesn't this seem out of proportion?
> (*YL* 103)

But his China Watch scans along some oddly independent
angles:

> A protest against still another
> empty-minded choice
>
> I've acquired this political problem
> since I returned to North Beach
>
> Every day now, for a while,
> I've been handed a yellow piece of paper
> which tells me to normalize
> and just last week I saw
> a banner spanning Grant Street
> over in the China section
> which told me to *not* normalize
>
> I'm just a simple american*
> which means that I don't *object*
> to the normal, yet
> the *not* normal of course interests me more

> ————————
> *I.e., a fate-torn traveller.

(YL 97)

Normalization of U.S.-Chinese relations, recycling, Nadarism; Dorn goes to some trouble to goad his readers—mainly liberal, of course—into examining their pieties skeptically. His trick is to write in a manner than makes his readers feel like insiders, at the same time that their sacred cows are being rendered a little swinish.

In order to engage civic beliefs, Dorn keeps his poetry specific in its reference. Of course, much of his work has always been occasional, but now it is tendentiously so.

In Defense of Pure Poetry

> The guards can say what they want
> And so can Vernon and so can NBC
> But whatever it is they have to say
> Nobody can fault the King
> For squeezing the trigger on Robert Goulet.

(HLJ 30)

Than which, no verse is less pure. Elvis Presley, of course, was the king of rock 'n' roll. After his death, a number of stories, originating with his father, Vernon Presley, his bodyguards, and others, appeared in the papers about the king's quirks. One story had it that he was once so annoyed at watching Robert Goulet that he fired a pistol at the television set. Dorn's joke has to do with the pop culture's appetite for what seems suave: Goulet, Streisand, Barry Manilow. The programmatic point is that when such taste prevails, poets who try to write purely surrender one of the traditional (and now urgent) offices of their vocation—the correction of taste.

That correction, Dorn presumes, begins with attentiveness and ends in judgment, not emotion. Goulet, Streisand, and Manilow sell great swells of feeling to a culture that needs the lance.

The Word (20 January 1977)

Moved was a bit too classy
to be used to note an emotion
and I doubt that it occurred to him.
And who knows, it might
have seemed too Lowell-like
if it had crossed his mind

Sentimental, to be sure, cheap,
imported and ordinary
(YL 71)

January 20, 1977, was Gerald Ford's last day in office. *The New York Times* ran an article entitled "Farewells and Tears at the White House," but Dorn is referring, with outrageous specificity, to a remark by Henry Kissinger in an interview about his service as secretary of state: "Finally I was terribly moved when President Kaunda [of Angola] got up at the end of my [1976] Lusaka [Zambia] speech and embraced me. I thought that was a moving occasion." Dorn suggests that perhaps the interviewer, not Kissinger, came up with that claim to have been moved; Henry the world-shaker is more hard-nosed. For all of Lowell's interest in the ways of the powerful, Dorn doubts that he truly understood such people at all. Lowell, in Dorn's eyes, was the Goulet of poets: he was always presenting the powerful in terms of emotions that are reassuringly familiar. The powerful (even J. Edgar Hoover), Dorn believes, are stranger than they get credit for; they bear watching closely. That point is made, with these last two books, in sentences that are rawly polemical and topical—and usually amusing.

> Environmental carcinogens
> and large bowel cancer
> go together like marble steps
> and fancy dancers
> (YL 18)

"Go together like" is a formula made famous by Frank Sinatra ("Love and Marriage") in the 1955 television version of Thornton Wilder's *Our Town*. Dorn is a Juvenalian connoisseur of American mass culture.

Dorn shows rather little of Lowell's ambition. He has never attempted a *summa*, like *History*, and these last books suggest that he is unlikely to do so soon. The case for Dorn as a major poet may one day be strong; certainly his work cannot be adequately represented—as Eliot said that of a minor poet can be—by a small number of single poems. His accomplishment, however, will not be properly assessed if his engagement with ideas becomes the main measure. He himself has said expressly that his use of Heidegger and Lévi-Strauss is playful, light (*I* 50–51), and the categorical discriminations that count heavily for didactic poets—between honorable and pernicious behavior, say—double back on themselves and dissolve in *Slinger*.[39]

39. For an excellent discussion of how crucial categories in *Slinger* break down, see Michael Davidson's essay in this volume.

Judgment and understanding are not, for Dorn, ends in themselves; they are vehicles of wit, which is his true muse. In *Slinger*
and these last two books, Dorn has become something of a
notetaker: he watches the fantasies and distractions of American popular culture from the sidelines. He has been "covering"
the mass culture for the last decade—taking the role of com-
mentator, not teacher, surely not prophet. This is a modest
form of writing, always secondary, though his subject matter,
the mind and manners of the nation, is major indeed. His poems
are not particularly deep, nor wise, and few are moving (in a
pathetic sense), however unsettling they are. Above all, they are
spirited. And that, especially now, is a fine thing for poetry
to be.

# Internal Resistances:
# Edward Dorn on the American Indian

## PAUL DRESMAN

Edward Dorn's poems, essays, and fiction about the American Indian have a common theme: internal resistance. This phrase can be defined both in relation to the culture and history of the Indians themselves and in relation to the poet. For the Indians, internal resistance has found its historical expression in their opposition to conquest by the dominant white culture. This resistance, as described in the historical materials of Dorn's *The Shoshoneans* (1966) and in the sequence of poems in *Recollections of Gran Apachería* (1975), involved open warfare in the past century. Apart from such times of warfare, and after the close of the American frontier, this internal resistance has taken other forms that are also part of the history of the interaction of Indians and whites. In Dorn's view, this history reveals much of both the contemporary American Indian and the contemporary white American. Even the foreign policies of the United States government, Dorn argues, are prefigured by this internal resistance.

The gulf between the white and Indian cultures has amounted to the difference between a rising industrial power and scattered tribal groups, often nomadic, whose cosmologi-

cal ideas predate the birth of Western civilization. In the face of
these extremes, the survival of Indian culture itself becomes a
form of resistance. Dorn's portrayal of the resistant qualities of
Indian culture celebrates the Indians' difference from European
tradition particularly in terms of the ideas the two cultures have
of private property and of the role of the individual in a post-
tribal world. One form of internal resistance for the Indians is a
spiritualism that refuses to separate tribe, person, and land.
While this may be culturally expressed in many ways, one of
the possibilities Dorn recognizes is in the traditional song, especially that of the singer Willie Dorsey, whose chant is described in the opening pages of *The Shoshoneans*. The traditional song, as it reclaims a heritage for the Indian, can be seen
as a point of such extreme difference from the dominant white
culture as to become a form of resistance—arising from the
innermost being of the singer.

As Dorn says in an interview, one of the obligations of the
poet is to the divine (*I* 66). This obligation may be seen as a
point of resistance that the poet partly shares with his more
marginal Indian comrade. An obligation to the divine has a
quality of resistance in a materialist culture where religion is
often practiced as a social rather than a spiritual obligation.
Dorn defines the world of the poetic imagination as "what is
not evil," and therefore all external authority is suspect and
must be expiated (*I* 52). One means of expiation is through the
affiliation of civilized with primitive song.

Arguably, America's historical divergence from its European
culture-hearth has been predicated on its contact with Indians,
leading to a desire to validate an experience outside European
knowledge. European rationality does not account for the experience of figures like Cabeza de Vaca and others who were
changed by their contact with the Indians and with the American wilderness. Many of these figures, explorers and outlaws,

came to share with the Indians a status apart from the dominant culture. Dorn is attracted to such figures precisely because of the way their marginality implies a resistance to established authority. Even in Dorn's lifetime the outlaw, black, and Indian retain their privileged and paradoxical status.

However, Dorn understands the distance between the conquering culture and that of the Indians, and he does not share in the attempt by certain of his contemporaries to recreate Indian cultural expressions. He acknowledges the otherness that exists between the two cultures, a distance that equally exists between certain university-trained Indians and their own people. For Dorn, attempts to think and write as an Indian are doomed from the start—they are even condescending, given the history of oppression and cooptation. Dorn practices a recognition of difference rather than a romantic identification, then, even as he is sympathetic. This necessary qualification is consistent with Dorn's total approach, as discussed in the other essays in the present volume, which show Dorn's transcendental lyricism to be generally modified by a Swiftian commentary.

One of the earliest examples of Dorn's thought about the American Indian can be found in his essay on Charles Olson, "What I See in the Maximus Poems" (1960).[1] At the time he wrote this essay, Dorn was living in Santa Fe, New Mexico, and the place itself becomes a substantial part of his argument. The local Pueblo Indians are seen in their well-defined roles as purveyors of artifacts of the indigenous culture; their accommodation with the white culture is specifically contrasted to the resistance of a lone Navajo, who is screaming in the main plaza where Pueblo women conduct their business and are retrieved each evening by chiefs in pickup trucks. Even as it is irrational,

1. Edward Dorn, *What I See in the Maximus Poems* (Ventura, Ca.: Migrant Press, 1960). Also included in Donald Allen and Warren Tallman, eds., *The Poetics of the New American Poetry* (New York: Grove Press, 1973).

the Navajo's incoherent anger penetrates the illusion of accommodation and reveals the difference between apparent and actual reality in Santa Fe.

Expanding his argument from the city to the region, Dorn discusses the one author of the area for whom he has regard, Haniel Long. Speaking of Long as a "great minor writer" (whereas Olson would be major), Dorn refers to Long's most significant work: the recasting of Cabeza de Vaca's original letter to the king of Spain in the book *Interlinear to Cabeza de Vaca* (1936).[2] Describing the sixteenth-century conquistador's trek across North America, Long's version particularly emphasizes the spiritual breakthroughs of de Vaca and his companions. Stripped of civilization's forms and institutionalized roles and beliefs, the survivors become healers, medicine men, or shamans. They practice heresies such as faith healing, first as a matter of survival but later, if we follow Long's version, as a consequence of their spiritual awakening. Through their experience with tribal people and with the most primitive of environments (they are the first Europeans since the Ice Age to see bison), the intended quest for plunder and gold becomes transfigured as a realized quest for the spiritual self.[3] The experience is thus taken as an object lesson for what the civilized European might gain through contact with the primitive Indian and his world. Using Long's interpretation, Dorn portrays de Vaca as "a wandering Christ figure, who traversed the Southwest . . . and cured, cast lovely spells, who had long hair, was a man full

2. Haniel Long, *Interlinear to Cabeza de Vaca*. Originally published by Writers' Editions, 1936, the most recent available edition is: New York, Frontier Press, 1969. The original Spanish edition is *Naufragios* (Zamora, 1542). See Fanny Bandelier's 1905 translation (New York: A. S. Barnes).

3. De Vaca and his companions were perhaps prototypical of American experience. Upon this odyssey, there were the three Spaniards and a black, a Moor, Estevanico. Is there any previous record in world literature where the three races made significant contact, as occurred here—the Europeans, the Indians, and this lone African?

of grace and humility, a violent kind who talked too much, walked, was lonely, and had meaning and cognizance, was followed, there was an awe."[4]

Whether we are speaking of a search for mythical cities of gold or for the quite real wealth of later land acquisitions by the United States at the expense of the indigenous tribes, the Western European search for Cíbola can be seen as a quest to satisfy not only material needs but also a yearning for spiritual fulfillment. As crudely as this yearning might be portrayed or suggested by James Fenimore Cooper or throughout the dime novels of the later nineteenth century, it remains a force in the white American mind. Charles Olson invoked it in his dialectic of the primitive and the civilized; many modernists and postmodernists have also invoked the yearning for spiritual fulfillment through a union with the primitive—some scarcely understanding the implications. In the most unreflecting expressions of this seeking, the idea of spiritual union is conflated with cultural and material colonization. The actual history of white relations with the Indian therefore has to be recognized before the spiritual possibilities on this side of romantic aggrandizement can be considered. To his credit, Edward Dorn shows great care here and can, on occasion, be outspoken about the possibly extravagant and therefore limited quests:

> The blood does not flow from a red vein
> as Lawrence through Cooper had it,
> and it does not flow from a pale, beautiful
> white vein, as Wyndham Lewis had it, and it does not
> flow from a black vein as Malcolm X would
> have it, the blood does not flow at all.
> The land is stained, and it is true
> it is stained black, because black is active,
> red, the first color of that stain, before black

4. "What I See in *The Maximus Poems*," in Allen and Tallman, eds., *Poetics of the New American Poetry*, p. 298.

had washed out and sunk into the ground
and now comes up secret, inward, resistance
(*CP* 104)

The above passage comes from "Inauguration Poem #2," a poem on the occasion of Lyndon Johnson's inauguration and possibly numbered "2" in relation to Robert Frost's poem at John Kennedy's inauguration in 1960. Bearing more resemblance to a LeRoi Jones poem than to Frost's, "Inauguration Poem #2" is largely a diatribe. The second section of this poem speaks of a spirit in the Algonquian Indian religion, the Manitou: "a spirit or force underlying the world and life, understood as a nature spirit of both good and evil influence."[5] This combination of good and evil stands in distinction to the Western European religious tradition. In a parallel way, the rational premises of the United States government, and, by extension, its progressive tradition of expansion derived from Europe, are opposed in this poem by an assemblage of nonrational explorers and outlaws. Dorn contends that the explorers of America, those who came into contact with the wilderness and with primitivism, were driven by this nonrationality, as were fugitives such as Billy the Kid and de Vaca's black companion, Estevanico. Like the spirit of the Manitou, these figures were beyond the promulgated and accepted limits of rationalized religion and social order.

Americans, you were that stupid from the beginning the rest of the
    world
stood with their lower jaws dead with amazement at you, and you
    never
never did get that the point from the beginning, Columbus, Cabot,
Nuñez, LaSalle, Estevanico, the Kid, was precisely nonrational, you really thought you had to annihilate the Narraganset
which means people of the small point, oh god, the moon, is the body

5. *Webster's New World Dictionary*, s.v. "Manitou."

of the small point, your whole concern is of the small point, the war
saw concerto seems to your crossed eyes a song of great emotion
But you missed it, they made no images; their divinities
were ghosts; they were extreme spiritualists. Plenty of gods
The Sunn
      Moone,
         Fire,
Water,
   Earth,
      The Deere,
         The Beare,
           &c
And &c is the most important gods you missed. For they
were the Manitous, they dwell in you at different
    times.
      If they choose.

                         (CP 104)

One can perceive how the fugitive and nonrational explorer
figures (like the social outsiders and strangers in many of Dorn's
early poems) become prototypes for the mythical figures of the
later *Slinger*. The Gunslinger himself is godlike, beyond good
and evil, a transcendent Billy the Kid, a Maximus of the American
West who stands in sharp opposition to the prevailing
culture.

"Poets of Exploration" might be a rubric to describe the
Gunslinger, the members of his troupe, and the persons cata-
logued in "Inauguration Poem #2." Mythical American figures
in legend and literature share the nonrationality of their quest,
and the quest can be seen in relation to American writing itself,
certainly in the Black Mountain School in which writing becomes the journey, the opening of the field. Robert von Hallberg points out how Olson exemplified this role for Dorn (a
role clearly emphasized in the *Bibliography on America for Ed
Dorn*, which Olson gave to Dorn in 1956).[6] Von Hallberg

6. Charles Olson, *A Bibliography on America for Ed Dorn* (San Francisco:
Four Seasons Foundation, 1964).

speaks of how Olson approaches his content by ranging "over a wide terrain that encompasses nothing that might be construed as inherently poetic. . . . Convention demanded that he always seem to start in unfamiliar territory; his poems are meant to repeat what he called 'the first American story,' 'exploration.' "[7]

Yet if Dorn's poetics were clearly based on Olson's example (especially in the continuing use of materials from American history), it is also true that Dorn expanded on his mentor's premises (or went in completely other directions, such as in the dramatic narrative and comedy of *Slinger*). Dorn's residence in the American West allowed him a longer connection with Indians than Olson had known in the relatively brief and removed circumstances of Yucatan, and Dorn observed the Indians in a much more direct fashion than any of his contemporaries in the New American Poetry pantheon. Gary Snyder and the later ethnopoets such as Jerome Rothenberg largely depended on traditions of myth and ritual gained from textual sources as opposed to primary observations. Perhaps following Olson's urge for a Herodotean approach to history, a history to be apprehended immediately by the senses as a primary way of knowledge, Dorn often observed directly and then wrote of contemporary Indians on or from the reservations. This method certainly argues against the romanticization of native materials, especially where those materials apply to a way of life that no longer exists or that belongs to a few shaman figures rather than to the large majority of the Indians. The method also allows for a recognition of the real relations between the dominant culture and the reservation or near-reservation people, and it admits as well the multiple and often subtle ways that Indians resist that dominant culture or succumb to it.

7. See Robert von Hallberg's essay in the present book, especially for his establishment of relations between Dorn and Olson and between Dorn and LeRoi Jones.

In "The Land Below" (*CP* 57–73), Dorn's longest early
poem (1961) and a precedent for many later poems, he meditates on the substratum of America's historic past and America's unexplored present conditions. At the end of this poem a
light, partly witty interaction occurs between the author and a
family group of contemporary Indians as Dorn observes them
in a park on the Fourth of July. The passage does have a symbolic relation to the earlier argument of the poem. In contrast
to both his own family and to the white world that the author
represents, the old Indian man with traditional hair personifies
the land below:

> I marveled at the beauty
> of men who have long hair. Yes, it is quite
> different. Their world. I am sure they tread
> upon an Earth I don't. And I would like to.
> Not facilely, or for long, but to be with them
> for a spell, the chatter
> of the women really distraction, everything
> they had, gone up in smoke.
>
> (*CP* 72)

In the early 1960s Dorn moved from Santa Fe to another city
frequented by Indians: Pocatello, Idaho. During this period he
published poetry and prose related to the Indians, and much of
it derived from direct observations on journeys throughout the
Great Basin. In "Idaho Out" (1965, *CP* 107–22) a journey
through this "land above" contains much the same exploration
of past American history in relation to present conditions in
Western America as Dorn conducted in "The Land Below." In
"Idaho Out," however, there is no direct contact with the Indians; rather, their historical vestige is contrasted to the aims and
cultural limitations of the white settlers, a contrast that anticipates much deeper explorations of cultural differences in *The
Shoshoneans* (1966) and *Recollections of Gran Apacheria*
(1975). More primary observations of contemporary Indian

life than are afforded in "Idaho Out" occur in other poems of
this period, such as the newspaper-direct "Fort Hall Obituary:
A Note," a bitter account of the death of two reservation Indians in a Pocatello jail, complete with a coroner's absolution of
any guilt on the part of the authorities involved (*CP* 146).

The lengthiest portrait of an individual Indian in Dorn's
writing can be found in the novel *The Rites of Passage* (1965;
retitled *By the Sound*, 1971).[8] *The Rites of Passage*, a low-
keyed, domestic narrative, centers on three working-class families in the Pacific Northwest during the 1950s. The straightforward prose style of the novel stands in contrast to Dorn's later
collection of prose, *Some Business Recently Transacted in the
White World* (1971), which is much more oblique and experimental. Among the central characters in *The Rites of Passage*
there is Ramona McCarty, of the McCarty family. Ramona
(her name ironically invoking Helen Hunt Jackson's romantic
heroine of the nineteenth-century novel of the same name)
suffers much more quietly desperate circumstances than any
other character in the book. If she is subject to more social
oppression than the other major characters, it is because she is
an Indian. A tubercular Eskimo living in migrant housing with
a drunken (although usually well-intentioned) white husband,
she has two of her five children taken from her by the state. Yet,
as with the white characters in this book, Ramona exhibits an
individuality beyond any symbolic role as an Indian woman.
Her personal history and her unique personality are portrayed
with an evident compassion. At the same time, she and her
husband are shown in some of their worst moments, such as the
New Year's dawn when, stumbling drunk, neither of them can
open the doors of their car. Their children, locked inside, are
crying, and Ramona and James McCarty curse one another in
a stupid but vicious way. The scene becomes symbolic when

8. For Dorn's explanation of the retitling, see *I* 56–57.

they finally enter the car and James attempts to back up. But he continually forgets to shift gears, and the car goes slowly forward, again and again.

The main family of the book, the Wymans (Carl Wyman is Dorn's alter ego), interact with the McCartys throughout the narrative. In poignant scenes, Mary Wyman cannot practice the most minimal charity for Ramona because of the woman's pride, and Carl witnesses a redneck's crude verbal brutality reduce Ramona to tears in a neighborhood tavern. While the families' relations are superficially warm and certainly genuine on one level, inevitably events express the distance between the Indian woman and everyone else, including her own husband.

At the end of the novel, as the Wymans prepare to take a train south to San Francisco, there is a memorable scene involving Ramona and a visitor in the Wyman house. Even as the Wymans prepare to depart and escape the circumstances of others in the region, the McCartys have suffered several setbacks. They have been forced to return to the migrant housing in the pea camp, which they had escaped briefly; James is arrested for drunken driving and must accept near-indenture to the owner of the pea camp in order to pay the fine. Their income tax refund never arrives (this is left purposely vague: perhaps it was stolen, perhaps it went for drink); Ramona's shame has grown overpowering. In the scene involving the visitor Ramona turns a final setback into a small victory by her comic response to him. Yet, even in victory the point of her position as an Indian woman in a hostile culture remains the real difference between her and the others. The visitor who comes to see Carl is described as a loud, arrogant, bearded poet from Seattle.

The poet found many things wrong with the world. And he expressed himself freely, as though his experience and learning could carry him even into areas that were foreign to him. They all sat at the round table in the Wymans' kitchen. . . . Pierce, the poet, was talking about Paris to Carl. Ramona and Mary were talking between themselves. Ramona was telling Mary that she had gone down to Seattle that morning to try to get the kids and that there seemed no hope at all, now, the welfare people said the children were happy in their homes, attachments had been formed and that the families had adopted them. Ramona's consent was not needed because she was considered derelict. Pierce overheard the last of this and broke in, What do you mean? They can't do that! Ramona turned a bleary gaze on him as if she had just discovered him. She stared at him for some time. He asked, in a lower voice now, How old are they? POOP! she said in a low steady voice. Poop on you! Poop to you, you poop. Pierce withstood this barrage like a man. He settled back into his chair and looked from Ramona to Carl and from Carl to Ramona. I'm sorry, he said, very deferentially. Sure, you're a poop!

(*BS* 195)

Ramona's resistance, however, remains a futile gesture in the face of the circumstances of her life. Finally, her story remains typical of many American Indians in this century. But American writing generally has failed to make this kind of portrayal. In partly redressing that failure, Dorn demonstrates his own resistance to the usual standards for fictional subjects. And by not sensationalizing the mundane lives of his characters, he also resists the usual treatment of such characters given by novelists to portray marginal persons such as Ramona.

Certainly, his calm and deliberate approach to the reality of the contemporary American Indian carries over from *The Rites of Passage* to *The Shoshoneans*, even though the method of *The Shoshoneans* is quite distinct from fiction and involves wider applications. As Dorn said, "You *don't* have to talk about Vietnam. You don't have to talk about South America. You can talk about Nevada. That's much closer to home."[9] While this short passage conveys one of the strategies of *The Shoshoneans*

9. Edward Dorn, *The Poet, The People, The Spirit* (Vancouver, Canada: Talon Books, 1976), p. 6. This is a tape transcript of Dorn's lecture at the Berkeley Poetry Conference, 1965; he was then writing *The Shoshoneans*, and several asides and addenda about the book are present throughout this transcript.

(1966), the book's documentary collaboration between Dorn and Leroy McLucas, the photographer, justifies itself on several other levels. It escapes easy classification because it combines several genres: documentary, history, impressionistic anthropology, new journalism in advance of new journalism, and the lyrical essay. Yet with all that variety, the writing is remarkably even. The main line of the book is a journey across the Great Basin from Idaho to Nevada and back. The writer and photographer seek out the Shoshonean people in a variety of ways, presenting materials ranging from individual portraits to Basin landscapes, from accounts of historical vestiges such as graveyards to descriptions of present conditions in Nevada towns and cities, where Indian sections are unabashedly termed "colonies." While much of the photography centers on the interaction between white and Indian culture, and particularly on the degradation of Indian motifs as billboard icons, much of the writing moves from the present to the historical background.

While the individual tribes within the Shoshonean language grouping have distinct differences, ranging from the Bannocks in southern Idaho to the Northern Paiutes in western Nevada, the geography of the region has long determined a necessary similarity. With the exception of the Eastern Shoshoneans, who lived east of the continental divide, most of these tribes experienced a history of scarcity; they were rabbit hunters and seed gatherers, and they often dwelled in temporary wickiups of brush and sticks. Even today, with irrigated farms on the reservations, the Shoshoneans contrast with other Indian groups such as the Pueblos in the Southwest by the nature of their geographical situation and the lack of a long and inherited cultural tradition. Dorn assumes this to be an advantage, since there is a stronger contrast between the Shoshoneans and other Indians and particularly between the Shoshoneans and the prosperous white culture that has come to dominate.

One problem arises from this assumption, related to the

premises of the book. Particularly in its use of photography but also because of the vast extent of the region portrayed, *The Shoshoneans* is occasionally superficial. The writer and photographer are on the move, and as a result a large part of the book is impressionistic. Documentary photography always bears this problem of the relationship between the photographer, who is an "other," and his subject. Largely outside the lives of their subjects, the writer and the photographer seem to be cosmopolitan, even voyeuristic at times, in relation to both the Indian and the white culture of the region. The night spent with the drunken Indians on the Duck Valley Reservation stands out as an instance of such voyeurism. There is a lurid feeling to the record of this event, and this section of the book approaches the manner of new journalism; it verges upon cultural exploitation in its sensationalism.

On the other hand, because Dorn deepens the treatment of his subject by including background history, because the extent of his sympathy is obvious, and because he penetrates surfaces with incisive observations the impressionism is mediated. These possibilities either are denied to the photographer or must be expressed in infinitely subtle ways due to the nature of the medium. In McLucas's favor, many of his photographs are portraits, and these do not suffer from superficial impressionism; rather, depths belonging to the individual are expressed.

The opening chapter of *The Shoshoneans* displays the collaborators at their best. Dorn and McLucas visit a one-hundred-dred-year-old man, Willie Dorsey, and his equally old wife. As if to answer, at the outset of the book, the problems of documentation and distance I have raised, Dorn proceeds to acknowledge and enlarge upon his own role as an outsider:

I was then preoccupied with what was going on, and coincident was the feeling, quite strong and un-comfortable, that I was thinking about it, again the psychological double mirror.... Should we be there. There was in me an oppressive thrill over the idea of my own presence.

I thought of it as a ruptured cord in the consciousness, a strong confu-
sion of the signals of my culture. I think I failed to see this as a pure
event having nothing to do with *me* as such. I felt intrude the foolish
insistence of the conception of myself, the content of my own particular conception of history raced past my head and I must say I thought
of my government's relationship to this man, I felt I would "realize"
him somewhere in the cache of all *my own* sentience. For one thing, I
smiled at the man and he smiled back, and this led each time to a new
attempt to make him understand me. Did he need anything? Could we
bring him something, anything possible, would he tell us what they
needed? Shouted into his ear so close my face was nearly touching his,
the deep texture of his rich skin an untranslatable brown geography
suddenly printed on my own eye, locations I would never have to cross,
the hundred years were so laid out they included my own perishing
flesh. And I felt some embarrassment over the difference of our two
charities.

(*SH* 13–14)

Willie Dorsey's extreme age and his connection to a past that
he alone, of all his people, embodies in the most fragile of ways
serves to exemplify the distance between Dorn and the infor-
mant. This exaggerated situation functions very well as a beginning illustration of the awesome gulf that exists between even
the best-intentioned of whites and the least hostile of American
Indians. The situation also begins to illustrate the enormous
distance between anyone (white or Indian) in the present and
someone who was born into a world before contact with
whites. It must be emphasized that there are no longer any such
informants available in North America. The so-called "vanishing American" has not vanished, but the last witnesses of indigenous culture have gone. It is therefore obvious why Dorn feels
the power in the presence of the man and why, in one of the
book's most poetic moments, he describes Willie Dorsey's singing in an exalted fashion:

He is the spirit that lies at the bottom, where we have our feet. The feet
which step between the domains, the visible sign, the real evidence of

the coming event, and which one can see on the Humboldt fragments
from Mexico, or on a linguistic map where this man's low, incantatory
verbs spill down across the plateau and basin, between the mountains
into the final plexis [*sic*] of the great Uto-Aztecan image of the world
he sings in his daughter tongue.

(*SH* 13)

The spirit arises from the land below, geographically speaking,
and in the singing of the old man's doddering tongue.

McLucas's photographs of the visit to the aged couple cor-
roborate Dorn's account. Documenting the poverty and clutter
surrounding the Dorseys and making portraits, especially of
Willie Dorsey, the photographs embellish the prose description. Where Dorn's account is accurate, the photographs
underscore that accuracy. Also, the extraordinary circumstances are given credence by the camera; this is not only to the
reader's advantage but to the writer's advantage, too, drawing
attention beyond the question of veracity and toward poetry. In
one of the portraits of Willie Dorsey, McLucas abandons the
usually sharp contrast of his camera work. The portrait brings
us Willie Dorsey in a most direct and intimate way, revealing
the inner qualities Dorn pursues.

As with any collaboration of photography and prose, in
many stretches of the book the collaborators have almost nothing to do with each other. Specifically, this variance occurs
when the writing establishes itself as a medium, as in the following passage where we hear of the region as a cultural geography,
as a land above:

There is an open pit copper mine west of Salt Lake City. The biggest on
earth? Probably. Every operation is the biggest on earth in somebody's
mind. Once I saw the Kennecott thing from the ridgepole of the Wa-
satch fifteen thousand feet over the Ute country, over Huntsville,
across the Colorado Plateau, past Ship Rock, floating to Albuquerque.
Now in the blackest of night the thousand lights hover off the ground
a vibration of insects, anonymous busyness has come into the desert

and possessed it. The contract is a superlatively soundless hum ex-
changing men and materials for men and material, leveling mass to
one interchangeable, the Chilean copper night is the Utah copper
night, come and go, see nothing, be nothing, on call. The valley, the
flats, the Basin, have come into other hands.

(SH 28–29)

Throughout the middle chapters of the book, which involve
Dorn and McLucas in a search for the Shoshoneans, much of
the commentary (as in the description of the Kennecott mine) is
about the dominant culture. In one passage about the ironically
named Lovelock, Nevada, the description moves from the tor-
por of a small desert town, with its attendant police and mean
provincial behavior, to its overt connection with such things as
presidential assassinations, water rights, and the suppression
of women. As strangers moving through this region, Dorn and
McLucas share the perspective of the Indians they are documenting, particularly since McLucas is black. The Indians remain strangers to the culture above them; they are ignored,
harassed, dislocated. In summarizing their relation to the white
culture, Dorn also summarizes the history of white and Indian
relations in America at large, relations that have echoes in
American foreign policy:

Questions of sympathy, outlook, ethic, point of view, attitude or whatever seem to me to be wholly beside the point. So what if one "feels"
for the Indian? So what if one doesn't? The real ameliorative effect of
civilized on uncivilized has so far not shown itself to be much. The
history of relationships has demonstrated that the "best" men were
wrong, that the disposition of evil was finally never vivid enough to be
remembered seriously except as a mark of our redolent capabilities.
Indian and white hearts were broken, white lusts satisfied, but that did
not make anyone more Indian or more white. What it comes to in our
day is this: Who are the most habitually useful people? Who are the
most vivid members of any given people? It is all back in the street.
Even in small towns. There the distinction is clear in the East as well as
the West. An Indian family crossing the intersection of some dusty

main street in a 1952 Ford. Or a negro just released from a Utah prison trying for the life of him to find out, with all the dangerous sense of nuance a delicately experienced man has, how to get from this corner to the restaurant in the next block without becoming too precise in the eyes and nose of the indigenous loafer—whether he be businessman or town bully or cop, and the prisoner never has to sort the differences. Or a white bum wondering if, as he passes through Pocatello, he can get a job in Cheyenne as a dishwasher. If he gets to Cheyenne. Of course he can't. They can't. Nobody should have to. If one thing is clear today it is that the prevailing structure of supply is dead and has been dead from the beginning of the Industrial Revolution. All that gain was unavoidable but nonetheless wholly mistaken activity. The grain grown on the appropriated hills of Idaho is used to buy off the Indian still—now it is shipped to India to secure the sub-continent against the ambitions of a China. Any stranger, passing along the ghostly sidewalks of our towns and cities, instinctively knows that he lives in a "permissive asylum."

(*SH* 83)

Within the highly generalized level of argument in the above paragraph (moving from the Indian "question" to its connection with external policy), the author also presents a near-narrative of the Negro recently released from prison and his white counterpart, the bum. (This persistent identification with the outcast is one rationale for considering the Shoshoneans in the first place.) The liveliness of the paragraph, with its appeals to both specifics and generalities, marks some distance between Dorn and, for instance, the professional ethnographer or historian. Bound by the requirements of the discipline, just as the journalist is usually limited to a narrow range of speculation, the professional must often omit the most engaging core of knowledge of a particular subject. Yet what seems to be digressive may well be the essence of the subject.

In an exemplary digression in this book about Indians, Dorn speaks of the cowboy and of what the cowboy has become. He notes the ossification of what were once thought to be virtues: "1. wide open spaces, 2. independence, 3. a special freedom from corruption (usually the imagined corruption of the 'city' . . ." (*SH* 31). The "innate, dynamic fascism" of the earlier cowboy was "an extension of pure ego uninhibited by any hint of the reflective or decisive moment" (*SH* 31). This reading of the cowboy has a relation to *Slinger*, which Dorn began in the next few years after *The Shoshoneans*. As Michael Davidson contends in his essay in this volume, the Gunslinger character and the character of the nemesis, based upon Howard Hughes, share qualities similar to those mentioned above, even if the *Slinger* characters are largely mythical extensions.[10] In fact, the term Dorn uses in *The Shoshoneans* to describe the current condition of the American West, the "neo-wild West," begins to describe the world in which *Slinger* occurs.

Similarly, in *Recollections of Gran Apacheria* (1974), the book coincident with the completion of *Slinger*, there is a subtle reflection, perhaps even a self-criticism, of the documentary process of *The Shoshoneans*. In the important final poem, "La Máquina a Houston," Dorn's commentary explains how the photographer stands for our civilization's consistent "otherness" in its relations to the Indians. He recognizes the problem of distance between even the best intentioned of reporters and the Indians. Of course, the evidence for this distance is continual in the documentation of *The Shoshoneans*. The Indian cultures and their vestiges are continually transformed and debased through contact with the white world. Dorn defines the various Shoshoneans encountered in terms of the degree of their assimilation or resistance. The spectrum ranges from traditional figures such as Willie Dorsey and the "dark" Indians—the Indians of the land below who display long hair and sullen attitudes—to managerial Indians on reservations who are inseparable from their white, corporate counterparts. Cultural nationalism becomes a strong point of resistance, leading Dorn

10. See Michael Davidson's essay in the present book.

to speak favorably of the then-recent pronouncements of LeRoi Jones (Amiri Baraka) on this subject. Coincidentally, a slogan ("those who are not part of the solution are part of the problem," which was widely employed a few years later in the 1960s) by a politicized, activist Indian, Clyde Warrior, comes at the end of *The Shoshoneans*. As Dorn says, the Indian now deserves the last words, especially the Indian who resists. Most importantly, this Indian combines spiritual knowledge of the old culture, and of the land below, with necessary political action in the present. The possibility has certainly occurred in sectors of the American Indian movement since *The Shoshoneans* was written. Coincidentally or not, since much of what was in the air in the mid-sixties found its way into this book, *The Shoshoneans* anticipates what has come to be. Moreover, the book provides, with only a few exceptions, a model for a white author's approach to the Indian, an approach based on a recognition of "otherness."

"Otherness" is the basis for the final book Dorn has written about the American Indian, a book of poems: *Recollections of Gran Apachería*. "Otherness" is exemplified in the front cover illustration of the comic-book format of *Recollections*: a man in bow tie and roller skates sits astride a very strange steer, complete with a gas tank cap on a rear flank; he is loaded down with the detritus of civilization, including golf clubs, a telephone book of greater Chicago, a flashbulb news camera, motel towel for saddle blanket, a canteen case where, in place of a canteen, a clock has been enclosed. Michael Myers, the illustrator who worked with Dorn at this time, presents the white man as a complete "other" against the surrounding desert. Of course, Myers himself is quite different from McLucas, the photographer of *The Shoshoneans*. Myers's drawings express symbolic possibilities and a wit beyond the means of photography; this reflects the extent to which *Recollections* may even stand as a partial criticism of *The Shoshoneans*. The economy of poetry, particularly the epigrammatic poetry of this book, contrasts with the prose of *The Shoshoneans* as much as it differs from the poetry of *Slinger*, a comic epic of the white West where scarcely an Indian appears and the poetry is anything but epigrammatic. Quite probably, the distance in time between *The Shoshoneans* and *Recollections* resulted in Dorn's deviation from the manner of his earlier book. Authorial revision and self-criticism are characteristic of this poet of shifting genres.

"Otherness" is ultimately a dialectic between the Apaches and the whites, and the poetry of this book depends upon that theoretical basis. Where the Judeo-Christian creation ("the alien church" in *Recollections*) has an omnipotent creator at the beginning of time, the Apache creation myth contains several agents, including a Night Girl, laughing animals, and a Little Boy whose birth coincides with the opening of the world (*RGA* 32–34). Also, the Western European tradition emphasizes causal thinking leading to distinctions of thought, to an abstract sense of time, and to the predication of the future. The Apache tradition lacks a predicative mind, the abstract sense of time, and the "mechanic of the future"; it proposes instead an identity (including clan names) with the land itself (*RGA* 36). These qualities are said to demonstrate "the superiority of Native over Alien Thinking," given the successful resistance of the Apaches: "The longest run / of external resistance: / the Apache Wars" (*RGA* 35).

While the dialectic of "otherness" pervades this book, the poetry itself, especially in the sequence of Apache portraits, presents this "otherness" through metaphor and by relating historical incidents. Indeed, *Recollections* achieves its balance through the constant interplay of specifics and generalities; the specifics include individuals, particular places in the geography of Gran Apachería, and vivid accounts of usually violent incidents in the warfare. More generally, the author employs wry wit and ironic humor to underscore the gap between the contending cultures. In "The Provoking Figure of the Horsewoman," for instance, the portrait of Luzon, the warrior sister of the Apache chief Victorio, begins with a line that contrasts her to the prototypical Indian woman of American experience: "Victorio's seester was no pocahontas . . ." (RGA 17). While the line has its humorous overtones in the Spanish-dialect English, it is also intended to remind us that no symbolic marriage between the two cultures, as occurred with Pocahontas, can occur between the Apaches and the whites; as the poem continues, Luzon's difference from the mythical Pocahontas is made manifest as her hatred and the violence of historical events are recalled. In another of these portraits, "Nana and Victorio," there is perhaps the best expression of the Apache otherness: their tenacity, even when terribly wounded; their opposition to white cultural institutions such as the Christian church; their union with native geography; and their distance from ourselves in time. In this short poem, Dorn uses archaic English spelling (winde, Jewell) to suggest the arcane realm of the Apaches, as opposed to the modernity of their conquerors and ourselves:

> Along this spine of dragoon mountains
> the pains in Nanas bit off leg
> a wound inflicted by the vicious teeth
> of the Alien Church, their thin line
> moves north then south
> across the rio bravo del norte
> the winde driving the wild fire of their loyalties
> and in the cruel vista
> I can see the Obdurate Jewell
> of all they wanted, shining
> without a single facet
> upon our time
> and yet the radiance marks everything
> as we unweave this corrupted cloth
> (RGA 14)

The "Obdurate Jewell" is the land that cannot be separated from the Apache identity; the "Jewell" no longer shines since the Apaches were overwhelmed and their land divided by the conquerors. Yet the "radiance" of their realm marks everything about this clash, this ultimate corruption by historical forces. Two poems conclude the portrait sequences. In one, "Assorted Compliments," we are given an assemblage of sentence-long comments on the Apaches from various observers in several languages; these comments generally reveal as much about the prejudices of the observers as of the nature of the Apaches ("Geronimo is the worst Indian who ever lived," General Miles reports; *RGA* 27). In the other concluding portrait, "A Period Portrait of Sympathy," Dorn speaks of a commander of the Apache scouts (the scouts were used against their own tribe, a common feature of warfare against indigenous people). The "sympathy" of the title contains some irony as the poem unfolds:

> Captain Emmet Crawford,
> Commander of the Apache Scouts
> is sated with German Romanticism
> his eyes are sunk deep
> in centuries of masturbátory introspection
> on his chest two ranks of buttons
> and a complicated rigging of braid
> he has a dark lost look
> in the style of Poe
> and the scouts love his weirdness
> (*RGA* 25)

Following the portrait poems, the poem "Reservations" opens the final section of *Recollections*. In "Reservations" we are told that the otherness between the two cultures was seldom, if ever, acknowledged. Even the first ethnographers are included as being part of the "dung and piss / of Warfares invariants" (*RGA* 28). The Bureau of American Ethnology cannot be separated from the framework of the destructive civilization (a point of historical accuracy, since the Bureau was founded partly to supply information to the War Department). In light of these conditions, necessary "reservations" must be acknowledged. Among these, Dorn points to the inability of the United States government to propagate a "central thought," a condition that has made *internal* policy a *foreign* policy. Enlarging the scope, the poem speaks of the inability of Northern Europeans to live on earth with others—hence the whites' derisive treatment of the thoughtful ethnologists Adolf Bandelier and Frank Cushing during the period of this warfare with the Apaches. Manifest Destiny disallows cultural mingling of the conquerors with the conquered. The conquerors presume to go onward, even into outer space, while their "biggest footnote / is an apocalypse prior to themselves" (*RGA* 29). This apocalypse, such as the destruction of the Apache culture, becomes a premonition of the conqueror's forthcoming apocalypse, which may occur when the fabrications of our polluting technology promote "the early return of the glacier" (*RGA* 29). Or, as "Reservations" continues, the destiny may be "absolutely nowhere," suggesting the vacuity of the conquering culture, its lack of a central thought, since, even as it abolishes other cultures, it does "not even yet / know what a crisis is" (*RGA* 29). As another poem, "The Slipping of the Wheel," says, the Apaches "embody a state / which our still encircled world / looks toward from the past" (*RGA* 41).

The major poem of *Recollections* is the final poem in the book: "La Máquina a Houston" ("The Machine to Houston"). Among other things, the poem presents the moment when the final solution to the Apache problem was enacted: the forced exile on a railroad train from Holbrook, Arizona, via Houston to immurement in Florida. This solution to renegade Indians who would not tolerate the confines of reservations (and the frequent starvation that attended this confinement) literally forced the Apaches to become part of the alien culture they had long resisted. The railroad train is perceived as a representative object of the linear culture, and it is also aligned with "the particulates of the English language / Itself the agent of frag mentation" (*RGA* 44). As the poem proceeds, the Apaches are shown to be on one side, as they represent their particular culture's ordering of time and space, and the whites are shown to be on the opposite side, accompanied by another object of frag mentation: a camera and a photographer. "We are with the man with the camera," the poet reminds the reader, while the Apaches must be prodded out into the light, out of the unknown of their world and into the recording frame of our world (*RGA* 44). Their world is "indivisible," while for us "that is a philosophical implication" (*RGA* 45). The contrast continues throughout a long stanza of comparison between the captive Apaches and the observing soldiers, between the indivisible and the divisible at this "important terminal moment / In the Rush Hour begun in this hemisphere" (the end of any external resistance within the eventual contiguous states; *RGA* 45). This is the moment before the leg irons are locked, before the Apaches are fixed into the finite—the moment when "they look good" in ways we never will, since "we are too far gone on thought, and its rejections" (*RGA* 45). A final portrait of the Apache, Natches, appears in contrast to the faceless soldiers, whose eyes we look out from. At the conclusion of the poem and the book, the Apache dogs follow the departing train:

> And some of them followed the cars
> for forty miles
> Before they fell away in exhaustion
> (*RGA* 46)

Edward Dorn's writing on the American Indian has appeared in several genres. He has ranged among the past history and present state of various tribes, from the Pueblos of the

Southwest to the Shoshonean language people of the Great Basin, from an Eskimo woman in the Northwest to the Apaches of the Southwest. Always he has acknowledged difference and distance between the American Indian and white Americans. And yet Dorn has allowed not only the obvious bitterness but also the occasional lighter moment, since he is a poet of considerable wit. In the internal resistance of his thought, Dorn has been able to understand the American Indian more deeply perhaps than any recent writer, scholarly or poetic, who is not himself an Indian. In these works, as in the larger body of his writing, Dorn makes marginal figures, as they resist external authority with an indivisible spirit of self, land, and history, morally central to the inner life of American culture.

## 4

# "To eliminate the draw": Narrative and Language in Slinger

### MICHAEL DAVIDSON

> *any man*
> *can't understand*
> *what gravity is*
> *that he has an*
> *ordered and*
> *endlessly transferrable*
> *place*
>
> ("The North Atlantic
> Turbine," *CP* 182)

When Charles Olson set out to delineate texts and contexts about America for his Black Mountain student Edward Dorn, he emphasized those works that invert the traditional terms for personal, spiritual, and political life. Olson proposed, rather than the study of the purely physical universe, a study of the "human universe," stressing that for any historical study, "it is not how much one knows but in what field of context it is retained, and used."[1] Obviously the "Bibliography on America for Ed Dorn" was intended to do more than provide a reading list. It suggested a radical rethinking of "place" as characterized

---

1. Charles Olson, "A Bibliography on America for Ed Dorn," in *Additional Prose: A Bibliography on America, Proprioception & Other Notes & Essays*, ed. George F. Butterick (Bolinas, Calif.: Four Seasons Foundation, 1974), p. 3.

by its linear history, geography, discoveries, wars, and defeats. Authors recommended by Olson, such as Carl Sauer, Leo Frobenius, Alfred North Whitehead, Frederick Merk, Brooks Adams, or Katherine Coman, offered a methodology for studying and presenting historical data in some determinate relation to one's immediate concerns—the writing of poems, for example. As if to signal his awareness of how this methodology relates to a poetics, Olson signed the bibliography "me fecit January 7, 1955," recalling Pound's historico-economic interests in *The Cantos*. In Canto 45 Pound inveighs against an usurious economic system in which the stone carver may no longer sign his column "Adamo me fecit" and thus carve his personal and historical destiny into stone. The implications of such a fact for both economics and poetry are never lost on Olson or, as we shall see, on Dorn.[2]

Dorn responded to Olson's advice by taking the American West as his chosen area and by researching the lore of its discovery, development, and exploitation. His poetry of the mid-fifties to late sixties deals with the "iron locomotives and shovels, hand tools / And barbed wire motives" (*CP* 44) behind the settlement of the frontier. Its geography is projected as a component of the mind, possessing and terrifying the local inhabitant, who in turn alters the landscape to his own uses; what is "seen" becomes a matter of what frames the sight:

> the sky
>
>     is not
>
> bigger in Montana. When
> for instance you come
> from Williston
> there seems at the border a change

2. I have developed some of these ideas on history and methodology in another essay, "Archaeologist of Morning: Charles Olson, Edward Dorn and Historical Method," *English Literary History* 47 (Spring 1980): 158–79.

but it is only because man has
built a tavern there
(*CP* 115)

Dorn's researches into this area were aided by reading Carl
Sauer, one of Olson's recommended authors, whose geomor-
phological studies paid close attention to the tavern at the
border—that is, to the effects of man on the landscape. The
isolated river, watershed, or grassland does not exist separately
from man's use of it. To regard a landform as separable from
the "totality of its forms," as Sauer calls it, is to ignore the
relationships between adjacent areas—relationships that have
implications for social and economic mediation of the land.
Dorn's recognition of this mediation appears variously
throughout his early poems, and when he comes to expand his
vision to include the West as a global category in "The North
Atlantic Turbine," it is with the sense of how the local in America has been appropriated. The new westerner does not follow
a linear pattern but "goes anywhere apparently / . . . and space
is muddied / with his tracks / for ore he is only after . . ." (*CP*
115–16).

Olson's "local" is Gloucester, a single town in Massachu-
setts that becomes, in *The Maximus Poems*, a microcosm for
the nation. The historical transfer of the original governor's
mansion from Cape Ann to Salem becomes a metaphor for the
dispersal and transfer of place in America. For Olson, place is
specific.[3] Dorn's "local," as seen through such long poems as
"The Land Below," "Idaho Out," and "The North Atlantic
Turbine," gradually expands to include the West as a large
metaphor for modern man. According to Dorn, the local has
been lost; in its place is a variable fiction created by global
capitalism and manipulable by those few who have the cunning

3. This is primarily true for the first volume of *The Maximus Poems*, but
the second and third volumes of the poem introduce a more global perspective
and larger, mythic concerns.

and will to use it. The central recognition in these poems is that man has become a function of a series of signs, dispersed from distant data banks (economic, intellectual, scientific). One's ability to stand upright, once thought to be a sign of individuality, has been undercut; man's gravity is his "ordered and / endlessly transferrable / place" (*CP* 182).

This "endlessly transferrable / place" is the locus of Dorn's epic of the new West, *Slinger*, a poem that extends from Olson's *Maximus Poems* but that marks a significant break with it as well. Where Olson's Maximus is the embodiment of the potential inherent in any citizen, Dorn's Gunslinger is a problematic blend of existential outlaw, robber baron, and metaphysician. Where Olson focuses on Gloucester as, for better or worse, the American representative small town, Dorn's view ranges over the entire industrialized world as a succession of replaceable parts in what he calls "the cultural exchange." Despite Olson's despair over the gradual commercialization of American life, he is essentially nostalgic for virtues of self-reliance and independence visible in those early settlers, explorers, and fishermen who populate his great work. Dorn projects in the place of Olson's Leviathan-like representative man a cool and airy debunker, a gunslinger whose draw is faster than human intention and whose speech is as laconic and arch as that of any TV outlaw. And yet, as I hope to indicate, *Slinger* is as profound in its own way as *The Maximus Poems* in uncovering the cycles of greed and acquisition that have destroyed those qualities of individual strength and volition that Olson admires.

What Olson might have been disturbed by in Dorn's long poem would not be the historical-social critique but, rather, the method of its presentation. *Slinger* is a highly ironic work, full of puns, jokes, and verbal pratfalls. At times it proceeds by means of an arcane systems language that defeats the closest reading. For the literal-minded Olson, such playfulness must have seemed irrelevant to the task at hand, and yet part of

Dorn's task involves undercutting the high rhetoric of epic vision. At many levels the poem approaches the epic by its use of narrative passages, its conflicts between men and gods, its attendant poet who sings songs of comfort to the hero, its heroic epithets and its sustained social theme. It is, however, an epic closer to *Don Juan* or the *Dunciad* than it is to *The Iliad* or *The Aeneid*,[4] and the humor of the poem has a deadly seriousness behind it—one stated as such by "I" in the fourth book:

> Entrapment is this society's
> Sole activity, I whispered
> and Only laughter,
> can blow it to rags
> (*S* 155)

Laughter is the primary agent of Dorn's debunking power, although the humor in the poem is never of the rollicking sort but more the acidic variety that one associates with Swift or Blake.

In many respects *Slinger* resembles allegory more closely than it does the epic since the narrative moves by means of set dialogues spoken by characters who seem to step forth from a two-dimensional backdrop or "tapestry," as Dorn calls it. The world it depicts is one in which purposeful action has been severely curtailed; to travel from one place to another is unnecessary since all places are potentially the same. By the end of the poem, the journey that seems constantly underway gradually dissolves. Las Vegas, the ostensible object of the Slinger's search, is never reached; it becomes a "vast decoy," capable of providing an illusion of place while existing as an extension of Howard Hughes's empire. The towns encountered in the poem

4. Of the Don Juan figure in relation to the Slinger: "Strangely though, whatever ideas I had about my own figure came more from nineteenth-century poetry—more from the other Don Juan, Byron's, which I'm quite conscious of visiting at the time" (*I* 88).

are equally illusory. Truth or Consequences, New Mexico (formerly Hot Springs), has given up its original name in favor of the name of a TV quiz show. The fact that the new name illustrates the dualism inherent in the metaphysical West (and which the Slinger attacks) beautifully accommodates Dorn's allegorical scheme.

If allegory involves a flattening of narrative action and setting appropriate to the problematics of space in this poem, it also reduces characters to two-dimensional cutouts. The various personages of *Slinger*—Lil, the Stoned Horse, Kool Everything, Dr. Flamboyant, and the Gunslinger himself—are taken from the TV westerns, comic books, underground press newspapers and country music that represent the West to most of us. Dialogue in this poem usually involves cartoon-like patter or wry monologues on the state of contemporary culture. Lil's down-to-earth human concern and toughness are reflected through a rhetoric of the TV western saloon proprietress as fixed and absolute as that of any Puritan divine. Kool Everything's hip jargon comes straight out of Zap Comix. Characters do not carry on conversations; they assess, remark, rhapsodize, put down, scorn, send and receive messages, but they refuse to exchange ideas.

As I have pointed out, the space of the poem is the West in its largest sense. Not only is it the West created by television and movies; it is also the West of exploration and exploitation. The true heroics of this realm are seldom played out at high noon between two gunfighters but more often are performed in the offices and backrooms of merchants, traders, manufacturers, and financiers. For Dorn, wealthy entrepreneurs like Daniel Drew, Jim Fisk, and Jay Gould are the true western demigods, for they affect and modify the environment in ways that decisively alter the national consciousness. They speak in the high cant of a social darwinism that states that the more accumulated capital, the more evidence of a special place in an evolutionary scheme. Because the realms of economics and genetics are constantly becoming mixed, Dorn has seized upon the language of biological mutation and "genetic duels" for much of his characterization of western landscape.

Dorn's Slinger (in Britain the term means one who plays the stock market) participates in some of the high-rolling style of the robber baron. Like Howard Hughes, whom he sometimes resembles, he is mysterious and eccentric. He lives anywhere and seems able to appear in several places at once. His inscrutable actions confound all onlookers. He is to be revered and feared at the same time since he lives by laws totally beyond those of the average citizen. It would be tempting to read the poem as progressing toward a high noon duel between the Slinger and Hughes, but such a reading depends upon an outmoded fiction of absolute heroes and villains. If the Slinger's journey is perpetually "toward" Hughes, it is perhaps because the two characters are positive and negative poles of the same energy field. They represent two aspects of power in the western world, one that maintains cycles of acquisition and warfare and another that deconstructs the rhetoric upon which these cycles are based.

Behind the geographical and economic West, manipulated by Hughes, lies a more philosophical one: that metaphysical-theological tradition based on the primacy of Being as presence. The Cartesian separation of man from the objects of his knowledge, the divorce of being and thought, forms a topography every bit as decisive to western man as the plateaus and river basins of the geographical West. The Slinger is resolutely anti-Cartesian. He travels with a horse whose name alternates between Heidegger and Lévi-Strauss, two foremost critics of Cartesian rationalism. Heidegger's temporalization of *Dasein* and his radical critique of Being as presence in the Kantian tradition produce a dislocated subject whose being is endlessly deferred. Likewise, Lévi-Strauss's analysis of kinship systems in terms of their differential and categorical status violates the idea of a social contract with its attendant belief in the realm of inherent human values. Man, the Horse explains, has become a "classification," and his societies have become masses of data. To understand "what / you are" could not be accomplished "*without the aid of machines*" (*S* 35). The logocentric/Rousseauist view attacked from the perspectives of existential phenomenology and structuralism is an appropriate philosophical background for the West of Howard Hughes. His entrepreneurial skill has produced a world of centerless systems (computer banks, fast-food chains, corporate conglomerates) whose information is transferable and variable. Heidegger and Lévi-Strauss, as debunkers of privileged philosophical "centers" (the transcendental subject, a primordial Logos), become necessary "sidekicks" for the Slinger.[5]

Dorn provides a foil to such philosophical outlaws in the form of a character who stands at the pinnacle of western metaphysics: "I." "I" is both a pronoun and a name, "an initial" and a "single." "I" is the figure who interprets the meaning behind events, who needs to know what is happening and to whom. He is the last vestige of the self-conscious, rationalizing ego—a consciousness that understands the principles *behind* things and the ideals *toward* which events ineluctably move. He appears early in Book I of the poem as the constant interrogator of the Slinger's opaque language and attends the first part of the journey toward Las Vegas. He dies in the second book and is preserved in LSD until he emerges at the end of Book III as the

5. On Dorn's use of Heidegger and Lévi-Strauss: "My views of structuralism or Heidegger's phenomenology are not important to the poem at all. I want these characters to have the possibility of such names because they are widely understood and widely evokable intellectual signs. After all, this poem is addressed to the community in which I move, which is educated. My own audience might be small, but it's potentially comprehensive because the intellectual community is a mass community as much as the cotton picker's community, or the trucker's" (*I* 50).

secretary to Parmenides. From this point, "I" is the new man, capable of a consciousness appropriate to pre-Socratic and postmodern deconstructions alike. At the same time that Dorn kills off the ego he destroys the primacy of the first-person narrative. By creating a character who is also a pronoun, Dorn is able to illustrate the predicament of Cartesian ontology in which a man's being is defined by his thought and by his ability to call that thought into doubt. The reader becomes complicit in a double bind by following a first-person and a third-person narration at the same time. It is Dorn's strategic way of collapsing the subjective and objective poles without, at the same time, positing a transcendental principle. It is this monism that he admires in pre-Socratics like Parmenides, whose "it is" refuses a binarism of presence/absence, being/nothingness. As the singer explains, the "scenario" of this poem is the "redecoration" of the western mind:

> The scenario is all Emanation
> The nesting ground of number
> There are no *things* there as such
> Material is a not with the   K   detached
>
> All is transhistorical, functions
> Have no date . . .
>
> (S 98)

Dorn's ontological concerns in *Slinger* are flanked by a mock trinitarian theology. The Father is a kind of ultimate corporate captain named Robart, "the Valfather of [the] Race," who wages fantastic earthly wars and whose "enchanted Wallet" contains the oppressive "Cycle of acquisition" that maintains those wars. His earthly counterpart is the Slinger, half mortal and half deity, who searches every day of his two-thousand-plus years for a mysterious "third," the inscrutable Texan named Howard Hughes, Dorn's Holy Ghost. Since Hughes's middle name is Robard, we can be reasonably sure that Dorn is playing with the idea of God's suppressed or hidden name. Whether this allegory can support such a clearly defined triad is difficult to say. Dorn has left the supposed identity of such figures obscure. By the end, it is difficult to say *what* is happening since identities have changed hands many times, and Howard Hughes has long since disappeared from the Slinger's concerns. Still, the pursuit of a ghostly spirit who is capable of living everywhere at once, whose face is never seen and who contains the power to "buy Vegas and move it" (as Lil suggests), forms the ostensible purpose of the Slinger's quest and gives the poem its mythic dimension.

While the Slinger, Hughes, and Robart seem to live outside of physical space and sequential time, they inhabit all time and all space—both "inside real" (phenomenological) and "outsidereal" (stellar)—and gradually merge as a single mind. The coalescence of these three time travelers reminds one of Melville's "man in cream colors" from *The Confidence Man*, whose journey among swindlers, charlatans, and greedy citizens parallels the Slinger's movements through western towns. When Melville's shape-shifting figure appears briefly in Book IIII of *Slinger*, he speaks in the voice of Parmenides: "It is all one to me where I begin / for I shall come back again there" (*S* 174). This speech itself is framed within a song that celebrates the wonders of cocaine. Dorn's dense weave joins pre-Socratic cosmology to Melville's America and ultimately to postwar drug lore to create a completely ahistorical figure in whom resides a new consciousness. Dorn would be equally interested in Melville's creation of a mute figure whose journey along an allegorical Mississippi in search of "trust" parallels that of the Slinger along the Rio Grande.

The various characters of the journey form a conglomerate or, as Dorn calls them in an interview, a "constellation." They speak as various aspects of the poet's mind or as figures in a dream allegory. These "missionaries" observe mercantile civilization, its schedules and plans, and discover eventually that "time does not consent." Rather, "celebrations concur / and we concur To See / The Universe" (*S* 46). For time to "consent" it must be subjected to an order and sequence, and it is this limited, linear view of time that possesses the mind of "I." When "I" reappears at the end of the poem, he has assimilated the lessons of the Slinger (with help from LSD and Parmenides) and is able to live according to celebrations rather than schedules.

The other members of the party include Lil, the prototype of the dance-hall madam and a solid critic of the Slinger's more extravagant gestures.[6] The Stoned Horse is a parody of the cowboy's beast of burden, spending the bulk of his time rolling giant Tampico bombers and making oblique comments to all passersby. Since his name has become associated with the internal combustion engine (e.g., "horsepower") he now rides as passenger inside the very coach he used to pull. The next character in the party is the poet-singer, who offers interludes of song on his "abso-lute." His lyrics are a mixture of Shelleyan ode and cybernetic argot, the high and low styles fused in a manner not unlike Dorn's own earlier poetry. In addition to these central characters, we meet Kool Everything, a kind of sixties acid freak, and Dr. Flamboyant, whose researches into "post-ephemeral" subjects are the kind of far out scholarly work that the Slinger appreciates. Flamboyant, with his paradoxes, double binds, and unresolvables, is a comic synthesis of Whitehead, Parmenides, and Charlie Ruggles.

Along with the Slinger and "I," the "pleiad" of characters follows a path from Mesilla, a town on the New Mexico border, along the Rio Grande to Truth or Consequences and thence north toward Four Corners, site of the power plant that provides the focus for the last two books. In Book IIII the action takes place in Cortez, Colorado, a town near Mesa Verde in the

6. See *I* 71–72 for Dorn's discussion of Lil.

southwestern part of the state. Despite the appearance of a linear journey, the action of the poem occurs largely within the inner landscape of dialogues, monologues, and printed readouts. One might say that the poem traces a trajectory rather than a journey, for as I have indicated, "place" is transferable. The Slinger discovers early in the poem that Howard Hughes has moved from Boston to Las Vegas (a symbolic transfer of power bases in America, no doubt), and so the Slinger changes his direction toward the latter. But he by no means reaches Las Vegas, nor does he seem, in the interim, to actually move from place to place. The reader who becomes frustrated with the arbitrariness of the Slinger's movements must remember that the demigod moves outside of teleological motion. What is important is not *where* he goes but what he sees and does. By disavowing laws of sequence and causality, the Slinger may eliminate the contingent nature of times and places and thus penetrate time and space. He exists "in that warp of relativity one sees / in the backward turning spokes / of a buckboard" (*S* 27).

If the journey illustrates the mediation of space and movement, it is all the more appropriate that the Four Corners Power Plant near Farmington should provide a focus, since it represents one of America's massive industrial scars. The plant is built at a point where four states come together, and such demographic limits reflect the authority of man's economic concerns over those of the natural environment. Such arbitrary limits as state borders target areas of landscape for exploitation, and the power plant is a prime example of that usurpation. Dorn's cosmocrator, Robart, holds the gun that points at Four Corners: "And he has declared his crosshair / at 2 days minus 4 corners" (*S* 124). But the crossed lines of the gunsight also form a plus sign that becomes the indicator of capitalist appropriation. Speaking in a similar vein about Las Vegas, Dorn states that the magnetism of the plus sign creates the "psychological fact of a purely man-made, wholly abstract position" (*I* 34). The Slinger's journey then moves in the general direction of Four Corners or Las Vegas, but this northwest movement initiated in Book I gradually breaks down as the poem incurs the deeper ramifications of its own materials. In order to understand how poetic structure performs this thematic inversion, it will be necessary to understand how *Slinger* is constructed.

The poem consists of four books and two transitional sections, "The Cycle" (between Books II and III) and *Bean News* (between Books III and IIII).[7] The latter is a collaborative effort by Dorn and various friends to create the kind of newspaper that might be found in the Slinger's stagecoach. It is not included in the book proper but exists as a separate publication, thus extending the poem "vertically off the pages of the poem in a three-dimensional sense" (*I* 34). *Bean News* is printed in a tabloid format, but its news is made up of scientific-cybernetic jargon taken from technical journals. Both "The Cycle" and *Bean News* operate from within the highly codified, technocratic worlds of systems manipulation and can be read as oblique commentaries on the larger action of the poem.

The four books and two transitional sections were written over a period of eight years, a version of the opening lines appearing as a separate poem, "An Idle Visitation," in *The North Atlantic Turbine*, published in 1967. The years spanned by the writing are among the most turbulent in America's history, and yet the poem seems, at least on the surface, to be free of any specific historical reference. But beneath almost every line lies a specific, directed commentary on technological and industrial life. Of all the poetry written on social themes during the sixties, few individual works subject the historical moment to such extensive analysis as *Slinger*. Events concerning the Vietnam War may be absent from view, but they appear

7. On "The Cycle" and *Bean News* as transitional bridges see *I* 32–33.

obliquely through the filter of Dorn's economic concerns. Rather than focus on domestic confrontations, protests, or warfare in Southeast Asia, Dorn investigates the language of power brokers in high places: "We're scientists Al," says Robart, "Sometimes / we have to do Things we hate / Things that even sicken us . . ." (*S* 152). And rather than bemoan a generalized American evil, Dorn chooses to point out specific structures of imperialism and exploitation: the division of the plains by the railroad, the overnight accumulation of fortunes by oil monarchs, the co-optation of "straight information" by media and advertising, the racism of the "plain, unassorted white citizens," the mediation of experience by the "Literate Projector" (which projects the idea behind the object rather than the object itself), and the ravaging of the natural environment by industry. The fact that Dorn uses stiletto-sharp wit to undercut such systems never hides their insidious nature.

If the war in Vietnam is filtered through an analysis of capitalist systems, it is equally present through the so-called "altered consciousness" of the sixties. The four books of *Slinger* are each devoted to a specific drug, the first to marijuana, the second to LSD, the third and fourth to cocaine. Dorn is, after all, interested in the *mind* of an era, and the mind of the sixties was considerably affected by the context of drugs. The fact that "I" is preserved in Kool Everything's batch of acid represents the entire transformation of the ego made possible through hallucinogens. As the Slinger observes, the psychedelically reformed "I" will carry the "key to proprioception," which is another way of saying that he will become what he sees. The War becomes a dimension of human consciousness, and Dorn wants to suggest the ways in which drugs, during the sixties, were both a product of and a frame for viewing the War "as a way of thinking about a distant event which was obviously the most pervasive psychological problem the country was undergoing" (*I* 94).

Having provided these contexts, I want to summarize the events of the poem as it unfolds, taking as Dorn's theme the gradual dispersion of "place" from its specific geologic-historical locale and its mediation by entrepreneurial capitalism. The language of Book I is the easiest going of the book. The opening lines are written in a meter familiar to anyone who has listened to "The Streets of Laredo":

> I met in Mesilla
> the Cautious Gunslinger
> of impeccable personal smoothness
> and slender leather encased hands
> folded casually
> to make his knock.
> He would show you his map.
>
> There is your domain.
> Is it the domicile it looks to be
> or simply a retinal block
> of seats in,
> he will flip the phrase
> the theater of impatience.
>
> (S 3)

The question of the second stanza is central: is one's domain an empirical fact or a phenomenological projection? Subsequent questions by "I" and the Slinger's arch responses form part of a Socratic dialogue on the opposition between appearance and reality. The Slinger refuses the opposition by attacking the primacy of space over time:

> Time is more fundamental than space.
> It is, indeed, the most pervasive
> of all the categories
> in other words
> theres plenty of it.
> And it stretches things themselves
> until they blend into one,

so if youve seen one thing
youve seen them all.

(*S* 5)

And conversely, if you haven't seen something, don't talk about it—advice given freely (and often) to "I." Space, which Olson saw as the central fact of America, no longer stands as the defining character of the national psyche. Dorn substitutes time as more "fundamental" since it is the field of exploration for relativity physics and quantum mechanics—a world in which no volume or velocity may be fixed. The Slinger, as a time traveler, blends all individual moments into one. Space, viewed as an extended field of discrete areas, is closed; it has been bought up, appropriated, and modified. Time, then, becomes the medium of the new, postmodern, post-Einsteinean man. It is also the medium of pre-Socratic cosmology and myth, and the Slinger at times seems to be an atavistic reminder of that world.

The central scene in the first book occurs in Lil's cabaret. The presence of the Slinger's horse occasions some disgruntlement on the part of a local citizen who shouts,

Come on!
Who's the horse, I mean who's
horse is that, we can't have
No Horse! in here.
It ain't proper
and I think I'm gonna
put a halter on you!

(*S* 26)

The ensuing gunfight between the Slinger and the citizen exposes how fast a draw can be. Whereas the citizen's draw is based on "leverage" (the sequence of logically connected events between drawing the gun from the holster, aiming, and firing), the Slinger's is based on the principle of pure intention. By refusing the logic of cause and effect, the Slinger eliminates the draw and thus confounds his enemies:

> To eliminate the draw
> permits an unmatchable Speed
> a syzygy which hangs tight
> just back of the curtain
> of the reality theater
> down the street,
> speed is not necessarily fast.
> Bullets are not necessarily specific.
> When the act is
> so self contained
> and so dazzling in itself
> the target then
> can disappear
> in the heated tension
> which is an area between here
> and formerly
> In some parts of the western world
> men have mistakenly
> called that phenomenology . . .
>                    (S 30–31) .

What the Slinger is saying is that men mistake the attempt to synthesize the objective with the subjective world by developing the science of phenomenology—a study rigorously based in Cartesian dualism. Dorn would probably prefer to think of the Slinger's gestural synthesis as cosmology, a dramatic collapsing of time and space into one "dazzling" action. The citizen, by his exclusionary and proprietary attitude toward the horse ("that's even a *negra* horse," he says), has already "described" himself by his speech and so has already "drawn." He exists in an outmoded logic, one that the Slinger debunks by refusing to play by its rules.

To be "described" is the greatest danger in the Slinger's West. Once you have a name,

> you can be sold
> you can be told
> by that name leave, or come
> you become, in short
> a reference
>
>              (S 32)

To be described is to be bound to a single location or identification—a condition that, as the Slinger points out, defines mortality. The name "I," for example, stands for those assumptions about man that set him over against the world. When "I"'s name is missing from his shirt pocket in Book II, the citizens shout "monster" and "witchcraft" at him, to which the Slinger replies, "you are correct / citizen, your identification is the *same* / as your word for fear!" (S 70). Obviously, a name called may revert back on its user and freeze him for all to see. Howard Hughes, by adopting many names and many identities, avoids this danger and maintains his spectral authority over the world of ordinary citizens.

At the end of Book I the five "missionaries" set out for Las Vegas in a stagecoach pulled by six "driverless horses." The allegorical nature of their journey is established in the beautiful prelude to Book II, which defines the journey in terms of a "tapestry." The five characters are "estranged from that which is most familiar," to adopt Heraclitus' words, and they seek a unifying vision: "and we concur To See / The Universe." They will encounter the world of commercialism ("Tenders of Objects"), which presents a vision of time as a series of "separated events." Their desire is not for material or spiritual riches; it is, rather, "To See." Sight becomes the dominant argument against the "Vicious Isolation" of the local citizenry who "implore this existence / for a plan and dance wideyed / provided with a schedule / of separated events" (S 45). Dorn wants to substitute a temporality of the existential moment over that of the clock. The Slinger's party moves on the "selvedge" (or "self-edge") of time, inverting the terms for forward motion in the backward spinning spokes of their celestial coach.

Book II chronicles the ride along the Rio Grande to Universe City, accompanied at times by the poet's "heliocentric" songs. On the way the stage stops to pick up Kool Everything, whose "head has been misplaced" and who carries a five-gallon can full of LSD. He serves as a version of the laid-back, untroubled acid freak whose remarks are invariably a kind of ultimate cosmic reduction: "Man I dont know where youre At / I'm just hitchhiking / to Universe City and beyond . . ." (S 54). At the point where Everything enters the coach, "I" dies, and the Slinger wishes to preserve him "for a past reference" in Kool Everything's acid. The language here is brilliantly funny. For the first time in literature "I" can contain "Everything," an ontological (and linguistic) feat of no mean proportions.

Upon transfusing Everything's batch of acid into "I," the Slinger observes that

> we stand before an original moment
> in ontological history, the self, with one grab
> has acquired a capital S, mark the date
> the Gunslinger instructed,
> we'll send a telegram to Parmenides.
>
> (S 67)

It is entirely appropriate that Parmenides witness this "expropriation" since it was his view that self and other are one and the same—that in order for one to conceive of sensible objects at all he must be *part* of those objects as well. The "I" that Dorn kills off in the poem is the ego that detaches itself from the moment and anticipates, intuits, regrets, longs for, desires, and generally avoids what it experiences. The ego, Slinger says, is "costumed as the road manager / of the soul," but when preserved in Kool Everything's "autotheistic chemical" it is transformed into an allegory.

Universe City, where the group (including the preserved "I") decoaches, is the archetypal American small town. Its residents water their lawns, enjoy the "celestial repast" of lunch, and joke about "I"'s strange appearance. The law is present in the form of a narcotics agent (not too cleverly disguised as Dick Tracy) who follows the Slinger's entourage around town in a "bucket with crutches." Like most western towns, Universe City began as a wide spot in the road, but as Kool Everything explains, "Wide spots in the road / have a tendency to get wider / due to the weight and speed of the traffic going thruem" (*S* 71). As its name implies, the city is a microcosm for the nation. Unlike Olson's Gloucester or Williams's Paterson, Universe City is strictly propositional—an extension of its developers, commerce, and media. Like Truth or Consequences, New Mexico, it has changed its name to accommodate its anonymity, thus erasing whatever relation it may have had to its geography or history.

The theological center of town, as might be expected, is not the church but a movie theater that houses "The Literate Projector," the ultimate positivist tool. It turns an image into its script, thus transforming reality into the idea behind it. It is one of Dorn's most brilliant conceptions (although he has since questioned its usefulness), "designed for the stix / but works best in University towns / and other natural centers of double-talk" (*S* 79).[8] The Literate Projector is an extension of a logocentric universe in which each signifier is flanked by a primordial signified, in which essence precedes form and idea precedes image. Most insidiously, it may be used to provide ultimate rationales for unethical or immoral acts; it may "put funny music next to death . . ."

8. "It's [the Literate Projector] the most arbitrary thing in Book II. In some ways it violates the forwardness of the book. I was interested in the idea, at the time, and while I was writing I got into it. But I think it mars the poem because it's only an occasional idea. In fact, when I republish the whole poem I think I might extract that" (*I* 47).

Or document something
about military committment
and let woodchucks play the parts
(*S* 79)

Given the official government rationalizations for continuing the Vietnam War during this period, it would be fair to say that the Literate Projector was already in use. Its primary function is to reverse experience into text, to take complex issues and transform them into palatable substitutes.

Book II exposes the varieties of double-talk available to Universe City by means of the "Cycle of Robart's Wallet," announced at the end of the book. Its purpose is to liberate the paranoid citizens from their "Vicious Isolation" and expose the structure of global capitalism. The Slinger advises the citizens to realize their out-of-date materialism and begin to live under a new deific dispensation called "Sllab." If the new Logos of this postmodern world is to be Robart's global dollar, its New Testament is given in "The Cycle."

Trying to interpret "The Cycle" is a little like decoding glyphs for which no Rosetta stone has been found. Its language is relentlessly obscure, refusing at every point to fit into a readable context. Dorn's comments on this most difficult section of the poem indicate that, at one level, it is a "big speculation about [Robart's/Hughes's] habits and frame of mind and his furnishings which are anyway apparently like a battery of twelve TV sets or something" (*I* 31).[9] Robart's name, however, never appears; "[he] only appears as an echo . . . of the psychological condition of the United States of America. Therefore, the interior is a negative quantity, it's anti-gravitational" (*I* 31). I read "interior" both as a reference to the mind of Howard

9. A slightly more opaque definition of "The Cycle" appears in the poem itself when Dorn refers to the "language cleaner / [which] sucks up the negatives / From the cracks in the positive linoleum . . ." (*S* 99). Such remarks could as easily refer to Parmenides' philosophical position in which the negative proposition is rendered meaningless.

Hughes and to the nature of America, so that part of the difficulty in reading this section results from Dorn's attempt to activate the unconscious imagery of a psychic state.

At its most fundamental level "The Cycle" describes the journey of Howard Hughes (or as he is known in this section, "Rupert") from his hotel in Boston to Las Vegas, a journey that actually took place in the mid-sixties and that has already been alluded to in Book I. He disguises himself (in typical Hughes fashion) as a janitor and moves decoyed "as the cheeze in a burger" among the crowds at the railroad station. He is attended by his servant, Al, the time-twisting Atlante. Hughes/Rupert enters his private railroad car like many another high-rolling financier and ponders the cosmos while moving west.

The bulk of the poem concerns the "furnishings" of this railroad car as described by a mysterious "interior Decorator." One realizes after a time that the interior stands for what it contains: the mind of Robart in which "functions have no date nothing occurs / Dates have no function anyway. . ." (*S* 99). In this mind time cannot be compared to linear motion but rather to the imploding and expanding astral bodies in a periodic universe. The classical division of time into past, present, and future no longer holds in Robart's world, and his movements between Boston and Las Vegas can be compared to the alternating patterns of a star (or atom) within this steady-state system. When Robart's car moves west, it "Moves with a basal shift so Large / It would be a dream to feel time curve / For no masses so locked serve straight time" (*S* 100).[10] To remind him of the past, he maintains a giant urn in which rest the ashes of time, inscribed with the phrase "EMIT NO TIME." Since the reverse

10. The entire thematics of time in *Slinger* is discussed variously in *Bean News* (San Francisco, Calif.: Hermes Free Press, n.d.), especially on the second page under the heading "Determined?" On this page, ideas about "Beginning of time," "Direction of time," and "Personal time" are covered in relatively straightforward, textbook variety prose.

of the phrase ("EMIT ON TIME") would celebrate conventional, sequential temporality, we can assume that Robart and his Atlantes have performed certain violence on this outmoded idea. Around the base of the urn is written an equally significant phrase: "MADE IN JAPAN." The two phrases together offer an appropriate attack on Keats's Grecian Urn, in which time is frozen in mythic stillness.

Extending the theme of time is Dorn's use of Parmenides, whose great philosophical "Proem" presents an earlier discourse on the nature of the truth by means of poetic allegory. The opening lines of "The Cycle" appear to be a rough translation of Parmenides' poem, which begins as follows:

The steeds that carry me took me as far as my heart could desire, when once they had brought me and set me on the renowned way of the goddess, who leads the man who knows through every town. On that way was I conveyed; for on it did the wise steeds convey me, drawing my chariot, and maidens led the way. And the axle blazing in the socket—for it was urged round by well-turned wheels at each end— was making the holes in the naves sing, while the daughters of the Sun, hasting to convey me into the light, threw back the veils from off their faces and left the abode of night.[11]

Like "The Cycle," the "Proem" is an allegory depicting the stages from the world of seeming and illusion to that of truth, and both poems provide a circular or cyclic logic in which "what has been run thus far / Is what has been run before" (S 97). The nature of Parmenides' truth is similar to that of Slinger. For Parmenides, truth is a totality, "well-rounded" and capable of no division. Things are not created or destroyed but exist eternally. To say that something does not exist is to utter a meaningless phrase, since in order for something to be comprehensible it must already "Be." Mortals (Dorn's "lumpish lis-

11. G. S. Kirk and J. E. Raven, *The Presocratic Philosophers: A Critical History with a Selection of Texts* (Cambridge: Cambridge University Press, 1966), p. 266.

teners") have been deluded by the idea that a thing that exists may also, in time, perish and that something else may take its place. Time equally cannot be made of atomic moments that pass into the past; time and space are all one, "immovable" and "continuous." Parmenides' alternative to doctrines of flux and change is simple: "it is," and if it is not, it cannot be thought.

This philosophical monism provides the epistemological backdrop for "The Cycle," but the poem's *mise en scène* involves a blend of Parmenidean cosmology and Hughesean myth. The chariot and horses, the theological premise, the goddess, the spinning wheels of the chariot, the allegorical language all parallel Parmenides' poem. Likewise, the vision of Rupert wearing Kleenex boxes instead of shoes, his travel in railroad cars, his battery of antiseptic bodyguards, his demand for anonymity are all legends about Hughes no more fantastic than those told about other national heroes. Even his attendants, the Atlantes, appear to be demonic parodies of Hughes's army of Mormon guards. Such stories form the basis for legends (or "cycles" of legends?) sung by bards and used as exemplae in projecting the national character. Dorn's own "cycle" is an ironic continuation of this tradition.

To treat "The Cycle" as simply a code for a subterranean story would be anathema to Dorn's purpose. Rupert's journey involves "the Overhaul of the fucking mind," and the poem's language reflects that transformation by presenting meta-information, the source for which can only be traced to the computer bank named Robart/Rupert. Words are not tied to discrete meanings; they have only a differential function: "there is nothing more for now to know / Because the signals speak among themselves" (S 96). Language no longer constitutes or secures a primordial meaning but suspends it indefinitely within an infinite series of binary functions. What fragments of recognizable language one encounters in "The Cycle" come in the form of cliché, jive talk, scientific argot, and newspaper lingo—those elaborate codes in which a culture's unconscious life is inscribed. The effect is that of tuning in on a distant radio station that alternately fades in and out of one's range; the messages are recognizable in part, but their context is perpetually blurred. At the end of "The Cycle" Dorn alludes to the journey already in progress, that of the Slinger and his party to Las Vegas. Rupert and his number one henchman, Al, have "picked off" the telegram to Parmenides on their scanner. Al reports,

> I think this is it Boss
> The crack we been waitin for
> The scanners have picked off
> A telegram to Parmenides
>
> From a point on the arc
> 2 days minus 4 Corners
> We sure know where that's at Boss, um
> We can find it *in the Dark*
>
> (*S* 109)

A rough translation might read as follows: the moment in ontological history represented by "I"'s transformation (which has been detailed in a telegram to Parmenides) has become part of the geodetic record (the crack) of the (human) universe. The telegram has been sent from a point on an arc (the journey of the Slinger and his cohorts) that is two days from Four Corners. Presumably Al and Rupert will move west to meet the Slinger at the "crosshairs" of those four states. The death of "I" and his transformation through chemistry would ordinarily be described as a psychological-phenomenological event, but from the standpoint of such stellar travelers as the Slinger or Robart the event is part of the geological history of a universe in flux.

The railroad tracks that carry Robart's car become a metaphor for linear time. In the West they are the great equal signs, carving the history of exploitation into the landscape and col-

lapsing vast spaces into smaller and smaller units. Book III
chronicles the gradual merging of space and time by proposing
a third alternative, "personal time" or proprioception:

> There is no vacuum in sense
> connection is not by contact
> sense is the only pure time
> connection is a mechanical idea
> nothing touches, connection meant is
> Instant in extent a proposal of limit
>
>                    (S 115)

The last line suggests that, for Dorn, one moves in an "extended
instant," a moment of sudden attention or intensity that structures the nature of limit. This extended instant releases landscape from its sentimental associations and fuses it with human
attentions. "I have the sense that we know totality all the time
through our senses," Dorn says in a 1973 interview; "and what
part of that totality we can capture is the definition essentially
of our sensate capabilities" (I 46). The "outside real," seen from
passing train or stagecoach, becomes "insidereal," the human
assimilation of landscape or the incorporation of space by existential temporality.

Much of what occurs in Book III is an extension of what
(and how) the Slinger sees, but we begin to feel that his quest is
breaking down—at least in the conventional, narrative sense.
Books I and II follow an almost recognizable journey from one
town to another. Even "The Cycle," for all its opacity, is framed
by epic convention. Book III continues the playful, punning
quality of "The Cycle" but complicates the narrative by elimi-
nating practically all connectives and transitions. What appears instead is a series of cartoon dialogues. The journey to
Las Vegas has been subsumed by gags, puns, and elaborate
jokes. This breakdown in narrative continuity reflects the dis-
sociation of that causal logic on which conventional stories are
built. Since there is no place to go, why not intensify where one

is? The road that the Slinger's band follows is no longer "on the road"; rather, it "symbolizes our thinking process." It has moved entirely to the inner landscape.

The cartoon dialogues of Book III take on an impressive variety of subjects: Pindar's theory of light,[12] the horse as personification of knowledge, the relation of the poet to authority, the nature of "Sllab," Olbers's paradox,[13] game theory, the role of contingency in generation, and the nature of serial transmission. Each one of these subjects is covered by means of a verbal shorthand that transforms them into witty digressions. To take one example, Dr. Flamboyant's "Great Beenville Paradoxes" seem formed out of Deweyan epistemology:

12. Dorn seems to be referring to a book by Lionel W. Lyde called *Contexts in Pindar* (Manchester: Manchester University Press, 1935), which discusses Pindar's poetry in terms of light and the effects of light rays upon the Greek poet. Dorn's reference to Lyde on page 115 condenses a paragraph of Lyde's that reads as follows:

The description of φέγγος as Pindar's "medium" is due to a conviction that a large proportion of his work was done under the influence of the emotional light—in the early hours and the late hours of the day; and this conviction is based on a double comparison—a comparison between his short records of the actual exploits of the athletes whom he is nominally celebrating, and his long stories of the prehistoric heroes and heroines, and a parallel comparison between his lavish use of metaphor, i.e., of illusion as art, and his sparing use of simile, i.e., of comparison as science.

(P. 41)

13. Dorn speaks of the German astronomer, Heinrich Wilhelm Mathäus Olbers in *I* 99, and mentions his paradox: "The universe cannot be infinite *and* entirely visible." This idea seems to lie behind the lines on page 132 of *Slinger*:

> the world is absolutely finite
> and the cosmos is indefinitely finite
> whats that?
>
> a cross between a billiard table
> ana sponge cake the Horse whispered
> in Lil's piercèd ear
>
> (*S* 134)

Nature abhors a vacuum
but for nature, A VACUUM'S
GOT NOTHING AT ALL
(*S* 136)

But Flamboyant's attendant "pseudo paradox" quickly supplies the cultural referent: "Time and Life cooperate once a
week, or used to." If time and life can be said to "cooperate" we
begin to understand the nature of the previously mentioned
"vacuum." Obviously, the idea of nature does not make distinctions between time and life, but when these terms are names for
corporate entities, nature is suddenly severely mediated.

To treat Flamboyant's paradoxes as serious philosophical
problems would violate the sense of play that permeates the
book. Part of Dorn's intent here is to expose the faulty logic of
much philosophical reflection while maintaining some of its
serious tone. Flamboyant himself, while a sympathetic character, is a satire of the academic whose researches into esoteric
subjects (the "Tensile Strength of Last Winters Icicles" is one of
his projects) lead nowhere. But hidden behind many of the jokes
in Book III is a further exploration of the proprioceptive view
announced at the end of "The Cycle." The prologue to the
book, to take one example, frames those laws that unite man to
the cosmos. "The Lawg," as the prologue is called, is a capsu-
lized record (a log) of the "human universe" that Olson valued
over against the strictly objective or empirical. Olson had pitted
himself against the older humanism of the Greeks, based on
Plato and Aristotle, and on their tendency to abstract man from
his literal, biological condition. "There are laws," Olson admits
at the beginning of his "Human Universe" essay, but they are
laws of man as organism, not solely as egocentric, reflective
mind. The laws of this organism are those of the body, the
senses, the musculature responding at every moment to the
world. It is this dynamic participation with the so-called
"outer" world that replaces the concept of law as Mosaic and
Deuteronomic and that forms the basis for Dorn's comic inversion:

> Here Kums the Kosmos
> Dont just stand there! (lookin dumb
> Stick out your thumb.
>
> (S 113)

Participation in the Cosmos is, apparently, as immediate as hitching a ride.

Such cosmological banter makes up most of Book III and is continued in *Bean News* where we hear, for example, of the "Conference on Nothing" taking place in Notsuoh, Texas (or Houston spelled backwards), where the central question is "when (and where) is Now." Or we read of the arrival of "Sllab" in a "Cloud of Adobe Dust and Chicken Feathers" or of the first "macro transplant" (i.e., of a whole body). The language plays with recognizable information channels but debunks them at the same time by extending real conferences, geodetic occurrences, and organ transplants into their absurd potentialities. The inversion of terms for "Time" and "Life," however humorous, is not funny to Dorn. Behind the arch debunker is a social critic who understands the deeper implications behind physical laws and media dissemination as they are subsumed by economic interests:

> you know why everybody
> in this state's fat?
> They're convinced torque
> is a relationship
> between the tongue and the fork
>
> (S 124)

If Book III has a central event, it is the delivery of the "night letta" from Parmenides via "I" disguised as a goggled biplane pilot (another Hughes persona). He hangs from his biplane into the window of the Slinger's carriage and hands in a letter that reads like a computer printout. The only recognizable information appears at the end of the letter: "Expect Materialization at Precisely 4 Corners," a reference to the long-anticipated incarnation of Robart. The rest of the message is in code, which, as the Slinger observes, is "Sllab." This is the first appearance of that deific principle by which Robart operates. Since the word is "balls" spelled backwards, one can assume that this deity works through an inversion of the male sexual principle by which father is replaced by son, a transmundane God by a mortal Christ. Sllab is not "past-trapped" but is a "perfectly proceeding, but irregularly worn Cube, imbedded 5 quarters into the hypersurface of Eternity."[14] Dorn has spoken of Sllab in terms of Stanley Kubrick's giant monolith in his movie *2001* (which also proposes an inversion of temporality) and has described it elsewhere as an ultimate Rosetta stone upon which the key to deity is inscribed (*I* 54). Its appearance *in absentia* at the end of Book III suggests that Book IIII will be a mock Revelation, a last judgment in which the key to Robart (alias Rupert, alias Slinger, alias Hughes) will be revealed.

Book IIII does provide a kind of last judgment, but its terms are economic rather than eschatological. It is the book of Robart's "Shortage Industry," the manipulation of which keeps the world in a constant state of turmoil. The book's locale is southwestern Colorado near Cortez and presumably within range of Four Corners. In the "Superior Air," beyond this area resides Robart, who unrolls his "Global Report," attended by his aide, Al, who plays Rochester to Robart's Jack Benny:

> Plaise the Lord
> and pass the municiones Al chortled
> Have you read that nasty note from the Xah?
>
> Shadup you impudent slave Robart grinned
> and balanced a kleenex on the tip of his nose
>
> You the onliest man in the world
> can do that boss, Al sang
>
> You say that because it so true, Albert

14. In *Bean News*, under the heading "Where Is Now," p. 5.

> No patrón I say that
> because you got the only special
> rigid kleenex in the unit
> (S 149)

Behind the banter lie the insidious terms of global economics, complete with munitions sales and correspondence with the Shah.

Robart's "Global Report" includes information about his earthly warfare between the "dreaded Mogollones" (the name taken from an Apache tribe) and the "Single-Spacers" ("your Glorious Low-Violence Army") that he keeps alive by playing one side off against the other. Such diabolical management keeps everyone in an uncertainty that only Robart can transcend. The "Shortage Industry" creates the illusion of limited supplies in order to drive up prices, a condition felt acutely during the oil crisis, which occurred during the time that Book IIII was being written. When Robart talks about turning a car into a chile relleno or when Flamboyant drives up in a "green 1976 Avocado" we witness the transformation of our immediate needs (foodstuffs) into cars, a ratio that exists at every level of the economy. The shortage industry, maintained by international cartels, creates relationships that, when seen in Dorn's comic strip, are perhaps humorous but that, upon reflection, are ominous indeed.

The ethic of the "Shortage Industry" is preached by a giant hill of beans that the "pleiad" of travelers encounters outside of Cortez, Colorado. This hill is Sllab's messenger and has been made, like much else in the West, by the Hughes Tool Company. Its message is all too clear:

> Achievement comes thru absolute power
> and power comes thru strength
> . . . . . . . . . . . . . . . . . . . . . . . . . . . . . .
> this nation is the product of reason
> & corn
> (S 164)

And, one might add, beans. Only to a privileged class does a "hill of beans amount to nothing." To poor Indians in the Southwest, for example, the trope is meaningless, and "I" notices this fact by paying attention to the figure of speech, "not the hill." Those who are in a position to indulge themselves in such a figure are the same who hide behind a rhetoric of humanist concern—who abhor

> the excessive opulence & waste,
> the blatant commercialization
> on which society is built,
> the selfish introspective approach
> to world affairs . . .
>
> (S 165)

Sllab, speaking through its talking hill of beans, has appropriated all symbol systems and rhetorics and feeds it back, like a juke box, to anyone willing to deposit a dime in the slot.

Robart and Al, as lesser deities in the configuration of this new Logos, operate from a similarly lofty vantage. In "The Cycle" they occupy a celestial railway car, but in Book IIII they are clearly residents of the astral realm. Like their earthly counterparts they exist in a state of war, but their opposition is never named. Warfare at this level involves the implosion and explosion of galaxies, comprehended by Robart's scanners in terms of red-shifting and blue-shifting. The warfare between the Mogollones and Single-Spacers, which Robart maintains on earth, is a microcosm for the large-scale stellar movements comprehensible to us in terms of the Doppler effect. We read Robart's movements by means of varying frequencies of light rays, but we feel his effects in the form of perpetual global turmoil. Dorn sustains the various levels of warfare by blending one into the other until Robart's super radar scanner merges with the Slinger's telescope.

One of the central events of Book IIII is the return of "I," who has been on a "tour of Cumulus" and who is now apprenticed to Parmenides. Life in his post-LSD manifestation feels like "trying to read a newspaper / from nothing but the ink poured into your ear," a clear formulation of "I" 's transformation from questioning ego to cybernetic intelligence. Information is poured straight in; it is no longer mediated. "I" has become an observer of the contemporary scene like the Slinger, "one eye out / for the prosecuters of Individuality / and the other eye out for the advocates" (S 162). His gift to the Slinger is a bag filled with "all the known species of Cant," which, when thrown on the stagecoach, sails over the top and lands in the desert, whereupon a geyser of oil springs up. Apparently Dorn intends a satire on the relations that exist between oil and the diplomatic jargon involved in procuring it from the Middle East (the bag is decorated with "fine Iranian tooling"). "I" 's indifferent observance of this incident indicates that he has come a long way from his earlier confusions.

In addition to "I," several new characters are added: Taco Desoxin, the "best / environmental modification man / in the business," and his partner, Tonto Pronto. Both are parodies of TV western characters. Taco Desoxin is a new-age Speedy Gonzales (Desoxin is a type of amphetamine), and Tonto is the Lone Ranger's trusted Indian. As "speedy" types they are adept in interpreting Robart's movements. Along with Dr. Flamboyant and a fourth character, Portland Bill, they form a quartet of Luddite anarchists who destroy technology from within. They

burn telephone poles
slice permutationes thin as baloney
nothin complex
we also kick the perpendiculars outa right anglos
eat fur coats

suck air thru white sidewalls
but thats a Zen Act, extra
and, we do Blowtorch pretty good
we just Blowtorch Vegas from the kitchen . . .

> We also supply Hi-grade lunatic information
> *you can get it here* & so forth
> also do Pre-pourd Scorn . . .
>
>                   (S 167–68)

Such subversion is prepared by Flamboyant for conflict with the Mogollones, "the new machinists / Masters of the wedge inclined plane screw."

The projected battle between the Mogollones and Single-Spacers never takes place as such but serves as a metaphor for the battle between technology and the environment. Dorn's satire is as black as that of William Burroughs, whose Nova Police and mind-control experts are comic projections of entropic disorder. The Mogollones have neither virtues nor vices; they are "totally anti-Darwinian," living on octane fumes since they cannot breathe the pure desert air. The Single-Spacers are "anythingarians" (i.e., "opposed to nothing"), capable of torturing animals and altering the "subduction zone." Robart, as cosmic mediator, provides each side with "peste bubonica" to make the stakes even higher. The Slinger and his comrades view the coming battle from a mesa high above Four Corners—a false Pisgah before which Robart will finally fulfill his ambiguous covenant.

When Robart finally appears, it is in the form of an overheard conversation picked up on Flamboyant's radio (called a "reduit," presumably because it "re-does" what has been done already):

> Krackle Krackle Krackle
>
> *Incarnation is bunk*, Al
> *Get that Punk outa here*
> *And send for the Hydralicx*
> *we're in a fracture*
> *surprise is no longer the mode*
> *We gotta get as big as we can*
> *as fast as we can, that's the game plan*
>
>                   (S 195)

He then descends from his railroad car, riding a cow, and takes off for Chile. The cow is perhaps that "longhorn bull" for which the Slinger searched in Book I, but if this is Dorn's incarnation scene, its grandeur has been diminished by the rapidity of Robart's withdrawal. The moment is wonderfully anticlimactic, deity reduced to an escaping bandito and the reverent multitudes transformed into wisecracking gawkers. Lil interprets Robart's sudden exit as his having been red-shifted (hence he moves *away* from the group), but Dorn provides no "textual tickets" to explain this event.

At this culminating point we might become intrepid "I"'s and ask a few questions: does Flamboyant's "reduit" actually receive Robart's messages? Are Robart's movements subject to unearthly forces beyond the Slinger's purview? What is the function of Taco and Tonto's "environmental modification"? What happened to the battle between the Mogollones and the Single-Spacers? Is the Slinger an antagonist to Robart or a part of him? In other words, to what pass has this poem brought us? By asking such questions, we fall into the pattern established by the western movie that demands a resolution, preferably in the light of the setting sun, at the end. But *Slinger* "ends" on an incomplete note; the action does not proceed from previous events. Instead, the party quickly disperses, the Slinger to his "timetrain," "I" to the "tachyon showers," and the rest to other states. In what sense, then, is this the end?

The answer has already been repeated many times in the form of a paradox: "Everything is prehensible / for from that which is not / we fall off." The Whiteheadean term, "prehension," describes the appropriation of elements within a cellular model. Each element in a system depends on (prehends) all other events for its existence. What Dorn has provided is a single cell (or solar system) made up of various atomic units whose interaction is total. From any point outside the structure (i.e., from Robart's vantage) the organism seems whole and

unified, but from any point on the inside events may be interpreted as threatening, friendly, encroaching, or departing.
Those who, by their vast control of media, technology, and
finance, are able to mediate the way in which these events are
interpreted may adjust how we perceive any individual event
(the war in Vietnam, say, or the oil crisis). Robart's control is
total; he adjusts the economies of the Southwest as easily as he
adjusts his own identity. "Vegas is a vast decoy," Lil says, but so
are the anonymous Chevrolets, airplanes, and hotel rooms that
hide Howard Hughes. Such absolute control creates a world in
which a handshake in America can effect a military takeover in
Chile or a business deal in Saudi Arabia (to use the two axes
most often invoked in Book IIII).

If *Slinger* seems incomplete, it is because it has viewed the
demand for closure as one of the oppressive features of Western
thought. Dorn refuses to tie things together in a mechanical
way; he refers to the progress of his poem in terms of a "Moving
Future" that is always at a selvedge between the finite and
infinite (*I* 99). Rather than fulfill the eschatological frame proposed from the first book, Dorn disperses his characters among
the western states as signs of a totally new awareness that has
evolved during the late sixties. The self-conscious, rationalizing
"I" has given way to a proprioceptive "eye" that has learned
how to see and read the world at the same time:

> Our Source is self refracting
> and when it rises it actually plays a tune
> on one's eyeballs, Maximum Deum
> and our birds have two heads and sing duets
> (*S* 199)

These lines seem to refer to Olson's valorization of the eye in
*The Maximus Poems* and to the maximal self that lies potential
(self-refracting) in any individual. At the end of this most un-
Olsonic comic vision, Dorn's homage to the older poet's sense

of *polis* as "eyes" is most profound. If Olson could not have anticipated where his bibliography would lead Edward Dorn it is only because his student so totally realized the methodological implications behind the study of American history. *Slinger* is not only a poem generated out of Olson's teaching and example; it is a truly American poem, "indirect" as Whitman felt the new epic must be. It is not content simply to reflect landscape and history but struggles constantly with its own precarious existence, creating a hero as problematic as Natty Bumppo, Huck Finn, Ishmael, or Isabel Archer. Its spirited language and acidic humor create an alternative tone to the epic tradition as found in Whitman or Pound, and yet its interest in "personal time" and heroic gesture are themes congenial to earlier American poetry.

At its most fundamental level *Slinger* provides us with a comprehensive look at language in the postwar era. Dorn invents a "language cleaner," an inversionary critique that transforms all talk into meta-talk, thus exposing the arbitrariness of sign production. He wants to keep language in "interesting repair" at all times by relentlessly testing its limits while at the same time exposing its vulnerability to forms of social control. His analysis of exploitation begins with the rhetoric of western romance and refers to theology, metaphysics, cybernetics, thermodynamics, comic books, rock and roll, biology, newspeak, technocracy, and high finance along the way. It is not enough to treat these areas as discrete, metaphoric subjects; Dorn must incorporate them as semiotic systems embedded in the surface of modern American life. The Slinger indicates that it is no longer possible to look from any privileged vantage at a landscape that has not already undergone modification—if only by rhetoric—and it is this heavily encrusted topography of signs and dollars that compels his heroic search.

# 5

## *Art Rising to Clarity: Edward Dorn's Compleat* Slinger

### WILLIAM J. LOCKWOOD

When in "Oxford, Part V" two "loose . . . stringed" lads complained that everything had already been said, Dorn's speaker tautly suggested they start naming themselves and "this / 'rock from which the language springs' " (*CP* 210). When Dorn declared his "mystique of the real" for American poetry, he did so in the context of an appraisal of "HDT" (Henry David Thoreau) within a poem of subterranean reflection; that poem, titled "The Land Below" (*CP* 57), was itself a kind of "sheer[ing] off" archeological expedition. When, toward the close of his four-year residence in England, Dorn "looked" across the Atlantic, his mind picked up and projected in "An Idle Visitation" (*CP* 226) his image-dream of "the long plains night" of that continent where Texans were said to "carry on / and arrange their genetic duels / with men of other states." (The latter stage involved a somewhat metaphysical shifting from the opening line of "A Epic": "HE STOOD BEFORE THE DARKLING PLAIN" [*SB* 10].) And when, the idle visitation having by that time blossomed into the three-quarters-evolved *Slinger*, Dorn had the poet recite the "Song of Cocaine Lil" (*S* 171ff.)—alias "Erythra with a wig of roots"—he insisted on tracing her elaborate genealogy back to her roots in ancient Peru. "Rock" (signifying dwelling place), shearing off (as with a geologist's hammer), and "roots" (both vegetable and racial)—such a word list supplies a selective index to the history of Dorn's mind as that history gathered toward the heroic and hilarious compleat *Slinger*.

The angle of approach I shall adopt here is based on two central perceptions the foregoing "index" seems to invite: that *Slinger* is predominantly grounded in the mode of song and that that mode of song is grounded in Dorn's sense of the "intensity" (in-tensity) of places. The modes are various in this long, leisurely, and variously furnished poem—as, indeed, are particular moments announced as "songs"—and yet it is the presence of song, more than of satiric, declamatory, or meditative forms of speaking, that supplies the poem's reader his most stable point of reference. Engaged in the journey through surprising, unpredictable, multireferenced territories, the reader-as-fellow-traveler comes to rely on the recurrence of song, and on the always present possibility of its recurrence, as a means of getting his bearings or of trusting that he will get them. Undulating rhythms sustain the reader's involvement in "Idaho Out," as I have elsewhere argued, and so it is in *Slinger*, only in a journey-poem that is considerably more complex because it is much longer, more comprehensive, and more artfully sustained.[1] Thus Dorn speaks of his recent interest in language songs more than music songs—songs that go straight to the ears and knock directly on the brain. Language, its derangement and recombination, he sees, is needed to act like a honed wedge to cut through the grain of cultural resistances toward aliveness, and yet it is song-language, he sees, that is needed if the poem is to be sustained in its flight. Attuned to the announced "mission" of a journey finally concluded in the heart

1. William J. Lockwood, "Ed Dorn's Mystique of the Real: His Poems for North America," *Contemporary Literature* 30 (Winter 1978): 58–79.

of the Colorado Plateau, that "absolute" song, enabled by the scarred but living rock of the bright dark plains and by the flora that inhabit them, would bring the long poem to a satisfactory close.

The approach here will thus differ from Michael Davidson's in his *Slinger* essay, and it will also suggest that Donald Wesling's view of Dorn's checking of lyricism needs to be qualified in light of what strikes me in *Slinger* as Dorn's most extroverted piece of writing (more extroverted on the whole even than its prose companion piece, "The Sheriff of McTooth County").[2] Davidson's underlying assumption that all places have been appropriated and that, consequently, Dorn's poem consists of a play of gestures and tensions operating within an elaborated system of signs seems to me an appropriate angle of approach to "The Cycle" and to "The Winterbook" (Book III). But I do not think it adequately accounts for the poem's wider attentiveness to those selective, relatively pure flashes of landscape that appear at crucially timed intervals; and it does not take sufficiently into account the ecstatic effect of the imprint of those flashes upon the travelers' minds. What I think needs to be more fully recognized is that the Slinger's stylishly metaphysical gestures in Book I seek answering forms, what Dorn's Poet speaks of in his "Poem Called Riding Throughe Mádrid" (Book III) as "matter" sheared off from the reclaimed Southwest locale in which and through which the alert travelers move. Dorn's strategy of gradually dispersing the Slinger's commanding presence as the journey evolves through successive stages calls, if it is to stay coherent and lively, for more than metaphysical pretensions. Rigidity, in all its possible manifestations, cannot be

2. "The Sheriff" is from *Some Business Recently Transacted in the White World.* Its connections with *Gunslinger: Book I* and *Gunslinger: Book II*, earlier versions making up the first half of *Slinger*, are elaborated in Lockwood, "Mystique of the Real," pp. 77–78. Books I and II were published by Black Sparrow Press (Los Angeles) in 1968 and 1969.

risked. Style itself must take on the permeable and permutable quality of song, sung not in a purely verbal sign system but in the shifting context of a landscape or dwelling place, itself *eterne in mutabilitie.*

In a related way, then, the poem Dorn first envisaged in "An Idle Visitation" could not be held together and sustained by wit alone, or by wit only aided by song and laughter. The originary elements of *Slinger* as set down in that seminal fragment would have to be elaborated: the "cautious Gunslinger / of impeccable smoothness" will gather about him a diverse assemblage of congenial comrades; his unrolled "map," disclosing a "theatre of impatience," will become a magnified sequence of images projected onto the poem's "screen." Local interferences will be encountered along the way: dollar signs, petrochemical installations, and so forth; they will, on nearer inspection, lie in the path of such elaboration of the visual drama picked up from across the Atlantic. Such information will need to be dealt with: vigilance and resiliency will be required. But a capacity for utterance in the mode of song will have to sustain the original vision and constitute the bright threads in the poem's fabric; a capacity for diversifying the kinds of songs, including parodic versions of song, will ensure its resiliency.

In general, I submit, wit increases the elasticity of *Slinger,* supplies it a kind of malleable, tough membrane. Thus in Book II the coming of dawn in the desert is presented as a sublime occasion: a raga, a rock song, and a version of the traditional dawn song name it. The raga is preludial; the "Rock Oh Light" provides an enthusiastic though parodic version of a sacred hymn set to the words and rhythms of rock music, and the dawn song, "Cool Liquid Comes," internalizes the virtues of approaching sunlight. Heard in sequence, the effect is one of an increase of lyric expansiveness. The parodic "Rock Oh Light" tempers with broad humor the tendency toward celebration, and yet that very tempering lends greater weight to the shared exhilaration and even tenderness expressed in the ecstatic Slinger's warm thanks for the Poet's timely performance. At first sight, similarly, the Horse's "Equestrian Song," earlier in Book II, recalls the parodic mode and its both tempering and intensifying function. What a horse sings of is grass, especially a talking horse who habitually smokes giant rolls of marijuana, and especially when, upon the coach's arrival in Truth or Consequences, that horse is astonished to find only the grass you can mow in small rectangular lots. Wit seems, at first sight, the obvious business of this "Equestrian Song"; still, what sticks between our ears, after all, is the impression that what we have heard is also a version of a Blakean song of a green paradise promising a time when

> the fair yong sor-rel
> lies in the green green tow-own
> and para-dice will floo-rish
> . . . . . . . . . . . . . . . . . . . . . . . .
> We'll *Flash* on our own legs then
> and nev-er-more come dow-own
> (S 64)

In context, too, the song fits within a wider occasion: a pause in conversation created by Kool Everything's adjusting the tubes attached from the can of liquid preservative to "I"'s recently deceased body. In the established context—of the dreariness of the town set in a splendid landscape on the one hand and of the death of "I" on the other—the Poet, the Slinger, and Lil are all visibly moved by the Horse's recitation of another version of reality: "*I'm al*right Lil whispered / when the hand of Everything / touched her shoulder, *I'm* / just *looking for my handkerchief*" (S 64). Such moments of contact between the "inside real" of pure mind and the "outsidereal" of the pure cosmos (glimpsed in such "flashes") deserve songfulness and Dorn supplies it.

To return to that angle of approach that finds *Slinger*

grounded in song and song grounded in the "intensity" of places, I would observe that such triggering moments of contact like the foregoing ones generally arise whenever the attentive travelers shear off vital forms discoverable in *particular* locales and identifiable by *singular* topographic phenomena. Song signifies the triumph of the living mind over deadening matter, but such triumph occurs within a selective spatial field having its own local regionalisms, geological histories, landforms, and so forth. One travels through them in a quest for purity of mind but without the innocence of immediate being, which is to say that one travels in a deliberately defined context. For Dorn has never been interested in blowing words into a vacuity but rather in inducing in his society a cognizance of itself: in America art needs to rise to that kind of clarity.

The approach argued here approximates that which George Steiner advocates in reading Dante's "Gossip of Eternity" as set down in the *Commedia*. We need to read it, he suggests, attentive to the "axes of relation" that support its elaborate structure and that give it its "crystallographic integrity." The satisfaction that that poem can give to the attentive reader, if he will bestow himself upon it, lies in full recognition of the anchoring of the "spiritual motion" of Dante's text in its "literal specificity":

*Spaces are densely material and topographical* . . . making of the narrative a laboured voyage into concreteness, into mine shafts, marl-pits, rock galleries and up gritty moraines toward flares and crenellations of celestial light themselves palpable. . . . *The voyage has a twofold mapping: internal and North Italian. These two are knit by a tactic of constant references* . . . to sites, often minute . . . exactitudes, pedantries, regionalisms which stabilize the leap of the visionary arc and posit authority. . . . *The text is timeless, universal, because utterly dated and placed.* [Italics mine][3]

3. George Steiner, *On Difficulty and Other Essays* (London: Oxford University Press, 1978), p. 213.

It will be apparent in extended sections of *Slinger*, when "civil interferences" intrude, that Dorn's investigations of the outer limits of language become so far-reaching that they will seem to have been written in a code only the adept or the ideal reader could crack. And yet it remains true even in such instances that Dorn's text remains "a laboured voyage into concreteness, into . . . rock galleries and up gritty moraines toward flares and crenellations," that it involves a "twofold mapping" of internal and regional-continental territories, and that its unfolding song proceeds by "a tactic of constant references . . . which stabilize the leap of the visionary arc."

■ I ■

*Entrapment is this society's*
*Sole activity, I whispered*
*and Only laughter,*
*can blow it to rags*
(Book IIII, part 2, *S* 155)

*Gunslinger: Book I*, first published in 1968, offered a wry and lively twist upon the standard treatment of Western materials. It appears that from his transoceanic vantage Dorn perceived in the figure of the Westerner adrift in the American continent a mysterious presence. In the course of thinking about that presence, which had somehow survived beneath the trappings of national myth, he evidently began to attribute to him a specifically vitalist identity. The poem's plot then evolved from that attribution: for in the spatial field of the Southwest corner of the North American continent he imagined a collision between the vitalist principle embodied in the Slinger and the romanticized mechanistic principle figured in the capitalist entrepreneur named Hughes.

By the time the whole poem appeared in 1975 under the title
*Slinger*, in four books (plus an interlude called "The Cycle") a
series of metamorphoses had occurred—as, significantly, in the
hero's name, which shifted from the "Gunslinger" to the
"Slinger" to (in his farewell) the "Zlinger." What the whole
*Slinger* invites attention to, then, is the way in which the stylized
mode of Book I yields to the allegorized mode of Book II as the
poem initiates its arching trajectory. That trajectory gets inter-
rupted in "The Cycle," reaches its zenith at the close of Book
III, and then splits off into two motions in Book IIII, toward
the sun (the Slinger's home) and toward the earth (ours). What
Dorn teaches us to see and how he beguiles us into that seeing
in the opening books thus needs to be viewed in relation to that
wider perspective toward which the journeying poem finally
unfolds. It is the track of that trajectory—a journey of the mind
authenticated by a close mapping out of the life we live and of
the places given to us to live in—that I have nominated in this
essay's title as the "compleat" *Slinger*.

The stylized mode adopted in the opening scenes beguiles
the reader and so involves him in the subsequent journey.
Dorn's deliberate stylization builds upon the reader's pleasurable recognition of the familiar Western hero and surprises him
into new recognitions of what remains alive, retrievable, and
culturally enabling (as against that which is dead, rigidified,
and disabling). The allegorizing mode to which it gradually
yields constitutes an extension and amplification of such recognitions. *Dulcere* precedes *docere*. And to a degree that sets
his poem off from those of other poets of his generation, Dorn
supplies the reader a full measure of accessible pleasure here.
The pleasure centers in the figure of the Gunslinger and it
radiates outward. It extends, notably, to the incidence of song
and to the activities of the Slinger's horse, and also to the hero's
dress, his affection for Lil, and his preference for drink. Though

tempered by the almost tongue-in-cheek tonality Dorn's language generates, such pleasures are secured by the equilibrium of the semidiós that the reader discovers beneath the Slinger's stylish displays.

One encounters in the opening frame, then, a hero who seems, by virtue of his single-mindedness, impeccable smoothness, and exquisite manners, familiar: his slender hands are encased in gloves imprinted with the Queen of Hearts; he has traveled without sleep the dusty, alkaline route from Nuevo Laredo (across the Texas border) to Mesilla (across the Mexican border in New Mexico); craving cool refreshment in the local saloon, he drinks tequila; he chats with his old friend Lil while tipping his chair back and shadowing his eyes with his hat; and so forth. Soon, however, one's initial sense of this familiar gunslinging hero alters: he begins to seem a marvel, after all, a kind of faerie creature, like the Green Knight. Consequently, when Lil, the saloon girl, slaps the Slinger on the back and speaks of how the sight of him makes her shake (and how she twists her Kansas City parasol only in order "to keep the dazzle of them spurs outa my eyes"), Book I's mediating figure named "I" objects to her offhand manner. And the reader, as witness of the occasion, tends to concur with his respectful view:

> I think the sun, the moon
> and some of the stars are
> kept in their tracks
> by this Person's equilibrium
> or at least I sense some effect
> on the perigee and apogee of all
> our movements in this, I can't quite say,
> *man's* presence
>
> (S 8)

That assessment will be confirmed elsewhere in the ongoing narrative, as for example, in the Slinger's thumbing through his "galactic notebook" just before the recitation of the "Song of Cocaine Lil" in Book IIII. Still, agreement with "I" about the Slinger's cosmic presence remains tentative in light of Lil's subsequent inquiry concerning this greenhorn, "I":

> *and* who *is this*
> *funny talker, you pick him up*
> *in some sludgy seat of higher*
> *learnin, Creeps! you always did*
> *hang out with some curious refugees.*
>
> (S 8)

The hero's origins remain an elusive matter, and if in Book II doubt about his authority persists in the reader's mind, it persists by virtue of this tone of comic irony. The Horse's response to Slinger's comment that since he is "extra-terrestrial" he has "no practical sense of smell" illustrates the point: "More likely you can't keep your nose / out of those $50. bags" (S 59). Wherever directed, laughter is an essential ingredient of this poem; it is indeed an elemental quality of "this Person's equilibrium." The generation of laughter may be delegated to the Slinger's companions because the Slinger's presence remains determinative. The whole matter of "smell" is related to the subject of what to do about the body of the recently dead "I," i.e., before it begins stinking. Dropping him off at the bus station in Albuquerque is the Horse's suggestion. But the Slinger finally intervenes with these quietly spoken words:

> I would urge you, friends.
> I is a reference to the past
> and cannot be So dropped
> If I stinks, it is only thus

> we shall not so easily forget
> his hour of darkness.
>
> (S 59)

That intervention thus precipitates the alternative, more decorous solution the Slinger's companions finally arrive at, namely
to pump him full of the hitchhiker Kool Everything's can of
LSD preservative. But, beyond the question of authority and
beyond matters of practical decision, it needs to be recognized
that the initial center-stage treatment of the hero has already
begun to shift toward a poem conceived of as "a multiple conversation between half-a-dozen people" (I 99). The allegorizing
mode has set in. It lies implicit in Slinger's words, on the foregoing occasion, that his mind has begun to zero in on the
poem's mission.

That mission, one senses, lies beyond the figure of Hughes,
who eventually, like Las Vegas itself, will simply drop out of the
picture. Before the Slinger himself vanishes into space with a
farewell to his friends at the close of Book IIII, he will have
taken the reader on a remarkable journey. It will have been a
journey approximating On Nature, Parmenides' versified philosophical journey employing the allegory of a chariot drawn by
driverless horses and escorted by the daughters of the sun moving from the realm of darkness to the realm of light. The eventual reappearance of the metamorphosed "I" as the messenger
of Parmenides indeed hints at the possibility that Dorn may
have had the structure of that poem's journey in mind, but more
centrally, the relevance of Parmenides' travel poem to Dorn's
lies in Dorn's determination to resist the possibility of rigidity
setting in anywhere, as for example in his hero's describable
identity. For the essential Parmenidean propositions he means
to enact in Slinger are these: that objects of thought are ungenerated and indestructible; that reality lies not in objects but in
the mind's lively conception of them. Dorn's initial stylized

treatment of the Westerner, registered in a persisting comic-ironic tonality, thus aims at projecting a "new stance toward reality," one conformable with the Parmenidean proposition incorporated into the Slinger's mode of vision.[4] Having anticipated that that very stylization is itself becoming familiar to the reader, Dorn turns the Slinger into an allegorical figure, an abstracted version of the drifting Western hero. And more generally, I submit, this shift from stylization to allegorization expresses Dorn's crafty intention to keep the long poem in motion by never allowing it to become susceptible to the dead weight of paraphrase.

Dorn's treatment of his hero in Books I and II has an initially delightful and beguiling, and then increasingly instructive, effect. The device of equipping his hero with a self-parodying mechanism, one capable of anticipating and exploding all possible objections on the ground of everyday reality, may be illustrated in the Mesilla saloon episode (Book I) and next, in a more lesson-oriented occasion, in the Universe City Plaza episode (Book II). Both involve the erstwhile familiar subject of gunslinging.

The Mesilla episode includes two related scenes, and in the first a local fracas breaks out. With bullets flying about the saloon, the gunslinger simply smokes and contemplates the action, offering brief commentaries upon the event, from his quiet corner of the room. Only after the smoke clears, and Lil asks for some music, is his gun brought into play:

> he looped toward the juke then,
> in a trajectory of exquisite proportion
> a half dollar which dropped home
> as the .44 presented itself in the proximity
> of his hand and interrogated the machine

4. Charles Olson, "Projective Verse," in Robert Creeley, ed., *Selected Writings of Charles Olson* (New York: New Directions, 1966), pp. 24–25.

> A28, Joe Turner *Early in the Mornin'*
> came out and lay on the turntable
> His inquisitive .44 repeated the question
>     and B13 clicked
> Lightnin' Hopkins *Happy Blues for John Glenn*,
>     and so on
> the terse trajectories of silver then
> the punctuations of his absolute .44
> without even pushing his sombrero off his eyes
>                             (S 23)

His "inquisitive" and "absolute" gun, one perceives, is no ordinary piece of reality, even as one recognizes "without even
pushing his sombrero off his eyes" to be an echo of the familiar
tall tale. Just so, in the scene that develops next, Dorn treats his
reader to what seems to be a classic Western confrontation, and
yet it is twisted, turned into a satiric commentary on the rigidification of old forms in the New West. When a voice suddenly
speaks out of the crowd demanding to know what the Horse's
business is in this place

> the length of the bar froze
> arms and legs, belts and buckles caught
> drink stilled in mid-air
> Yea! You! You're a horse
> aincha? I mean you!
> and, "looking around", *Horseface*!
>                             (S 25–26)

Again, only after leisurely attention to that stranger's elabora-
tions does the Slinger's gun go into operation, but when it has,
it is, as Lil notes, pointed straight out of town, giving the
stranger time to unload. But the purity of the Slinger's act, as
registered in the slow-motion exactitude of the language, out-
matches the efforts of the stranger as noted by the heaviness of
the description:

        the disputational .44
    occurred in his hand and spun there
    in that warp of relativity one sees
    in the backward turning spokes
    of a buckboard,

                then came suddenly
    to rest, the barrel utterly justified
    with a line pointing
    to the neighborhood of infinity.
    . . . . . . . . . . . . . . . . . . . . . . . . . .
    the greenhorn pulled
    the trigger and his store-bought iron
    coughed out some cheap powder,
    and then changed its mind
                    (S 27–28)

Standing fixed with "one eye wandering," the stranger finds
himself *described* as a "plain, unassorted white citizen."

   In Book II a like episode recurs, but in the shifted context of
an allegorized on-the-road journey ascending north along the
Rio Grande. At Universe City, alias Truth or Consequences, a
black stallion unhitches itself from the post in the Plaza, heaves
its saddle through the door of the local saloon, and runs off.
That action wakes up the stallion's owner, who appears in the
Plaza ferociously gesturing:

        And in its wake,
    with a punctuality almost
    beyond relief, appeared the Owner
    of the saddle
    and the horse
    guns in both hands
    cigar between teeth
    hat on head sideways
    his face a miracle of undocumented
    attention
                    (S 73)

In the earlier gunslinging episode, one recalls, the hero handled his gun chiefly as an exhibition of his supranatural speed and metaphysical stylishness, but here he does not bother to take his gun out of his holster (and beyond Book I it is in fact never used again). Instead, he uses pure words as ammunition. The Owner is simply "described," and as a consequence of that description he grows so heavy that he begins to self-destruct: his bullets jam and fall onto the sidewalk, the gun disintegrates in his grip, and at last his body petrifies, shifts weight, and settles into the earth in the form of an "Old Rugged Statue of the good ol days."

If Books I and II were bound up as the first issue of a new magazine, the article on the stallion's Owner might brightly illustrate the principle of rigid stasis set off against the principle of easy dynamics. ("This can only be / *materialism*, the result of merely *real* speed" [*S* 74], notes his antagonist.) Our familiar Western hero has thus turned into an unforeseen figure of allegory. In this increasingly abstracted role, he will teach us to thread our way through the vicissitudes of the both real and unreal world we inhabit.

The general shift from a stylized mode in Book I to an allegorized mode in Book II may next be illustrated through Dorn's elaboration upon the Westerner's taste for song. His preference for tequila, that "last / dwindling impulse of the sun," anticipates Slinger's taste for those specifically heliocentric songs pervading Book II. He sings once himself. As he climbs the steps of the Mesilla saloon he is heard reciting a fragment of a song about a woman from La Cruz ("she stood and she stared like a moose / and her hair was tangled and loose . . ."). But Dorn intends to supply a new twist on the old singing cowboy. For from the time a Drifter-Poet-Singer enters the saloon, it becomes evident that the function of singing in the poem's journey is to be awarded to him who prefers, as he says, to sing absolute songs to the accompaniment of an "abso-lute" (which ordinary people mistake for a guitar). His "Song about a woman," a blazon which ends with a celebration of

> her swelled black mound
> her startled fawn
>
> which has the earthy smell
> of slightly gone
> wild violets
>
> (S 44)

is greeted with a rare expression of enthusiastic delight from the Slinger: "O Fucking Infinity! O sharp organic thrust / the Gunslinger gasped / and his fingers / spread across the evening atmosphere." It is this absolute song, moreover, that prompts the Slinger's attention to the fact that the "24th hour" of midnight has approached and that the Sun's position dictates their setting out upon the journey to Las Vegas.

The matter of song, especially of absolute, heliocentric song, firmly underlines the allegorizing shift that appears in Book II—both in Dorn's treatment of his heretofore stylized hero and in his handling of the narrative development. The travel north along the Rio Grande valley now provides a leisurely occasion for more songs by the drifting singer (who is, significantly, henceforward spoken of as the Poet), and the journeying poem itself begins to unfold in the manner of a celebratory song. As recorded in the preludial verses of the opening of Book II, the Slinger and his companions appear now as simultaneously unmoving and moving figures in a narrative woven into a tapestry:

> This tapestry moves
> as the morning lights up.
> And they who are in it move
> and love its moving
> from sleep to Idea
> born on the breathing
> of a distant harmonium, To See

> is their desire
> as they wander . . .
>          (S 45)

Not until twenty-four lines later will the reader's ordinary understanding of what his mind has been receiving become clear:

> Our company thus moves collectively
>      along the River Rio Grande.
>                    (S 46)

The use of the final *e* in "Grande," reminding us that the river
was named by the Spaniards, corresponds to the frequent use
of archaic English noun forms in the poem. It functions, as
George Gugelberger points out, as one of several linguistic
means of figuring reality in the poem.[5] The large image, clarified
by these lines, sustains some of the both unreal and real quality
of the initial conception as located, notably, in the particular,
metaphysical image of their moving "from sleep to Idea." They
here wander, as do figures in an allegory, on a quest "To See"—
not objects but an Idea (traceable to a "distant harmonium"),
the Idea underlying the objects of perception. The narrative
embodying these wanderers has thus begun to work on two
levels, depicting both an actual trip by horse-drawn coach and
an intellective journey. Although the occupants of the coach are
still asleep, their deep-sleep state itself represents a journey
toward a Supra-Reality. Thus the foregoing passage, excerpted
from Book II's prelude, advances further toward an unpunctuated and seamless close:

> they wander estranged
> through the lanes of the Tenders
> of Objects
> who implore this existence

5. George M. Gugelberger, review of *Slinger*, *The American Book Review*
1 (Summer 1978): 2.

for a plan and dance wideyed
provided with a schedule
of separated events
along the selvedge of time.
(S 45)

A "selvedge" ordinarily denotes the edge or border of a fabric, and the word reminds us of Dorn's elaborated conception of the poem now—as a kind of tapestry of moving figures. Thus the word "Tenders" here elaborates upon the action expressed by the image: the coach moving along its path, parallel to the Rio Grande, is like a ship supplied by tenders, that is, by small vessels that bring the main vessel supplies from shore. They are the tenders of objects that lie on the "selvedge" of the ship's journey, and they implore the sleeping voyagers on the metaphorical ship for a "plan," that is, for a place in conceptual reality. For only in the attentive minds of such voyagers may they truly exist.

As the journey proceeds, the singing of songs, hitherto conventionally viewed as a familiar element of the popular Western, approaches the condition of songs-within-Song. Coincidentally, the Singer/Poet himself begins to serve a new function: he acts the role of intermediary between the cosmos and ordinary mortals, that is, between the Slinger's cosmic consciousness and that of his travel companions. The Poet's dawn songs, earlier alluded to, for example, fulfill that function. His combination of Protestant hymn and contemporary Rock music is applauded by the Slinger as "a roll of Solar Reality," as product of a mind marvelously heliocentric. "Cool Liquid Comes" (a title that, we will see in retrospect, anticipated the appearance of Kool Everything with his five-gallon can of LSD) denotes the synaesthetic effect of the sun's first light upon the cooled early morning air of the desert; next, however, it refers to a heavenly flow of "cool liquid distilled of the scalar astral spirit" (S 51); and finally, it signifies a spiritual influence, "the great plaining zodiacus / . . . coursing / the country of our consciousness" (*S* 50). The poem has become rather Joycean. Essentially, "Cool Liquid" announces the travelers' approach to the margins of the Colorado Plateau, that landform conceived of as a relatively pure piece of the cosmos viewed at its purest moment in time. The occasion thus anticipates the Slinger's declaration that

> Our mission is to encourage the Purity of the Head
> pray we dont lose track of our goal.[6]
>
> (*S* 63)

The shift from a kind of stylized metaphor (focussed in the Slinger) into an extended metaphor (more generally elaborated in the coach's motion through the rarely beautiful forms of the Rio Grande valley) finally appears in Dorn's treatment of the hero's horse. I have argued that Dorn's song of Slinger is grounded in the literal specificity of places flashing upon the travelers' minds, and that the consequent inclination toward song is aided by the resiliency of wit. But another, remarkably extroverted resource arises out of the poem's trajectory, and it takes the form of a new amalgam of pure song and pure laughter.

In Book I the remarkable horse talks, smokes marijuana, flirts with ladies, and is generally gregarious. In Book II, he becomes the Stoned Horse of "pure head" and acts as an agent of liberation from forms of mental entrapment. Sometimes

6. It might be further noted that in the figure of the Poet may be inferred the voice of the poet behind the creation of the poem itself. Thus, in the later "Winterbook" section the Slinger speaks words that Dorn himself employs in an interview published in *Contemporary Literature* 15 (Summer 1974) and reprinted in *Interviews*. There, Dorn speaks of the poet as one who expiates the evil of external authority. Evil, in that classical sense, is what Dorn declares everybody has—"except that there is that kind of potential in the poet not to have it. . . . That's the connection with the whole burst of glow in the cosmos" (*I* 52).

referred to as Heidegger and Claude (Lévi-Strauss), the Horse not only embodies the philosophical clarity of his namesakes, but also, energized by a kind of Blakean vision of the universe, he becomes an evangelist and clever practitioner of the art of subverting external authority. The action in the Plaza of Universe City involving the problem of the runaway stallion's owner was thus precipitated by him. He spread the news of liberation among the hitched horses, inciting a white mare to run off and then the black stallion to kick up his heels.

> This horse laughed out loud
> and tore the finely tooled saddle
> off his back by hooking the belly strap
> on a knot in the hitching rail
> whereupon he seized the pommel
> with his Great Teeth and pitched
> the whole affair thru the swinging doors
> leaving one of them banging
> off one hinge. A loud
> vacuum of pure silence
> flowed suddenly forth
> from that busy place.
>
> (S 72)

The plain unassorted white citizens of this misappropriated town are *served notice* here as well as in the Slinger's subsequent handling of the Owner, as later they also are, in the book's close, when they are strongly invited, by public notice, to hear a recitation by the Poet.

Laughter allied to song constitutes a powerful new combination in the poem's progress. The shift into the leisurely and abstracted condition of an allegorized narrative in Book II has not then incurred a loss of the broad humor of the highly stylized Book I. Rather, refined to the essentials of pure song and pure laughter, that humor has only become more precisely directed and more lethal. Indeed, given the more complicated difficulties and subtle negativities that arise in the unmapped territories subsequently encountered in "The Cycle" and Book III, humor *must* be thus precisely directed. If the intended journeying toward a retrieval of cultural aliveness is to survive the deadly, monocultural forms of entrapment programmed to engulf it, it must furnish rectitude of mind with an unparalleled resiliency of spirit.

■ 2 ■

*There are some people who have power and a certain kind of means at their disposal who are trying to get the society to think a certain way, to do a certain set of things, and so forth. I think any responsible writer is never that. No writer is ever trying to get anybody to* do *something; what they're trying to create is a cognizance in the society of itself, to furnish the means— through clarity of language—for a self-appraisal and self-evaluation.*                          (I 109)

Could one look forward to the Slinger's farewell and from that vantage recall the two opening books, one's memory would likely furnish images of hijinks and high spirits attuned to song-fulness and tempered by a subtly governing principle of decorum, by that measuring force embodied in the marvelous hero upon whose flawless exactitude and singularity of mind the equilibrium of the local cosmos seems to depend. But what if, in the later books, that hero, whose glance had been of a force sufficient to alter a local situation or general mode of thought, were moved away from center stage so as to allow to society the means of a more direct self-appraisal and self-evaluation within a broadened and more variously furnished scenario? What if, say, that scenario involved a scene shift to a Boston railroad station where another mysterious, literally disguised, and weirdly sinister figure were glimpsed making his way onto a special car that was to be coupled to a train heading West? Set off in the mind against the preceding account of a relaxed, apparently random mode of journeying on the part of the Slinger's group, the identity of that mysterious figure and of his company would become an object of present curiosity. Why, we should ask, are they traveling on a vector that will intersect Las Vegas, with what intention, and furnished with what mental habits?

Between Books II and III Dorn in fact interpolates, in the form of "The Cycle," such an intentional discontinuity. "The Cycle" sets off weird reverberations antithetical to the ecstatic tendency of the poem's preceding evolution toward the condition of a serene and leisurely allegorical journey. It is heavily referential, directing explicit attention to the phenomena of capitalist entrepreneurism—and, in particular, to the jargon and mental programming that have emerged in the recent history of its activity. In general, the intended effect of this attention is to demystify the mystique that surrounds romanticized American entrepreneurs here figured in one particular Texas entrepreneur.

Howard Hughes himself, the announced object of the journey's mission, will in fact be treated only obliquely in "The Cycle." Instead, it will be the *effect* of the Hughes mentality as embodied in the race of "Atlantes" who surround him that will be chiefly delineated. Thus the intentional indirection and weirdness of "The Cycle" will constitute a field of disturbance in the poem's journey, just as the exploitative petrochemical industry constitutes a threat to the Southwest locale in which the journey takes place. This field of disturbance may be noted by the condition of "linguatilt" ("I"'s phrase in his nightletter at the end of Book III): for "The Cycle" represents, through the invention of a new-languaged universe, a nightmarish un-reality, the closest approximation of that invention perhaps lying in the sustained, supraphenomenal reverie of Joyce's *Finnegans Wake*. Its pace jerky, its language distorted and non-human, it stands as the antithesis to the earlier established principle of coherence identified with the Slinger's mind. If in the poem's central journeying Dorn seeks to reproduce the condition of a group of men hanging around together, here in the interpolated "Cycle" he deliberately juxtaposes its opposite: an elaborated image of a static assemblage of functionaries for whom alternatives are closed off, whose desires are wired into the systematic entrapment of the society they function in.

The Slinger's company of travelers as a group will first directly observe the approach of Hughes's Atlantes in Book III from a point along the edge of the Colorado Plateau. The Atlantes' movements will be picked up by scanners: by "I" in his new role as secretary to Parmenides and later, in Book IIII, by Tonto Pronto, the ear specialist, who will hear them coming. Hence the plotted motion of Hughes's Atlantes appears within an elaborated framework, their advent first foretold in the Poet's predestinarian lyric called "The Cycle" recited back in the Plaza of Universe City, and subsequently in the centered consciousness of the Slinger group on the road into the heart of the Colorado Plateau. And so, by virtue of this conjunction of poetic vision, centered consciousness, and the approaching awful forms of the Colorado Plateau, the incursion of this race of Atlantes may be critically measured and placed in an authentic perspective.

Such an elaborate angle of observation as this conjunction supplies constitutes an observation point or command center for the ongoing poem that is perhaps most accurately described by Dorn himself when he speaks of "The Cycle" as an instrument panel, with its speedometer, odometer, red and green warning signals, etc., facing the driver: "In the road sense, it's like an instrument panel in front of my nose" (*I* 34). Even so, "The Cycle" narrative is further refracted by the Poet's decision to recite the words of the Interior Decorator, who originally designed the car and gave in two stages a rundown of its scenario and of its actual furnishings. Again, such an elaborately framed point of view and such a complex transmission process tend to heighten the contrast between "The Cycle" and the previous books. They intensify the qualities of hyped-up negativity associated with the Atlantes, and they create a mood appropriate to a heavily iconographic style of presenting the static microsociety of Atlantes.

"The Cycle," standing strangely alone between Books II and III, is, as noted, actualized by the announcement of the Poet's address, at the Tanner's Yard in a corner of the Plaza, to the citizens of Universe City. Marking a radical shift in the poem's unfolding, it captures and projects the Atlantes' state of mind as one of creative inversion. For they represent, in microcosm, an entropic society—a kind of traveling "black hole" that sucks into its negative energy field all objects in its path. Technological apparatus of a computer-programming variety objectively identifies this black holism, but the nature of those objects is essentially revealed by the "neo-electronic jargon" that permeates the speech habits of the Atlantes who preside over their workings. Thus "The Cycle"'s initial rendering of Howard Hughes, alias "Robart," disguised as the cheese in a burger and carried on a long white stretcher onto his special car, sets off a set of weird reverberations that are heavily amplified by the telectronic language that occasion triggers off:

> The scene thus leans the way of the stretcher
> As His guard of AntiBasins teleglance
> The Gate and *guard the shuffle* as Save the Cheeze
> Programs through their simple relays
>
> And they push all buttons Close all gratings
> Revise all functions Review the digits on The Move

> Repunch the possible Locate the Im
> Feed Back the pragma of the plan Itself
> (S 91)

As the car is coupled onto the train on the main track we seem to be getting an allegorical line of description that comes through as a vision of a hyped-up world of national conglomerates coupling with multinational conglomerates. The object of the destination we pick up as the discovery of "A New Crack"—possibly denoting a geological fault system—and not an old one like the one in Pennsylvania but a new one—"a crack from a society without a history." The negative effect of such a journey upon the citizens along that route is here obliquely indicated. It is to be inferred from a passage that parodies Thoreau's allegory of "sleepers." Thoreau asked:

Did you ever think what those sleepers are that underlie the railroad? Each one is a man, an Irishman, or a Yankee man. The rails are laid on them, and they are covered with sand, and the cars run smoothly over them. They are sound sleepers, I assure you. And every few years a new lot is laid down and run over; so that, if you have the pleasure of riding on a rail, others have the misfortune to be ridden upon.[7]

Dorn's parodic rendering of Thoreau here offers a similarly critical, harsh, and sharply honed piece of satirical writing (the lines are reminiscent of the more surrealistic prose pieces in Dorn's *Some Business Recently Transacted in the White World*):

> The click of their coupling is as startling
> And as urgent and as quick as a whisper
> Into the ear of a corporate being
> With a perfect background, The shrill scream
> Of metal to metal across the switch-yard

7. Henry David Thoreau, from "Where I Lived and What I Lived For," in *Walden*, ed. J. Lyndon Shanley (Princeton: Princeton University Press, 1979), p. 90.

> The scream of the Accomplished Present
> A conglomerate of Ends, The scream of Parallels
> All tied down with spikes These are the spines
> Of the cold citizens made to run wheels upon.
>
> (S 96–97)

If Dorn's initial conception of Hughes was triggered by his curiosity concerning a glamorized instance of the powerful magnetism of money and, specifically, of Las Vegas—a purely artificial construction built upon that abstraction, money—the original conception appears to have shifted by the time he came to "The Cycle." For at this point the poem's kaleidoscopic succession of images turns up a singularly sinister set of phenomena. The Atlantes' great leader, Robart, for example, is rendered as faceless, ambiguous, and dangerous. His eyes are never seen behind his shades; he emits ambiguous signals; and his motives are hidden in a booby-trapped safe:

> He whispers and folds His hands
> Nor do His eyes flash inside the Amber
>
> They emiT, and the emissions brake
> They turn hot red to cold green
> . . . . . . . . . . . . . . . . . . . . . . . . . . . . . . . . . . .
> Each datum is caught I got em
> And stored cold in a special future
> And sent to the floor below
> . . . . . . . . . . . . . . . . . . . . . . . . . . . . . . . . . . .
> The prescription of His Amber shades
> A mysterium as booby-trapped with counter-locks
> Perhaps,
> As the multiple entrances to Ft. Knox
>
> (S 97)

Some baroque glamor, derived from the old Howard Hughes myth, is allowed to persist in this rendering:

> Rupert's view of the planet is as
> From directly over the N Pole

. . . . . . . . . . . . . . . . . . . . . . . . . . . . . .

. . . I located an aperiodic compass
Under that chair He sits in—
Also He's got some primitive touches

Like the sundial
Mounted in the palm of His hand
And I don't Know, But They Say
He's got a Star finder in the head of His cock

Or used to have.

(*S* 101)

But that sort of *Star Wars* strain, which somewhat recalls the
broad humor of the opening books and anticipates the interpolation of a comic-strip mode in Books III and IIII, is relatively suppressed here in favor of the poem's concern with
investigating the pure intensity of the negativity that is identified from the outset with the elusive, blank mysterium called
Hughes. For the most part, the poem's steady attention remains
fixed on "the instrument panel," that is, on the direct visibility
of Robart's henchmen—Al (his clone) and the faces of the
technocratic automata Al presides over. Robart's hypothetical
existence and its force can, to some extent, be extrapolated out
of these secondary and undifferentiated slaves, but on the
whole "The Cycle" functions as a magic mirror in which the
ruling principle of the denial of identity, and hence the condition of Absence, may be reflected:

The scenario is all Emanation
The nesting ground of number
There are no *things* there as such
Material is a not with the   K   detached

All is transhistorical, functions
Have no date . . .
. . . . . . . . . . . . . . . . . . . . . . . . . . . . . .

For inside is no-One
There is indeed inside only
The No No No
(S 98–99)

This "Scenario"'s broad iconographic representation of the Atlantes as a corporate technocracy (addicted to a strange kind of nonlanguage) yields next to a somewhat more particular satiric elaboration of their characteristic behavior, a stretch of writing informed by broadly comic tonal parameters. The Atlantes' behavior, which is determined by the whimsical Robart (alias Hughes) from his control tower, exhibits an instance of "programmed" behavior. In a mode reminiscent of "The Land of Laputa" book of Swift's *Gulliver's Travels*, this subsequent section of "The Cycle," titled "The I.D. Runs the Actual Furnishings," begins with the observation that there is no principle of gravity in this "uncentered locus." It goes on to comment further on the Atlantes' strangely limited language. And then it closes by observing the Atlantes' latent hysteria, a condition that becomes active whenever they are presented with negating contradictions, here personified as the dreaded "Vice-Versas":

When they speak they say simply Shit!
Or thanks! though sometimes they whine
Could I have the pickle when youre done with it?

Their conversational English is limited
Yet they mimick its rehearsal very cleverly
They fear one thing and one thing only
And that is the avaricious Vice-Versas

An obscene and gluttonous order of rat
The Supreme janitor unleases on the floor
After Lunch where they destroy themselves
With madness

> When they find nothing
> But their Raving Expectations
> . . . . . . . . . . . . . . . . . . . . . . . . . . . . . .
> And Rupert cackles and grabs for Breath
> (*S* 103)

Even Al, Rupert's favorite, who possesses some flexibility and as a sign of it holds the Atlantes spellbound by his recitation of a past they are cut off from, stands as an iconographic representation of the Vice-Versa principle. The urn of the ashes of Time he holds itself carries the inscription: "EMIT NO TIME." But it wildly disturbs the Atlantes because if read backwards it commands "EMIT *ON* TIME." Indeed, it becomes evident that Al is himself beginning to crack under the strain of this ambiguous role as he is pictured pathetically addressing the group as his "stunted glories," his "frozen beauties," and shedding a tear—which, like a ball of jasper, "rolled / Into the mouth of a Vice-Versa and disappeared." Thus are all otherwise repressed natural tendencies finally gobbled up in this centerless, timeless, static world denoted in "The Cycle."

Rupert's ultimate control, on the other hand, lies in his sophisticated and systematic power of directly negating real objects:

> He cons the present to hustle the futchah
> By a simple elimination of the datadata
>
> Which was unpunched and resealed
> (*S* 109)

"Vice-Versa" itself seems to denote Rupert's power of treating all objects as data that can be manipulated, but finally even they may be just simply wiped out.

With his finger poised over the button that activates the Vice-Versas, Robart thus embodies the negative proposition that, in the poem's view, has so dangerously advanced itself in the history of Western culture, namely, the proposition that an object may be divorced from the mind that conceives it and so may be simply eliminated. Viewed in relation to the ultimately ethical implications of the epistemological concerns heretofore established in the poem, Robart and his race of Atlantes stand, we see, as the antithesis to Parmenides and those other pre-Socratic philosophers (elsewhere favorably alluded to) who held that the objects of thought are ungenerated and indestructible. And the sign of this intended antithesis appears in the dramatic suspension of "The Cycle" precisely at that point at which Robart is about to push the Vice-Versa button. For Robart's intended action is aborted by the reception of the news that his scanners have picked off "A telegram to Parmenides / From a point on the arc / 2 days minus 4 Corners" (S 109).

To again consider the wider relevance of this weird interpolation into the heretofore congenial narrative of Southwest journeying is to again note the significance of this juxtaposition: the sinister and destructive Atlantes set off against the rare and life-giving presence of the massive landform the Slinger's party has begun to sense their approach to. The juxtaposition shadows a possible crisis in the mental life of the continent's inhabitants; at least the warning signals on the "instrument panel" force clear attention to that possibility. It is worth noting that only after the characteristic behavior of the Atlantes is pinned down for careful examination are they explicitly identified in the final words of the frame that encloses "The Cycle" proper. Those closing words, spoken by the Slinger himself, arise out of a cosmic occasion, his notice of the setting of the sun. He interrupts the recitation—precisely at the point at which Robart is distracted from activating the Vice-Versa button by the news that the narrative will have to be continued at another time:

> Another time we will witness
> how this double hydrocarbon hustles the future

but for now,
Fresh *Distortions* have swept the screen.

(*S* 109)

"This double hydrocarbon," the organic compound of crude oil, thus specifically identifies at last what Donald Wesling has named the "unseen assailant" in Dorn's heavily political poetry: the hidden powers that, in capitalist entrepreneurism, control both the means of production and the mental outlook of the culture.[8] In the poem's Southwest scenario this means oil corporations, voraciously spreading over the face of the continent, uncreating the present while hustling the future. More generally they are identified with *money*, which is in turn identified with Las Vegas (whose existence, as noted, is wholly defined by that abstraction), where Hughes is rumored to be located.

The identification by means of the reference to hydrocarbon remains, nevertheless, incidental to that mental outlook whose weirdness Dorn has taken pains to measure precisely by means of the twisted and comic iconographic style adopted in "The Cycle." It is one thing to deal with a dangerous object and quite another to deal with the dangerous mental state in which that object originated. The latter needs to be comprehended precisely as no more nor no less sinister than it is; as Wesling observes, the unseen assailant is in Dorn's work dealt with by making him the subject of a "rich comic analysis, not a romanticizing in the terms the oppressors have themselves specified."[9] Further, the "weirdness" I have spoken of here may have an intentionally double-edged quality, mirroring the Atlantes' principle of negativity but also ironically observing our common fascination with men like Hughes and the world he moves

8. Donald Wesling, "A Bibliography on Edward Dorn for America," *Parnassus* 5 (Spring 1977): 143, 148.
9. Wesling, "A Bibliography," p. 148.

in. As Wesling suggests, "Such men of power control us even as we *love to hate* their crankiness."[10]

The foregoing examination of "The Cycle" might be usefully concluded by a qualification of the terms of it. That is, we may, recalling the resilient good humor that pervades Books I and II, notice that that mode of representation does not entirely disappear at this stage of the poem. I would note that the first separately published version of *The Cycle* (Frontier Press, 1971), in an oversized comic book format with drawings in the style of a ten-year-old working with felt-tip crayons, exhibits this "love to hate their crankiness" style. On the cover the long-haired Poet dressed in a cowboy outfit and wearing flowers, which stick out of his (otherwise empty) holster, is addressing an assembly of abstractly figured, dwarf-sized citizens; on the back cover a head and shoulders drawing of a short-haired, dark-bearded man of sinister regard holding a smoking six-shooter is identified as one of the Atlantes by the attributed words in the smoke over his head, words addressed to Robart in the text of the poem. Rather surprisingly, both the Slinger's companion and the Atlantes are presented in the same "Western" comic book style (albeit the one is obviously the figure of the good guy, the other the bad). Further, the occasional drawings on facing pages opposite the text of the poem itself present remarkably nonsinister representations in the same juvenile style. In one, Al, with long, overflowing curls, is holding the urn, while in the background stand an assembly of somewhat innocent-looking, half-sized figures of Atlantes with matching long, overflowing curls of hair. In another, Atlante number 19 looks like a kid in a classroom, raising his hand to say, "We've got a problem, Al." Even Robart himself, in a simple-lined head

10. Ibid.

shot with bow tie and amber-colored shades, presented against a chocolate-brown background, lacks the heavily sinister quality we picked up in the *Slinger* text (though, of course, the point is that Hughes, alias Robart, *is* attractive to most of us, on the surface).

At any rate the layout of the original publication of *The Cycle* offers a corrective to a too gravely intense reading of the poet's elaborate recitation of the Atlantes narrative. A drawing of a railroad engine and an attached coal car with "Blank R/R" inscribed on its side and also the picture of Atlante 19, which has the letters "Blan K" inscribed on a horizontal plane behind him, may underline the main point after all: this is simply a vision of *Blankness* whose sinister implications, if viewed in a comic perspective, may be appropriately neutralized. That is, once the code, which lies hidden beneath the neo-electronic jargon, is broken, "laughter / can blow it to rags."[11] Insofar as the jargon is a projection of the culture Dorn's audience has hitherto agreed to by its complicit passivity, however, the laughter must be to some extent self-directed. It is rather like looking into a distorting glass and seeing one's own image rendered as an other. Such an experience may be less agreeable than were the earlier experiences of Books I and II where it was the stuttering, petrified stomps that were the clear objects of laughter and where the Slinger's companionable authority served as a cue to such laughter. But the self-mirroring experience is nevertheless fitting within the framework of the established allegorical journeying (a form whose traditional business has been the problem of appearances *vis-à-vis* realities), and it is also beneficial in the sense that clear seeing as a self-reflexive activity may furnish the means toward an appraisal and evaluation of the society we agree to live in and with. And that, after

11. In Dorn's writings the difference between a "code" and a combination is significant. The one is rigidified and is there to be broken; the other is mysterious and is to be divined.

all, is what Dorn is trying to do here: to create a cognizance in the society of itself and to furnish the means for a self-appraisal and self-evaluation.

■ 3 ■

> I dare not say
> but while the coach was dark
> and I had, combined, the circumference
> of Our Mind, a stark alignment of the Sunne
> Ourselves and the Moon occurred
> And
> when the lunation was screened
> I had this vision which came in
> as a poem called
>
> The Poem Called
> Riding Throughe Mádrid
>
> I shall speak it—
> (Book III, "The Winterbook," S 128–29)

Precisely midway through Book III, named "The Winterbook," appear these words the Poet speaks in conversation with the Slinger as the coach passes through the "ghost town" of Madrid, just south of Cerrillos, New Mexico. Once a great coal-producing town and still today owned by the Albuquerque & Cerrillos Coal Company, it is imaged and projected in an instant anterior to the coach's actual arrival in Madrid. And this vision spoken in song (the song completed as the coach passes through the town) instructs us again how to see. (Note that the Poet's own mode of seeing, his "screening" of a solar occasion, triggers this prevision of the local place and its history.) Instructed by his glimpsed "stark alignment" of the sun, ourselves, and the moon, the reader as Wayfarer is enabled to become attentive to the essential objects to be located in Madrid, namely Trees. Not simply trees, but trees in the form of that ancient and all but vanished population that gave its energy to the creation of coal, and thus indirectly to coal extraction—and thus to the advent of the coal-mining town that, in its present static condition, merely carries the superficial sign of the proprietor, Albuquerque & Cerrillos Coal Company. The town's name (and the Spanish history that name carries) has itself been relegated to the status of a sign of that company sign. Thus, were it not for the Poet, our travelers (and we as the poem's fellow travelers) should have likely remained in the dark, seeing neither the "matter" of Trees nor the miners who spent their lives extracting that "matter."

Steiner's phrase "axes of relation," as applied to "difficult," because complexly cross-referenced, works of literary art, recurs appropriately to mind in coming to this implicitly political juncture in Dorn's journey toward "purity of the head." The nominated axes of relation, as defined by the language of outward reference, are cosmographical, historical, and political. The issue, i.e., the matter toward which they point, is, essentially, political: the coal company that still holds legal possession of this "ghost town" signifies another particular expression of "external authority"; whereas the Trees (now invisible), which gave their matter, and the miners (also invisible), who gave theirs in the process of extracting it, remain the definitive or authentic forms of authority, being literally indigenous to the living history of this locale. The making of such a discrimination, enabled by that rectitude of vision the Poet teaches, thus constitutes a political act. For Dorn, one begins to understand, politics centrally involves another matter of reference. It takes the form of this question: to which members of a given culture shall questions of wide human importance be mainly referred?

The reader thus at last is beguiled into an involvement in the political dimension of experience in the poem so engagingly initiated in the apparently familiar scenario of the desert-oasis town of Mesilla, with its refreshing and welcoming saloon at a bend of the Rio Grande. He has been drawn into a process of remapping old territory in a revitalized language. Such a remapping constitutes the initial phase of establishing what Amerigo Castro speaks of as a *morada vital*.[12] The poet begins by renaming, by staking his claim to territory appropriated or in the process of being appropriated by external, inauthentic forms of authority. His own authority must therefore be established through an activity that approximates the activity of the Madrid miners: he must tunnel through the signs (or "scars") overlaying the landscape of the "New West" toward the retrieval of local, indigenous, energy-yielding matter.

As they move through that portion of their "Winter" journey between someplace south of Albuquerque and Cerrillos, then, the travelers (under the now oblique guidance of the Slinger and his deputy the Poet) expend their attentive energy in "mining" and "picking up." Tunneling reflection on the one hand and sophisticated receptive alertness on the other to "the inside real / and the outsidereal" (Dorn's notation on the page announcing Book III) have become the twin activities of this stage in the poem's trajectory.

Leaving the citizens of Truth or Consequences and the vision of the Atlantes behind, heading into the higher elevations announcing the more varied and sublime landforms of the Colorado Plateau, the resumed journey may, initially, be characterized as a rebounding flow. The effect upon the travelers and the reader alike might be now compared (congruent with Dorn's

12. "A vital dwelling place." The phrase signifies a geographically identifiable cultural condition wherein subsistence problems have been solved and qualitative matters are deliberately addressed. See Amerigo Castro, "Description, Narration and History," in S. Gilman and E. King, eds., *An Idea of History: Selected Essays of Amerigo Castro* (Columbus, Ohio: n.p., 1977), pp. 287–88.

own characterization of the "bounciness" of the rhythms) to the fisherman's experience of getting his line snagged on a river bottom and then, after exerting twists on the line, of suddenly feeling the line's release as the current picks it up and puts it into the stream's flow again:

> [We] feel them rising
> into the realm of the surprising
> bent over what they say
> along the river Rio Grande
> 'earing the low chordes of the foothills
> spitting the seeds of the Sandias
> out of the corner of their eyes
> as they rise
>
> (S 116)

"Earing"—language song going to the ears and directly knocking on the brain—is what "we" first encounter in this preludial lyric turning upon the superlative, slightly off rhymes: "rising," "surprising," "eyes," "rise"—intertwined with "say," "Grande" (Grand-ay), "Sandias."

The journey poem, we discover, has retained its capacity for employing the lyric voice in order to sustain the aliveness of the intellective journeying and, at least momentarily, to inaugurate a sense of celebration. The resources of language may, as Steiner observes, be so extended:

Speech cannot identify, let alone paraphrase, even a fraction of the sensory data which man, blinded in certain of his senses and language-bound as he has become, can still register. . . . But we need not go immediately or entirely outside language. . . . Verbal signs . . . may . . . enter into various combinations with such [non-verbal sign] systems. The exemplary case is that of language and music or language in music.[13]

13. George Steiner, *After Babel: Aspects of Language & Translation* (London: Oxford University Press, 1975), p. 415.

Clearly Dorn understands the limits of those purely verbal sign systems identified with the tradition of lyrical verse and so checks it in the Madrid song by having the Poet "speak it" in the form of an essentially political pronouncement, the latter preceded by the implicit pronouncement that he is not waxing lyrical but employing the song form as a means of transmitting the "screened" image. All the same, Dorn understands the staying power of songful utterance, its capacity to allow authority to such a pronouncement. He could expect his readers to prick up their ears and become attentive to this pronouncement in Madrid because he was confident that they had retained between their ears an awareness of the Poet's demonstrable capacity to sing pure songs when he wished and when the occasion warranted.

The wider occasion set down in Book III involves encountering considerable interference in the form of the "outside real" processed in the language of neo-electronic jargon. The odds against envisioning a *morada vital* in the New West are here recognized to be heavy, both in the physical sense of that word and in the colloquial sense, in which heaviness signals mental rigidification and petrification. The poet's counter to those odds, his resistance to that heaviness, is, at this juncture, consequently mercurial. The modes of repartee and pastiche, varied with snatches of song and pronouncement, predominate here beyond the preludial verses and the Madrid Song. Dorn's travelers have become witty receptors, picking up a lot of neo-electronic jargon that they process through parody and instantly transmit. The art of the satirist intent in "The Cycle" upon creating a coherent mirror image of negativity, including the reader's, thus gives way in Book III to the art of burlesque. Everything gets picked up out of the air, apparently randomly. That principle of decorum evident in Books I and II, where the Slinger's center-stage presence required it, seems displaced now by a new strategy of causing all individual voices (all "I"s) to merge into a single voice or chorus, receiving and transmitting information. The jargon that mediates that information is summed up at the close of Book III in the coded nightletter "I," as secretary to Parmenides, sends from his headquarters in Houston: crammed with discontinuous words, numbers, and shorthand references, it strikes the ear, without penetrating to the brain, as a parody of a NASA command center communication.

In more explicit political terms, the poem at this stage of its metamorphosis may be thought of as a moving command center in its own right. It is equipped with subtle antennae for picking things up and with a version of the citizen's band radio for transmitting those things as "news" to its constituency: "Build Me a Genetic Louse Trap" is broadcast as the latest capitalist version of "Build me a better mousetrap"; the weatherman announces that "weather in the winter . . . is . . . the great policer of the glaciers"; and the overseas report on the "flashy scoreboard" is decoded and headlined as "The Out*of*Town Team is very Modal / therefore this Shit Could be TOTAL" (S 125). The "News," thus generally languaged as epigram, is not easy to decipher, but one sustained piece of literary news does lend itself to commentary, and I shall quote it entire in order to illustrate the shifted mode and strategy of this book:

> Thats an elegant geneology
> the Poet whispered into the ear
> of the risen morning Sunne
> as the stormclouds covered it
> and the Horse smiled perceptibly
> and asked the Slinger Do you Remember Me?
> dont you have something else to say?
> OH Jack, the Slinger prayed
> I want you to feel
> and in your feeling move your bones
> for the want we now have of your access

in this time so little beyond you
and which needs your moving nerve
as it dries tacked
on the warp of its own flat sedimentary internalism
    The divisions of hunger
        shut behind their Doors
    Pinned down by their Stars
    Kept going by their Rotors
    Waked up by their Alarms
    Attended by a Prose
        which says how Dead they are
    Frozen by a Brine
        which keeps them from Stinking
    It looks to me Jack
        like The Whole Set is Sinking
    and theyre still talkin œcology
    Without even Blinking

Ah Men, saith the Horse

*jivey*    Here comes Indica Jack
       He's got his gnosis in a sack on his back

*soberly*  Now, repeat after me 20 times
*falsetto*      I promise my mother
        I will not join the Sierra Club

Wild Horses! Everything promulgated
What kinda mother you got

Are you serious? She's a horse
Naturally

Of course, of course—
AND, you dont want none
of your sacred quatrapeds
packin no Honky Bi-peds
to the top of no sierras
for a look at whats
left of their more prominent hysterias!
                (*S* 120–22)

The passage poses difficulties and it cannot, of course, be "described," but I would point to a number of interesting refer-

ences and to interesting kinds of jargon being picked up, ironically de-ranged, and redirected to the ears. The Horse seems to be the center of attention in view of the Poet's declaration twelve lines earlier that "your horses personify the striving after knowledge / the road along which we drive symbolizes . . . our thinking process." It is the voice of the Slinger we pick up next then, launching into a eulogy of the Horse, a eulogy turning quickly into a parody of his (the Horse's) opposite: namely the "internalism"—dried, tacked up, flat, and sedimentary—of the current generation of minds and, specifically, it would appear, of the current generation of poets imaged here as shut behind doors, pinned down, alternately kept going and awakened by mechanisms incident to the mechanistic culture from which they proclaimed they have distanced themselves. Likewise, the state of prose writing is imaged as dead, frozen, and pickled, and, indeed, the whole state of letters seems to be sinking and, as it sinks, to go on talking about "ecology." Gary Snyder and such "Sierra Club" literary types seem to be the objects of this parody of thinking-turned-jargon ("gnosis in a sack on his back" possibly referring to the figure of the humpbacked flute player taken up from Hopi myths by backpacking poets like Snyder). Just who in the group sings the "jivey," "soberly," and "falsetto" notes in the above passage the reader cannot discover. The point is that the topic is being freely tossed about in the Collective Mind of this company of travelers, that Mind so in accord now that even Kool Everything may, without a breach of the poem's decorum, get the last word in his final reference to "Honky Bi-peds" climbing the Sierras.

The literary news supplies yet another instance of that generally static cultural condition so threateningly imaged in the vision of "The Cycle." It aids in establishing the collision between vital and static principles that Dorn evidently intends here, an opposition he likely picked up from recent findings of molecular biologists. One may incorporate such findings as relevant to the preceding discussion of Book III if only because the indicated use of cocaine has a chemical effect on the behavior of the brain cells. But more fundamentally, the radically new power of perception such findings enable allows us to angle out the creative premise beneath the "informational" poetics Dorn here employs.

The power of new perception appears in the *Bioethics* of Van Rensselaer Potter, who, perhaps surprisingly, stresses the role of disorder in the evolution of life-forms and of culture-forms as well. Combining aspects of traditionally opposed mechanistic and vitalistic views of life, he postulates that "man is an adaptive control system *with elements of disorder built into every hierarchical level*" (italics mine).[14] Disorder for the biologist of course signifies the history of accidental genetic combinations that result in mutations and so allow a life species to adapt in more complex ways to changing conditions. But Potter's language is broadened to include the words "variance" and "novelty" so as to imply that on the psychic level, as well, disorder is built into man's functioning, that, indeed, a high frequency of disorder-input constitutes man's most distinctive trait:

With a tendency in the molecule toward a nearly but not quite perfect replication ability, novelty (mutation: copy-errors) was guaranteed while gains were conservatively maintained. Similarly, cultural evolution would have been very slow were it not for the tendency of man to introduce novelty by sheer inability to learn exactly what he is taught. *This is not to say that the trick of creativity cannot be accomplished deliberately once we get the significance of it.* Man undoubtedly has a higher capacity for storing abstract information than any other form of life, but this fact is inevitably accompanied by the fact that *man has a greater tendency to introduce error or deliberate variance into his memory bank than any other form of life and hence the greatest opportunity to introduce novelty into his life.* [Italics mine][15]

14. Van Rensselaer Potter, *Bioethics* (New York: n.p., 1971), p. 12.
15. Ibid., p. 18.

Further, Potter goes on to argue, contemporary man, existing in a world of rapidly changing reference, needs to *exploit* this opportunity if he is to survive. And though it is arrived at by means of a separate intellective journeying, this view, I think, is precisely the one on which Slinger's insistence upon the power of laughter has all along been grounded.

But the spark that really jumps between the scientific and the poetic intuitions in this case lies in Potter's further argument that this built-in tendency toward variation may be consciously accelerated and that man's cultural evolution may thereby become an act of creativity:

> The role of disorder in biological and cultural evolution should be fully explored. Disorder is a force to be utilized, the raw material for creativity. The problem is to harness it.[16]

The displays of untempered ebullience and epigrammatic wit at this stage of the poem's trajectory thus arise, I submit, out of the condition of creative disorder Dorn has deliberately introduced.

If the poem's central intention (at the zenith of its curve) has been to enact the supremacy of the purified, hence liberated and literally ecstatic, mind over public referents identified with forms of external authority, then it needs to precipitate a mutation of consciousness adequate to that intention. By this view the close of "The Winterbook" represents the most rarely evolved stage in the poem's metamorphosis out of a flattening, freezing, deadening condition. In fact, "The Winterbook" supplies an ecstatic image bright with such an unforeseen mutation. I have said that the book closes with a transcript of "I"'s coded nightletter, but it needs now to be noted that the agent of that letter is a goggled biplane pilot. He suddenly materializes out of the air, and, while hanging from a rope attached to the

16. Ibid.

biplane, delivers it from his sheepskin-gloved hand. That utterly memorable *deus ex machina* occasion both recalls the Slinger's marvelous conduct upon his arrival in Mesilla and looks like a cameo appearance of Ed Dorn himself. Dorn's nostalgia for biplanes is implicit in the design on the letterhead of the stationery he used in 1974, and, more instructively, he had in an early, unambiguously autobiographical prose piece declared himself to be "a letter-carrier in a time when the post office has become obsolete."[17] The gist of Pilot's message, "Expect Materialization at Precisely 4 Corners," may be read, in this light, as Dorn's signal to his readers that the "darkling plain" of the poem's difficult passage would turn into the sun- and moonlight-filled world of Book IIII, that the journeying poem would be completed, and that Song would blossom again.

Beyond Madrid, we have heard no songs. They seem to have been wholly displaced by a necessary but heady brand of informational poetics. In truth, as we shall see, they have only gone underground as, indeed, it seems the poem's narrator and the Poet themselves have done. Their presence registers itself in what I have spoken of as the "tunneling reflection" that coexists with the "picking up." It is the narrator who sets down in the

17. "Driving Across the Prairie" (*SB* 55). The 1977 "Road-Testing the Language" interview with Dorn offers further evidence of Dorn's personal signature in the "Winterbook." He responds there to questions regarding the use of the "Iconic Notebook," which the interviewer footnotes as "a kind of workbook that Dorn used while composing some of the sections of *Gunslinger*. It contains drawings and captioned cartoons drawn by the poet . . . on napkins, matchbook covers [etc.] also notations . . . [and] clippings from magazines, newspapers" (*I* 106). Dorn describes one sequence of drawings among these "attempts to recruit the Real" as "landscapes of the West—with buttes, which are already a geographical representation in that direction." This "pasted" notebook (among the three notebooks he kept) was put together, as best he recalls, during the time of Book II and Book III of *Slinger* and supplied occasional "Quatrains of repartee" for the poem he describes working at "like a jigsaw puzzle" (*I* 73–75).

form of his brief "Lawg," preceding the "Winterbook" proper, his brooding condition of soul:

> The Body in winter is the hunting lodge
> deep in the forest sheltered, with a view
> overlooking the full metaphor of the hart
> · · · · · · · · · · · · · · · · · · · · · · · · · · · · · · · · ·
> the shadows a
> cross the top of your grand desk
> are the numbers of your Winter Book
> the tumblers of the opening falling
> opening the Gates of Capricorn, the
> days have decreased as much as they ever will
> snowe covers living things with quietude
>
> (S 114)

He seems to be brooding upon an impending turning of the year in tones not unlike those sounded at the opening of *The Waste Land* (his partial foreseeing the arrival of the biplane recalling Eliot's prevision of springing lilacs). He calls to mind, moreover, the subterranean narrators of "The Land Below" and "Idaho Out"—not idle but patiently "sheering off" retrievable matter bearing cultural aliveness along the route of his travel.

The Poet himself, we note, has likewise gone underground. His "Riding Throughe Mádrid" expresses a mind momentarily deflected from attention to the sun and toward tunneling reflection on matters fundamentally political. Noting that development, the Slinger addresses him in these words:

> Poet, me senses
> you have in you
> something Low this morning
> fewer stairsteps
> support your duel
> You stare out the window
> at the peasants gathering fuel on the hill
> have ye banked yor fires

wheres the Fairbanks
of your desires?
In your eyes I see
the underground
like a miner with his lamp
turned around
(S 122–23)

The "Winterbook"'s poet-narrator and the Poet in the "Winterbook" both take on, I submit, the function of miners with
their "lamp[s] turned around." While information is being
picked up and transmitted in the cockpit of the mobile command center, they engage in mental journeying along a lower
frequency or musical register. Alert to the signs of appropriation picked up and in the process of being decoded and sent out,
they give their more absolute attention to indigenous local
matter, to mining elements that, arranged in a new combination, promise a beneficial mutation of consciousness. The
"Winterbook" thus gives signs, as well, of a new blossoming of
song in Book IIII.

■ 4 ■

*My later books are more purely songs . . . language songs . . . I
use language to make things cohere . . . language that goes to
the Ears.*[18]  (Ed Dorn, in an interview)

Arcing along the journey's trajectory toward completion, Book
IIII of *Slinger* is marked by a more robust and rhetorical language. New kinds of language announce a new stage of this
shape-shifting poem. As registered in an altered tonality, new
language signals here a general displacement of comic irony by
broad comedy. Even the Slinger is briefly, amiably distracted

18. Material quoted in this epigraph is from *Vort*, no. 1 (Fall 1972), 49, 51.

from his "cryptaesthesic isolation" and so introduces himself
to the mayor's wife in Cortez in courteous fashion:

> He stepped smartly up to her
> and said Howdy mam
> and presented a large bouquet of
> Red Roses, expértly rendered in Solid lead
>
> And as she felt their great weight
> in her arms, a smile of regret
> raced across her superbly fastidious
> and disapproving lips, as she sank
> slowly through the boards, out of sight
>
> (S 161)

That occasion, so casually drawing on a nostalgia the reader
retains for the Slinger-centered Books I and II, merely elaborates the pervading, physical busyness of Book IIII. For the
stylized theater of impatience on which the curtain rose in
Mesilla here gives way to a close resembling the final scene of a
stage comedy wherein the whole cast of characters gets assembled in order to witness the untangling of complicated lines of
action and the announcement of a renewed society.

One must be content with enumerating the literary furnishings out of which the extraordinarily reverberating, robust-
languaged atmosphere of the poem at this point arises. Those
furnishings chiefly involve two elements: a rapid succession of
scene shifts and a continuous arrival onstage of colorful characters possessed of diverse language habits. The scene shifts
provide a kaleidoscopic and panoramic liveliness: from the
ongoing journey of the Slinger group to the approaching train
of Robart and his Atlantes, who talk of disguised vehicles
(among them a chile relleno with Akron Superslicks) and petro-
leum-based munitions ("brimstone/naptha and the other bitu-
mens"); to a scene in the Cafe Sahagún, downtown Cortez,
Colorado, materialized "out of the thin air" (where "I" daz-

zlingly reappears); to that scene outside the Cafe where the Slinger presents the mayor's wife a bouquet of lead roses; to a place outside of town called the Hill of Beans (locus of a fertility deity called Sllab)—to an evocation, through the Poet's song, of the history of Cocaine Lil. Section 2 finally slows down to a single scene on a hillside overlooking a deep canyon; it is from this vantage point in a geologically recent volcanic landscape that the Slinger's party, lounging around at siesta time, partly observes and partly hears reports of the battle between the Atlantes' local allies, the Mogollones, and a bunch of pure anarchists, the Single-spacers. Throughout this scene shifting the coming and going of a diversity of characters newly attached to the Slinger's company adds further liveliness. First we encounter the memorable figure of Taco Desoxin and his band of munitions experts, who have graduated from straightening fenders to blowing smokestacks or blowtorching Las Vegas hotels, Holiday Inns, and other such cultural landmarks. Next we meet Tonto Pronto, the ear specialist down from Toronto to solve Kool Everything's finger-in-the-ear problem. Then we hear Portland Bill, the booming-voiced, German-accented Northwest rough rider. And, finally, we make the acquaintance of the latter's compatriot, Cracker Barrel, a figure full of cracker-barrel gusto and free-form narrative wit. Each a great talker in his own right, in the aggregate they not only add a cosmopolitan zest to the poem's open-stage finale but signal, as well, a diversification of the forms of laughter in what we may come to think of now as an amplification of this microsociety's gene pool.

The possibilities of laughter, with its power of canceling the bonds of mental entrapment, have thus considerably expanded. This very expansiveness tends to upstage the Slinger himself, displacing outward the vitalism that originated in his definitive presence. And yet his very quietude engages us as Dorn manages to draw some exquisite tonal effects out of his reclusive posture. This gunslinger who punched the jukebox buttons without lifting the hat shading his eyes in Book I has become metamorphosed into the figure of a man apparently dozing (like a bat in the middle of the day), recumbent, hat over eyes, only remotely attentive to field reports coming in. And yet he is wholly in touch with what is happening and with what lies beyond that happening:

> Upon hearing this news the Zlinger
> lit up a Sullivan and leaned back
> his eyes fixed in a cryptaesthesic isolation
> His mind hung bat-like
> from the rafters of the Burlington Arcade.
>
> (S 185)

This sensor of otherwise hidden truths (as he lights up and leans back) we have come to admire, especially now that the materialization of the blue-shifting Robart and his Atlantes seems imminent. Further, I think, we have come to identify Slinger's absolute quietude and singleness of mind with the poem's rising to the fullness and clarity of song.

What the drift toward song signifies and how it corresponds to the vitalism attached to the Slinger may be best understood by looking back to an earlier moment, clarified now in the reflexive mind. I refer to the occasion, located beyond the terrible vision of "The Cycle," in the prefatory verses to Book III titled "The Lawg," when the time of the winter solstice coincides with the coach's rise into the heart of the Colorado Plateau. The occasion, underscored by references to the life of the local cosmos and by language going "to the Ears" with a remarkable force, precisely corresponds to the occasion of the shortest day of the year. The earlier-cited, relevant passage includes lines from the first half of "The Lawg," through "the / days have decreased as much as they ever will / snowe covers living things with quietude" (S 114). But the passage in fact continues in a rebounding motion in order to celebrate the paradox that the shortest day of the year also announces a new lengthening of days. For the sun, having reached the lowest point in its journey through the horizon, has begun its reascent, and its renewing motion announces a reaffirmation of the literally ecstatic principle of the living cosmos:

> Death rules over the visible, *then*
> *Life surges* with the *Sunne* out of decline
> the *Sunne moves northward* the light tauter
> *spring spreads* the *New Life* over *cool death*
> and the dissected earth includes the contrary
> . . . . . . . . . . . . . . . . . . . . . . . . . . . . . . . . . . .
> Dear lengthening Day
> I have loved your apparencies since you created me
>
> (*S* 114–115)

I have italicized Dorn's text here for the purpose of underlining the implications of the line's stresses upon the nominally cosmic and affirmative connotations of the diction. It was, one recalls, just such a combination of stress implications and word connotations that signaled the coach's timely arrival in the Sandias.

Rich tonal stage settings like that managed in "The Lawg" appear firmly anchored in observable cosmic conjunctions that recall the attentive reader to his citizenship in the world, a world dependent upon the local star, the sun. In the self-reflexive mind Dorn's poem induces, such tonal stage settings themselves define significant, memorized points of reference. Rhythmically spaced and gathered, they generate a condition of mind that discovers a liberated sense of harmony with the world of which it is a part. The opening verses of the Prolegomenon to Book IIII prepare for such a condition of mind, induced by a singular tonality arising out of such a foreseen conjunction. They strike our ears, familiarly, as a variation of Ben Jonson's "Hymn to Diana":

> Goddesse, excellently bright,
>    thou that mak'st a day of night.
>    You tell us men are numberless
>    and that Great and Mother
>    were once synonymous.
>
> "We are bleached in Sound
>    as it burns by what we desire"
>    and we give our inwardness
>    in some degree to all things
>    but to fire we give everything.
>
> (*S* 145)

This unforeseen address to the moon goddess (which, in view of the Slinger's lineage and of the heliotropic orientation of the songs, may seem heretical) is curious and instructive.

It seems intended to refer us back to "The Lawg" where the Parmenidean principle of the interplay of day and night, light and darkness, was dramatized—in the sun's rise at the moment of its deepest decline and, correspondingly, in the speaker's brightening out of his deepest wintry brooding. Coincidentally, however, that backward reference has the subtle effect of displacing the visibility of that immediately distractive reference point, the plotted collision of the Slinger company and the Hughes forces gathered under Robart. The moon's "excellently bright" clarification of the pure forms of the given landscape has, that is to say, reduced the Atlantes to an only dimly remembered distraction of the mind. Consequently, the reader as fellow traveler is enabled to see single-mindedly now, in its totality, that which is given to him to see here, namely the mass of continental upthrust carved by the earth's hydrosphere, the removal of purely local gradations of reality through the moon's effect, and the presence of the glittering trail of the Milky Way that canopies the coach's journey:

> We survey the Colorado plateau.
> There are no degrees of reality
> in this handsome and singular mass,

or in the extravagant geometry
of its cliffs and pinnacles.

This is all water carved
the body thrust into the hydrasphere
and where the green mesas give way
to the vulcan floor, not far
from Farmington and other interferences
with the perfect night
and the glittering trail
of the silent Vía Láctea

(*S* 146)

Earlier, brief flashes of the landscape—recorded at intervals
in "The Winterbook"—signified the emergence of pure song.
For example, while Kool Everything was getting the last word
on the subject of dead letters and Sierra climbing we might have
noted:

the light snowe
casually attracted to the earth
drifting blew
thru the perfumery of the piñon clad hills
which flash on the frames
of the windows of our journey
and cause the junipers to go by.

(*S* 122)

And later moments sustain it: implicitly by the Slinger's super-
natural attentiveness, explicitly by the increasing frequency of
celebrative verse. The former centers the generally animated
state of the assembled company in a present sense of assured
equilibrium; the latter, made resilient by broad comic effects,
impels the drift toward a condition of easy harmony, of feeling
at home. The following gathering of passages—from the opening lines of Book IIII, section 1, the opening lines of Book IIII,
section 2, and the initial announcement of the Slinger's leave-
taking—reveal then the final surfacing of Dorn's pretension to

heroic song in *Slinger*. The notice of local effects of meteorological conditions operating within the whole continental landform brings into play Dorn's capacity for a heightened lyricism:

> Then went through the Superior Air
> a descension in summer from the troposphere
> over the high mountains
> and along the Colorado Plateau
> dry and warm, the fairest
> and rarest mood
> of the southwest earth
>
> And the currents of fragrant oil
> disperse in the hills like greek wine
>     Only at the rim
>     does the day tremble & shine.
>
> (*S* 147)

Full recognition of the incomparable earth where she first bared herself in the local landforms triggers a declarative mode of celebrative song:

> mojones superboa, paisaje magnífico
> masculino, all thats left of the plumbing
> dikes, flues, the tubes of frozen magma
> Rico, a thing to contemplate
> Holly Holia, this is where
> the earth bared herself
> This is the old altar of fire
> This is San Juan reaching
> still sagrado and not consagrado
> this was once plasta
> now a worn and bitter fugue by Chaos
>
>     This is the quantus
> laid as bare as it can be laid
> It doesn't do to enter it
> its scale is revelátory
> not comparative. . . .
>
> (*S* 178)

And the Slinger's retrospective affection for the loveliness of the Southwest earth at sundown draws pathos out of his words of farewell:

> Many the wonders this day I have seen
> the Zlinger addressed his friends
> Keen, fitful gusts are whispering here and there
> The mesas quiver above the withdrawing sunne
> Among the bushes half leafless and dry
> The smallest things now have their time
> The stars look very cold about the sky
> And I have grown to love your local star
> But now niños, it is time for me to go inside
> I must catch the timetrain
>
> (S 198)

The diversification of kinds of spoken language appropriate to a healthy society, on the one hand, and the emergence of a shift toward celebrative, heroic song, on the other, have been the related subjects of my discussion of Book IIII thus far. I wish, finally, to argue the *confluence* of those effects appearing in the Poet's song of Cocaine Lil at the close of section 1. Cocaine Lil herself emerges as a fully developed character (an amplification of the southwestern American Lil we know), but, as a figure celebrated in song, she exists as well as a projection of the ideal possibilities of this place as they exist in the mind. She takes her place alongside Taco, Flamboyant, et al., as that colorful and vibrant type of character who might be expected to appear on the Western plain, but she enjoys Lil's distinction of being the only woman around and also of having her roots traced. As "Miss Americaine . . . a mountain thang / dressed in bright red calico," she is the most recent embodiment of "Bright Erythra" on whom "the sunne comes up in Cuzco" (S 173). The reference to Cuzco identifies her with the capital of the ancient Inca empire known as the City of the Sun. She was, we are told, married to Mescaleen on the edge of Lake Titicaca, that sacred lake located high in the Andes on the Peru–Bolivia boundary.

Despite her family resemblance to the traveling Lil, Cocaine Lil's ancestral history is thus more particularly exotic than Lil's, and her identity, derived from the local history of the Americas, seems mythical. Because she seems to enjoy a special place in the poem, in a space created by this most absolute of the Poet's visionary songs, I shall try to illuminate Dorn's intention in introducing her at this moment.

If Amerigo Castro is right in arguing that the possibilities of creative expression are at once circumscribed and enabled by the life of the culture out of which they arise—circumscribed by a culture's exclusive direction of energy into subsistence, on the one hand, enabled by a displacement of such energies beyond subsistence, into qualitative concerns, on the other—then Cocaine Lil's identity may be said to be rooted in the possibilities of an enabling culture, the poem's evocation of what Castro speaks of as a *morada vital*, a "vital dwelling place."[19] Viewed in relation to the trajectory of the poem's motion, she appears, it seems, as one in whom procreative flow triumphs over impotent stagnation, figuring forth the end of the traveler's quest for purity of mind and vitality of being. Associated with American indigenousness, she carries the female vitality of the life of the Americas, manifesting the history of its cultural transmission from the South to the North. One may recall that history recapitulated in the life work of the New Mexico novelist Frank Waters and in Carl Sauer's geographical explorations of the Southwest and Mexico. Thus she provides a many-centuries-long, archetypal backdrop to the Slinger's own journey out of the Land of the Sun. She is, of course, also the spirit of cocaine, a drug indigenous to the original northward shifting *morada vital* of the Americas. As such, she clearly embodies the oppo-

19. Castro, *An Idea of History*, pp. 287–88.

site of the static inwardness of the citizens of Truth or Consequences and of the Atlantes, those recent European migrants to
the region who have learned nothing from, or are determined
to suppress all traces of, indigenous ways of relating to the land.

To take from this song of 151 lines any one passage would
be to distort its quality, and hence I refrain from doing so
despite the "beauties" that emerge in its flow. The song does
confirm, however, the Slinger's later declaration in the poem's
crisis. When, at the pitch of battle—as the "inertia of the old
order / buckles" the plate underlying the mountains—the travelers cry out in chorus "Oh Zlinger are we lost[?]," he answers:

> No, we are crystals of gold
> along the axes of upheaval.
> (S 186)

The stylistic shift incurred by this lengthy interpolation of the
Poet's final song both amplifies the eloquence and intensifies
the declarative voice that has heretofore either been absent or
kept in check: the declaration that we are "crystals of gold." It
suggests that through a renewed contact with the "outsidereal"
and through a reduction of contaminated mental states, we
retain the possibility, at least, of recreating a *morada vital* in
this continent.

The poem's determinative axis of relation, as revealed in this
song and as embodied in "Cocaine Lil," turns out to be a
vertical north-south axis. If the originary vision was centered
on the dark plains night where Texans were said to wage genetic
duels with men of other states, it would, at last, be radically
shifted away from that horizontal plane on which the plotted
collision was initially figured. The high noon of America's present and future crisis could not be so simply circumscribed by
time, place, or moral paradigm. Once Dorn's point of view had
shifted from England to central North America, he began to
conceive of the genetic dueling as a collision of mental-cultural

outlooks that embodied a many-centuries-long conflict between northern transatlantic migrants, intent upon appropriating a land to their use and their mental habits, on the one
hand, and on the other, the indigenous populations of the western hemisphere, which, having shifted their dwelling place toward the north, fought to hold that place. The Southwest, Dorn
perceived, represented the last northern area in which the battle
might still be imaginatively waged. Historically, the Colorado
Plateau had defined an area inhospitable to appropriation by
northern races spreading from the Northeast. Should a cynical
observer remind him that that area has, nevertheless, been long
appropriated by Texas entrepreneurs and their confederates,
and should he supply quantitative statistics to enforce that
reminder, it may be noted that Dorn has anticipated that reminder and has incorporated it into "The Cycle"'s negative
measure of the appropriating mentality in its hustle for the
future. What those appropriating forces of a monocultural society lack is a capacity for excavating and retrieving vital matter. Their opposite, indeed, lies in Dorn's figures of the Slinger
and of his native counterpart Lil. In them resides the vitality
that slumbers in the Americas and remains locatable in the
Southwest locale Dorn has himself appropriated for his Song of
Slinger. If he were to establish a new foothold in this racial-
historical struggle, especially as it has shifted to the plane of
mental programming of citizens by a dangerous recent appropriation of language's power of naming, it would not suffice for
Dorn to express his view; rather, it would be necessary to so
stage his poem that it would be resistant to description and
hence to assimilation. He would have to stage a shape-shifting
journey of the mind, that mind nudged into accord with the
underground, rooted life of the given dwelling place and with
the local cosmos to which it is attached.

Although much of Dorn's work has been fraught with the
gnarled toughness of a working-class stoicism, I think he early

saw that song had the power to transact such an alteration of mind, to tap resources of inner resistance to stasis-defining externals. "I tell you," the speaker of the simply titled "Song" in *Geography* declared,

> I tell you the gleaming eye
> is a mirror of
>       the green hills
> where love struggles
>          against the drought
> in the desert
> in the spring
> in the quickness
> of the fresh bush
>      over the cove.
>
>        (CP 129)

It is just such a declaration, reverberating between our ears in the form of a song improbably sung out of our deprived cultural landscape, that finally sticks.

# 6

## Edward Dorn's
## "Pontificatory use of the art":
## Hello, La Jolla *and* Yellow Lola

### ALAN GOLDING

A Pontificatory use of the art
is both interesting & a lot of fun
the pope's got a really good role
                    (*YL* 31)

101

numbers are the only entities
which don't lie
                    (*YL* 65)

Juxtapositions(s)

1. Sure, there may be some interesting
*juxtapositions*, but so what    [Anat.]

2. *Juxtaposition* is ok if you can't do
anything else    [Sociol.]

                    (*HLJ* 65)

Shouldn't these "poems" appear on bumper stickers (as indeed one poem was titled when first published), on bubble-gum

wrappers, on TV commercials?[1] Is this work even poetry? I suspect that most readers of Ed Dorn's recent books, *Hello, La Jolla* and *Yellow Lola*, have asked such questions, and their bafflement has resulted in almost total neglect of those books. Even Dorn's largely ignored earlier work at least received reviews, but I have encountered only five reviews of *Hello, La Jolla* or *Yellow Lola* as individual books. Of these notices, one, on *Hello, La Jolla*, appears in the English journal *The Atlantic Review*, which few American readers will ever see, and a two-paragraph notice in *Sulfur* finds merely "a few chuckles" or "amusing snippets" in *Yellow Lola*.[2] One frosty review of Dorn's *Selected Poems* (Bolinas, Ca.: Grey Fox Press, 1978) ignores the work drawn from *Hello, La Jolla* entirely, while even George Butterick, a more sympathetic reader, sounds befuddled as he observes that "these later poems test the limits of obliquity."[3] But in reading a poet who dismisses "hard and fast distinctions between poetry and prose" (SL 93), we ask the wrong question if we wonder whether his work even qualifies as poetry. In this essay I would like to discuss rather what *kind* of poetry Dorn is now writing, to place the poetry in the context of his career and to advance some claims for its value.

Dorn himself shows little interest in justifying his recent

1. "Bumpersticker," *Chicago Review* 30 (Winter 1979): 112. The text reads, "RECREATION WRECKS THE NATION." It is reprinted, untitled, in *YL* 40.

2. Peter Ackroyd, "The Poetry of Public Statement," *The Atlantic Review* (New Series), no. 2 (Autumn 1979), 58–59; Bill Zavatsky, review of four books including *Yellow Lola*, *Sulfur* 1 (1981): 261–65. The other reviews are Kathryn Shevelow, "Ed Dorn's *Yellow Lola*," *Chicago Review* 33 (Summer 1981): 101–4; Robert von Hallberg, "Poetry Chronicle: 1980," *Contemporary Literature* 23 (Spring 1982): 229–32; and Donald Davie, "Steep Trajectories," in *Trying to Explain* (Ann Arbor: University of Michigan Press, 1979), pp. 13–17.

3. The review is Paul Breslin's "Black Mountain: A Critique of the Curriculum," *Poetry* 136 (July 1980): 219–39; for George Butterick, see "A Fist in his Heart: Edward Dorn's *Selected Poems*," *Chicago Review* 30 (Winter 1979): 157–62.

work as poetry. In the 1977 talk "Strumming Language" he discusses the work procedures that have produced *Hello, La Jolla* and *Yellow Lola*: "I spend a lot of the day monitoring the flow of news and so forth, watching how the language is being used. . . . I find it necessary to have a continuous stream of data pouring into my daily life" (SL 86–87). Thus he chooses to explain not how he achieved this poetry's form but how he arrived at its content, its "data." And he restrains himself from selecting that data—anything can find its way into a poem:

I hear an awful lot of what I repeat just on the air. That would be: radio, conversations on the corner, in a cafe, things my children tell me, reports of all kinds coming in from many many sources.

(*I* 101)

*Hello, La Jolla*'s first poem, "A for Ism," expands on this procedure. The poet arranges the words that his daily listening casts in his path:

A poets occupation
is to compose poetry
The writing of it
is everywhere
(*HLJ* ix)

Dorn acknowledges that his almost obsessive attention to language "reduces," "refines," or "granulates" it, resulting in the pieces (quite literally) that make up *Hello, La Jolla* and *Yellow Lola*: "shorter and shorter pieces of expression, which I'm not interested in calling anything, and I don't mean poems, but I mean anything. And yet I'm interested in formulating what the function of them might be" (SL 87).

Dorn sees questions of genre (is this poetry?) as resolved or unresolvable; he prefers to focus on content and function (what does the work say, and to what end?). This apparent sidestep of formal issues actually maintains a distinction to which Dorn has adhered throughout his career. As early as 1961 he expresses more interest in discussing content than form. Responding to the standard interview question about his poetic line, he says, "I don't think about measure and line, in a technical sense, that much. . . . It's a false problem. . . . It will become less important as the content of our speech becomes more important" (*I* 5). Much later, in 1977, he ironically conducts a mock debate on the formal nature of poetry: "Well, you can't really tell [a poem's quality], can you, and you can't really tell, because, well, is it really poetry, and is it really poetry because you can't really say what a line is" (SL 93). Such debates, Dorn believes, too easily afford an excuse for avoiding necessary value judgments: focusing exclusively on questions of form and theory allows a reader to wriggle out of saying whether a poem is good or bad. Dorn believes that to evaluate a poem as "good" or "bad" invites a formal judgment only in part; it also invites an assessment of content that might be fudged by a reader attending only to style.

Dorn deemphasizes stylistic criteria for discussing poetry more than most poets would do. For many of his contemporaries, style is the poetic man—style in the form of calculatedly unlikely images and a cute drollness of tone, a set of mannerisms that, in Robert Pinsky's words, has become "a kind of gaud or badge establishing that the writer is a poet."[4] At the same time it has become increasingly hard since the modernist era to define poetry by the formal characteristics of lineation (more and more poets now experiment with that hybrid, the prose poem); of diction (all levels and sources of diction have been up for grabs since Pound and Eliot); or of syntax (much of which, in contemporary poetry, is determinedly prosaic). Eclec-

4. Robert Pinsky, *The Situation of Poetry: Contemporary Poetry and Its Traditions* (Princeton: Princeton University Press, 1976), p. 8. For a similar perspective on contemporary poetry, see Paul Breslin, "How to Read the New Contemporary Poem," *The American Scholar* 47 (1977–78): 356–70.

ticism rules, sometimes obscuring distinctions between prose and poetry until the only one left is typographical: poetry is writing justified only to the left-hand margin. (Dorn seems to have typography in mind when he defines poetry by how it "optically occup[ies] its space" [SL 93].) This historical situation, and Dorn's own dismissal of the issue, provide two reasons for dropping the large-scale generic question "Is this poetry?" in reading *Hello, La Jolla* and *Yellow Lola*. But the smaller-scale question, "What *kind* of poetry is it?" can bear some fruit. The poetry's tone—satirical, sardonic, superior—combined with its brevity, condensation, and "slickness" (*I* 76) suggests a candidate: the epigram.[5] J. V. Cunningham's work aside, the epigram has fallen into disrepute in the twentieth century—so much so that, in Dorn's case, we fail to recognize it when we see it. But the mode enjoyed much favor in the eighteenth century, the period that has most influenced Dorn's poetry since *Slinger*. Prior, Gay, Pope, Swift, and Burns all mined the epigrammatic vein in that century, as did Pope's later disciple, Byron; Pope, "the great master of hatred," and Byron have both been important to Dorn's latest work.[6]

Dorn's later poems resemble both the classical and eighteenth-century epigram not only in their satiric tone and compression but also in their sense of audience. They feature a persuasive rhetoric that directly addresses an audience other than the poet himself. Many of the poems show a formal argumentative movement, from thesis to example. Like the traditional epigram, they are often occasional, culture-bound,

5. On brevity, condensation, and polish (Dorn's "slickness") as defining characteristics of the epigram, see Paul Nixon, *Martial and the Modern Epigram* (New York: Longmans, Green, 1927), p. 9; and "Epigrams," in Alex Preminger, et al., eds., *Princeton Encyclopedia of Poetry and Poetics*, enlarged edition (Princeton: Princeton University Press, 1974), pp. 247–48.

6. T. S. Eliot, "Andrew Marvell," in *Selected Prose of T. S. Eliot*, ed. Frank Kermode (New York: Harcourt Brace Jovanovich and Farrar, Straus, and Giroux, 1975), p. 162.

responding to contemporary trends and particular social situations rather than to ahistorical universals of human experience. And they continue a tradition of pithy insult traceable back to Martial. "What Will Be Historically Durable" exhibits all these characteristics:

> About Nixon there was
> Something grandiose
> Although this peevish society
> Failed to even blink at it.
>
> Nothing illustrates this
> More than
> When he stole the post office.
>                                    (HLJ 19)

This poem also demonstrates, in passing, one of the more distinctive features of Dorn's political vision: his capacity to adopt a surprising position that throws new light on a situation. He realizes that in a poem on the nature of political power in America "it is too easy to use one who's [sic] very name is a satire upon all government" (footnote to poem, HLJ 19), and so he refuses to align himself with the familiar, although justified, condemnations of Nixon. Dorn does not *defend* Nixon; he finds, however, "something grandiose" in Nixon's ambitions that the knee-jerk accusations of "this peevish society" can easily obscure. Hence the poem does something far more important than criticize Nixon. Like "The Death of Howard Hughes" (YL 50), in which "the story is not tragic because / [Hughes'] control is not to be seriously / questioned," it considers the possible and perversely fascinating range of one man's power.

In most of these late epigrams Dorn uses irony to define a position boldly and to simplify rather than qualify statements. His push to reduce subtleties of tone and feeling is one feature of Dorn's work that distinguishes him from J. V. Cunningham, the most accomplished traditional epigrammatist of this century. Cunningham's abstract diction and acerbic wit resemble Dorn's, but the diction makes reference to private and nonoccasional rather than public subject matter ("unsocial privacies obsess me"),[7] and the irony is used to qualify.[8] Also unlike Dorn, Cunningham writes in tight metrical forms. Probably influenced by his teacher Yvor Winters, Cunningham exploits irony and slight deviations from stanzaic and metrical norms to enhance complexity of feeling and meaning.[9] Because Dorn seeks neither emotional complexity nor qualification, however, he does not need a firm metrical ground against which to register subtle turns in thought.

In eschewing meter Dorn extends the epigram's formal possibilities. Free verse and the epigram are usually considered incompatible. Winters, for instance, asserts that "the satiric and didactic forms require of their very nature a coherent rational frame"—a frame reinforced by meter, with the particular kinds of control and closure it offers.[10] Dorn relies for closure on the reader's attention to the poem's argument and on fulfilling the expectations established by his formal prose syntax. Because a predictable rhyme or rhythm does not define the end of a Dorn epigram, the reader/listener is thrown back on syntax (listening for the completion of a sentence) and content (the punch line). Formal syntax and jokes, of course, offer almost as much predictability as meter. Since we can recognize, even anticipate, the end of a sentence and the end of a joke, Dorn's

7. J. V. Cunningham, "Epigrams: A Journal, #17," *The Exclusions of a Rhyme* (Denver: Alan Swallow, 1960), p. 76.

8. Pinsky, *Situation of Poetry*, p. 137: "This qualifying irony acts as a hairline indicator for meaning. . . ."

9. Yvor Winters, *In Defense of Reason* (Chicago: Swallow, 1947), p. 130: "The nearer a norm a writer hovers, the more able is he to vary his feelings in opposite or even in many directions, and the more significant will be his variations." Such statements form a cornerstone of Winters's views on meter.

10. Winters, *In Defense of Reason*, p. 121.

free verse epigrams offer as much reliable closure as the more traditional epigram.

The witty tone of Dorn's epigrams also provides a key to the poetry's function—a function rooted in the eighteenth-century view of wit. Eighteenth-century satiric poets saw scorn, the author's belief in his own superiority, as the basis of comedy. Scorn or wit aimed itself at the intelligence and understanding. Vicious and undemocratic though it may sound to twentieth-century ears,

the [eighteenth-century] theory of superiority had posited a real use for comedy and laughter: the identification of the immoral, the stupid, or the contemptible, with the suggestion that its comedy might be unpleasant in tone, but it finally promoted morality, prudence, and sanity.[11]

Dorn subscribes emphatically to this theory of comic superiority: "I do not share the current aversion directed at the words 'ironic' and 'sarcastic.' In fact, I value those modes . . ." (*I* 98); irony "is a thing I've always valued, against the current of my time" (*V* 12). The tone of his recent work holds words, ideas, and bits of cultural detritus up for sardonic inspection. Thus it has a didactic, or in his own words "exhortatory and pontificatory" (*I* 77), end. Dorn wants to create a "cognizance in the society of itself, to furnish the means—through clarity of language—for a self-appraisal and self-evaluation" (*I* 109). In other words, to purify the language of the tribe—not such an egregious goal at all.

Dorn takes a different approach, however, from modernist purifiers such as Pound, Eliot, and Williams. Claiming to go in fear of abstractions, these modernists preached (without always practicing) concreteness, devotion to the image—direct presentation of the thing, whether subjective or objective; the

11. Robert Bernard Martin, *The Triumph of Wit: A Study of Victorian Comic Theory* (Oxford: Clarendon, 1974), pp. 23–24.

objective correlative; "No ideas but in things." Dorn flatly
rejects, as did his early master Olson, this aspect of modernist
poetics. His 1960 essay "What I See in *The Maximus Poems*"
deplores modernism's programmatic "zeal for material effect"
(*V* 33), and in 1973 he asserts, "I don't want to say again what
Williams said ['No ideas but in things']—in fact I don't want to
say that at all" (*I* 47). As the diction and high level of generalization in all his work suggest, Dorn holds a philosophy of
language that allows conceptualizing and abstraction: "I've
always been confused by those attempts to make language the
same thing as the thing" (*I* 47). Even *Slinger*, which insists that
"we'd all rather *be* there / than talk about it" (*S* 24), is a densely
philosophical poem comfortable with deceptively jokey generalizations like "Time is more fundamental than space" (*S* 5).

In "The Problem of the Poem for my Daughter, Left Unsolved" (*CP* 94), Dorn writes, "The poem is an instrument of
intellection"—thus an instrument of diagnosis, explanation,
and judgment. This view of poetry explains his willingness to
move quickly between detail and generalization. In *Hello, La
Jolla* and *Yellow Lola* one such move often comprises a whole
poem:

A View, From 101

One flew over the Cuckoo's nest
Playing right next to
Trailer Park Village

The factory neatly retailing
Its product

(*HLJ* 77)

Here Dorn co-opts for poetry, as he does in the Nixon poem, a
technique of expository prose—drawing a general conclusion
from specific details. Dorn believes American culture "needs to
be examined by other methods than are ordinarily available
through the sociometrics," which merely yield statistics that
are not "converted . . . to intelligent reflection about the soci-

ety" (*I* 108). In his long, discursive early poems ("The Problem of the Poem . . . ," "Inauguration Poem #2," "The North Atlantic Turbine," "Oxford" [*CP* 92, 101, 179, 195]) he pursues an argument through all its ramifications to a conclusion. Thus the poem's movement embodies his "reflection." His more recent work teasingly suggests it: "Really, no kidding, I'm not trying to make you think" (footnote to poem, *YL* 68). In *Geography* (1965) and *The North Atlantic Turbine* (1967) answers were spelled out;[12] in *Hello, La Jolla* and *Yellow Lola* they lie waiting to be discovered: "It's not the content so much, but where the content might lead one" (SL 88).

To move from detail to generalization, from surface content to its buried implications, is to move from symptom to diagnosis. Dorn quotes Antonio Gramsci to discuss "what's happening" in contemporary America: " 'The crisis consists in the fact that the old is dying and the new cannot be born. In this interregnum, a great variety of morbid symptoms appear' " (*I* 113). Poets have often felt themselves situated in such an interregnum, so the idea itself is nothing new. Characteristically they have responded in one of two ways. They have bemoaned the perceived breakdown of a tradition that they then seek to revive (Pound, Eliot), or they have exulted over this same breakdown (Ginsberg, Williams) and sometimes celebrated their vision of the new order (Blake, Shelley; more recently Baraka, Rich). Dorn's response to cultural change, however, fits neither of these patterns. He detachedly accepts rather than celebrates "the fact that the old is dying" and remains skeptical about the new. "Don't Get Your Hopes Up" about the future, he says; maybe little will change:

> 1999 looks like they're
> On The Job

12. Both volumes are reprinted in *The Collected Poems*. They were first published as *Geography* (London: Fulcrum, 1965) and *The North Atlantic Turbine* (London: Fulcrum, 1967).

> Still drinking coffee
> From styrafoam cups.
> (*HLJ* 81)

And indeed little will change if we adhere to straightforward oppositions like "old" and "new." Part of Dorn's interest as a political poet (and one could say the same of Olson or the later Lowell) is that he refuses to posit any new order that simply defines itself as a "negative" of the old one. As the character "I" says in *Slinger*, "There is no negative pure enough / to entrap our Expectations" (*S* 155). Dorn has spent much of his career avoiding these polarities of political discourse. The poet's role, he believes, is not to offer schematic oppositions to the culture's "morbid symptoms"; rather it is to help his culture diagnose and explain these symptoms by offering a new language for the diagnosis. To reshape the language is to reshape the mind— hence to reshape, Dorn hopes, social policy, since the "crippled stem of this country is made with the mind" (*SB* 65).

This assumption that new language yields new thought and new policy derives most immediately from Pound and Olson. Both these poets took the path of exhortation, of earnest persuasion. The path led Pound to Pisa and St. Elizabeths. It won Olson, writing in a period when poetry rarely confronted public issues, a critical obscurity that has only recently begun to lighten. Dorn now works in a similar period, but he delivers a fresh twist on the relationship between language and political thought posited by Pound and Olson. Leaving behind his predecessors', and his own early, earnestness, he asserts that "Entrapment is this society's / Sole activity . . . / and Only laughter, / can blow it to rags" (*S* 155). *Slinger* embodies brilliantly this approach to the familiar assumptions about language and public policy. Its characters, "a society in trajectory" (*I* 33), talk in puns and neologisms. They spontaneously generate new language, until Lil proclaims the success of their venture: "*We've effected the saneamento*" (the sanitation, metaphorically, of the language) (*S* 197).

Dorn's goal in *Slinger* is to have this idiosyncratic habit of mind, this creation of a mutant language, generalize itself into a type: he calls the characters "our psychomorphs" (*S* 130). This goal extends into his latest poetry, where the poet works "to the end that the mumbling horde / bestirs its prunéd tongue" (*YL* 63). Like *Slinger*, *Hello, La Jolla* and *Yellow Lola* examine the language by isolating particular words for special attention: "Air Bag," "good" and "accurate," "represent," "the Gadsden Purchase" (*HLJ* 22, 59, 85, 88); "political," "hate," "moved," "Panama," "entrepreneurial," and "Booty" (*YL* 23, 54, 71, 102, 111). Only when we see how we abuse language can we change it, renew it, and hence use it to form the "Policy" and "Mind" (*I* 113) that we currently lack. *Hello, La Jolla*'s "Correct usages" (*HLJ* 64–67) explicitly undertakes to reshape words, to find especially soiled language and clean it up by trashing it. Dorn wrecks a word's tired contemporary meaning by debunking it; only when the word has been destroyed can it be remade. "Correct usages" scrutinizes, through a kind of *reductio ad absurdum*, "correct usages of some words widely misused or abused in modern conversation and poetry" (*HLJ* 64). One such word is that modernist shibboleth, "juxtaposition"—a poor substitute, intellectually and poetically, Dorn feels, for making connections. He connects ideas, not images, and does so rationally, not emotively: "I use [language] to make things cohere," he says, not to "dispel or exorcise" (*I* 102).

Emotional "exorcism" accurately summarizes the tone of much confessional and beat poetry in the 1960s and early 1970s. The cultural climate in those years frequently valued a poet in proportion to his apparent intensity of feeling. But Dorn recognizes emotional intensity in poetry as a rhetorical convention, all too easily contrived: "Happiness is a violent emotion / which makes it easy to fake" (*YL* 86). Ideas deserve the best poetic language, not feelings: "Moved was a bit too classy / to be used to note an emotion." Too classy, and also "too Lowell-

like," "sentimental, to be sure, cheap, / imported and ordinary" (*YL* 71). These lines, from "The Word (20 January
1977)," usefully illustrate the characteristic techniques of
Dorn's recent work. A surface of throwaway flipness conceals
serious thinking about appropriate poetic diction, the contemporary canon, and excessively personal poetry.

   *Hello, La Jolla* and *Yellow Lola*, then, favor a poetry of
intellect and judgment over a poetry of expression. Judgment is
a form of personal expression, of course, but in the satiric
epigram tradition that expression usually comments on, or
aspires to influence, public behavior. The tradition demands
more than a venting of personal spleen. Dorn see judgment, the
adoption of a polemic stance, as the proper end of intellectual
activity; what appears as prejudice in his work actually results
from rather than precedes reflection. The relationship between
intellect and judgment is a subtle, even contradictory, one in
Dorn's poetry, especially when the judgments take the form of
apparently unconsidered attitudes, prejudices, or insults: "At
least one increase has maintained itself / in the intermontane
West: / dumb fucks in pickup trucks" (*YL* 110). But insult recurs in the epigram tradition, and it is one thing that attracts
Dorn to the eighteenth century: "People were willing to insult
each other in that century. All the time. It was a total century of
insult. And it was a brilliant century. It invented the modern"
(*V* 22). Insult serves as a useful tool of literary and political
contention, both of which a culture needs to survive and grow.
Literary contention breeds "a higher degree of focus and perception" (*V* 22). Political contention encourages necessary
reevaluation of the social structure, necessary because it keeps
that structure healthy. According to Dorn, "It was always held
that democracy couldn't be healthy or even exist without contention. Contention is what democracy most needs" (*V* 22).

   One reviewer of Dorn's *Collected Poems* found the poetry

best when Dorn "transcends the prejudices of his ideology."[13]
This misses the point entirely, firstly because Dorn deliberately
avoids any fixed or summarizable ideology, and secondly because he turns prejudice into a conscious rhetorical strategy.
Early in his career (1961) Dorn felt the need to become "vulgar
and rough" (*I* 4) in his political statements. He acts out that
goal in a poem like "Oxford" (*CP* 195), where he attacks
economic imperialism via an erotic description of rich female
foreign students, bearing "witness to all it is possible / with
such instruments / as nations / and mellifluous boxes / to suck
up / the part of the world they may in any given period / have
wanted" (*CP* 196). Dorn uses calculated vulgarity to violate
those decorous norms of intellectual discourse that might in-
hibit or obscure a clear stance: "The metric system is as full of
shit / as the people who invented it" (*YL* 36). At the same time,
however, the insult stems from a comically phrased but genu-
inely thought-out position: that the metric system disrupts
commonsense ideas of proportion ("too small in the small measures / too big in the big measures") and that it may have been
taken up from a profit motive, "to push a new set of wrenches."

Cummings sometimes used this same strategy of vulgar insult, which may be why Dorn proposes that "some apprentice /
should take on / the revival of E. E. Cummings" (*YL* 58). It is
Cummings the epigrammatist who would appeal most to
Dorn—the Cummings who could write "a politician is an arse /
upon which everyone has sat except a man."[14] This deliberate
coarseness (he calls poets "we coarse ones" [*CP* 20]) is also one
area where Dorn leans closer to Byron's flouting of decorum
than to Pope's deceptive surface civility. Some of Byron's epigrams provide a model for Dorn's cheerful vulgarity:

---

13. Ben Howard, "Four Voices," *Poetry* 130 (August 1977): 288.

14. E. E. Cummings, *Complete Poems, 1913–1962* (New York: Harcourt
Brace Jovanovich, 1972), p. 550.

Posterity will ne'er survey
A nobler grave than this:
Here lie the bones of Castlereagh:
Stop, traveller [, piss][15]

Dorn has never shied away from name-calling. In his recent poetry, Ralph Nader, J. Edgar Hoover, Henry Kissinger, "Kennecott's auditors," and NBC, among others, all get it in the neck. Name-calling has always played a central rhetorical role in the satiric tradition, because it "reminds us of militant authorial presence."[16] This presence is what makes the fragments of *Hello, La Jolla* and *Yellow Lola* cohere. It emerges cumulatively, Dorn's interest in these books being to compose not individual poems but sequences. The poem is not a polished whole but a trace, an echo of Dorn's presence; its contribution to an overall set of attitudes takes precedence over its worth as a discrete artifact.

Jonathan Raban has observed how Dorn's voice works best over long distances, noting "the cumulative pressure of its inventions (which are locally often slight)."[17] Raban has in mind the longer poems in *Geography* and *The North Atlantic Turbine*, but his remark applies equally to *Slinger*, where any one pun may seem outrageously bad but where the level of sustained inventiveness is astounding. It applies further to *Hello, La Jolla* and *Yellow Lola*. Taken in isolation, some of these late poems sound facile or trivial: "I have an excellent, if unconventional, memory" (*YL* 100), to give a one-line example. But read as a sequence they pack considerable power, because they project a coherent and compelling persona. We value Dorn's mem-

15. Byron, "An Epitaph for Castlereagh," in J. Paul Hunter, ed., *The Norton Introduction to Literature: Poetry* (New York: W. W. Norton, 1973), p. 343.
16. Edward A. Bloom and Lillian D. Bloom, *Satire's Persuasive Voice* (Ithaca, N.Y.: Cornell University Press, 1979), p. 243.
17. Jonathan Raban, *The Society of the Poem* (London: Harrap, 1971), p. 127.

ory more highly a few pages later, when we are reminded that "the organ of memory is destroyed / systematically in our children / or teased with the meanest statistics" (*YL* 124). Together these two poems show Dorn's intellectual differences from his culture in a way that neither shows on its own. Poems explain and build on each other until meanings emerge from a whole book that are not available from individual pieces.

In addition to the "cumulative pressure" of barely suppressed anger and sometimes savage jokes, other stylistic features carry over from Dorn's early discursive poetry into *Hello, La Jolla* and *Yellow Lola*—declaratory syntax (the recurrent use of "There is/are"), abstract diction ("non-compliance / would be a repudiation / of their very own worst selves" [*YL* 82]), explicit moral judgments ("This device [the air bag] should not be permitted / General Motors was right to suppress it / and wrong to have relented / and Nader should stay out of it" [*HLJ* 22]). The recent poems, however, do not extend into argumentation. Whereas the early work often proposed a thesis and argued it through, the later work stops with the thesis itself or adds one brief example. The line in *Hello, La Jolla* and *Yellow Lola* refuses to be drawn into the subtle weavings and turnings that argument might involve. Dorn has come a long way from his pre-*Slinger* line, doubling back on itself, breaking unpredictably as it explores ideas. His recent line is consciously formulaic and uniform in its length and breaks, as if he considered any straining of line against syntax or sense distracting. Thus it grows naturally from his equally invariant central tone: "There's a certain characteristic way I want to say things, that isn't really deviated from much" (*I* 105).

This deliberately flat, consistent line is another means by which Dorn suppresses ambiguities of attitude or possible complications in the subject matter. Reacting against the bounciness of *Slinger*, Dorn "was trying for a tone to see how actually flat and rigorously final you could make a line" (*I* 77). A certain thematic truncation results: nothing gets developed. This trope leaves Dorn open to charges of oversimplification, but actually it forms a didactic strategy that shifts the burden of locating significant content from poet to reader. The strategy is not unfamiliar, deriving most recently from Olson and more distantly from Zukofsky and Pound. The poem becomes a code to crack for the useful knowledge hidden inside it. Dorn favors an almost scholarly use of secondary sources:

> Listen, if anybody's saying,
> you know, there's something new
> and something or other's not
> Well, they should look it up.
>                    (*HLJ* 57)

In a number of poems he specifies his expectations that the reader follow up on the clues he receives. "In defense of Quality," for example, hints that its significance lies beyond the poem, in a dictionary:

> I decided to look hate up
> and found it to be
> what I guessed
> before I walked over to the book.
>
> I won't presume to
> save you the trip, of course
> we know better than that.
>                    (*YL* 54)

He gives us a key to the poem's door: "I decided to look hate up." But we must turn that key ourselves: "I won't presume to / save you the trip." The door opens onto the *OED*, which tells us that the use of "hate" as a noun is "now chiefly poetical." Recording his hatred for his culture's backslidings remains as much the poet's business now as it was for Pope.

This sly, oblique exhortation clearly differs from the confrontive attacks of Dorn's earliest didactic poetry. By the time he finished *The North Atlantic Turbine* he "had become very convinced that the direct onslaught in that sober sense of the political poem was not only very boring but completely value-less" (*I* 26), and in fact *The North Atlantic Turbine*, Dorn's most overtly preachy book, is his least favorite, "the most un-comfortable of my work to me" (*I* 24). His rhetorical stance changes with *Slinger*, the hero of which has "no wish to con-tinue / [his] debate with men" (*S* 3)—but who still plays wise man to "the cultural collective" (*S* 146). And in *Yellow Lola*, amid mocking generalizations about his culture, and following a poem on the 1976 presidential campaign, Dorn disingen-uously denies the possibility of political poetry:

> You holding that little piece of paper
> up to me and saying it's political?
>
> Sure, it's as political as a gopher hole.
>     (*YL* 23)

Dorn gives with one hand and takes with the other in *Hello, La Jolla* and *Yellow Lola*: his serious side will assert a proposi-tion while his witty side pretends to undermine it. Yet one can hardly deny that this is propositional poetry. Sometimes the poems read as something even more emphatic than proposi-tions—as laws. Take "The Burr Quote":

> Law is anything which is
> Boldly asserted
> And plausibly maintained
>     (*HLJ* 84, *YL* 106)

Here Dorn advances his poems as laws themselves by defining "law" in terms that could equally well describe the poems. Bold assertions, however, do not necessarily demand an earnest tone, and a law can be plausibly maintained by irony. The satiric bite in Dorn's recent poetry often comes from affecting the same cultural ennui that he is attacking. Much of the venom of "Loose goose, tight shoes & cold igloos" derives from its title, which inverts the Secretary of Agriculture's notorious remark during the 1976 presidential campaign that "coloreds want . . . three things: first, a tight pussy; second, loose shoes; and third, a warm place to shit."[18] The text flirts with ennui:

> One mildly electric campaign
> the joke of 1976
> possessed one point of interest
> namely the amount of Euphemism
> generated by what were
> originally Euphemisms
>
> (YL 22)

One joke, one point of interest—a pretty low yield for an event whose outcome would determine the political climate for the next four years. In "Of Robert Creeley" (1978) Dorn finds the state of contemporary culture reflected in "a boredom throughout communications. In this condition, the wisecrack is about as great as the voltage gets" (V 122–23); in a poem title he remarks that "one of the increasingly urgent searches in writing today is to find an adequate exclamation" (YL 56). The culture needs a metaphorical storm to shake it up, to "loosen / a lot of rocks which would come tumbling down" (YL 56). But Dorn's hopes for this storm's outcome remain slim: "Expectations from the rain / overdue too long only breed the crass / and the people are aching to water the grass" (YL 56). Rain just provides enough water to turn on the garden sprinklers.

Watering the grass, and "the crass," is only one of the many social rituals that *Yellow Lola* takes to task; others include "group analysis" (YL 33), "The metric system" (YL 36), and recycling (YL 38–39). Dorn evaluates these activities by how much they contribute to the culture's life. He dismisses the

---

18. The quoted remark was made by Earl Butz, Gerald Ford's Secretary of Agriculture. For one source, see *New Times* 7 (15 October 1976), p. 27.

metric system because it makes no significant difference; it will simply allow some opportunistic manufacturer "to push a new set of wrenches." The system is an invention with no purpose beyond increasing uniformity. Recycling, meanwhile, "is an after-work recreation" (*YL* 38). Dorn has always treated skeptically the more self-congratulatory manifestations of social conscience. *Slinger*, written at the height of the Vietnam war, refuses to speak "about the war / in, well you know where the War is" (*S* 79). "Wait by the Door Awhile Death, There Are Others" (1967) despairs of a predictable liberal dinner companion:

> I thought sure as hell
> he is going down
> the whole menu
>
>       Civil rights cocktail
>       Vietnam the inflexible entree
>
> oh gawd what will there be for pudding
> (not another bombe
>
>                    (*CP* 218)

Social action, and talk about it, are too easily incorporated into the very culture that spawned their necessity. So "recycling has grown to be / a major part of the pollution industry" (*YL* 39), become part of "the rationale / of co-option parading as *cooperation*" (*YL* 44).

*Yellow Lola* finds American culture, then, in an "era of massive dysfunction / & generalized onslaught upon alertness" (*YL* 63). This onslaught has produced "an embarassed [*sic*] language" (*HLJ* 71), a language that has sunk to the bottom of the culture's scale of values. Poetry must revive and preserve the language; to do so is "the common duty of the poet" (*YL* 63). He preserves the language not just to have it for himself and other poets but to raise the common level of articulateness, "to the end that the mumbling horde / bestirs its prunéd tongue." This large ambition recalls a poem as early as "The Open Road" (1961), in which the poet strives to

> increase the
> daily imagery
> and bring within the ease
> of all, the powers anciently
> attributed and forthcoming
> from the muse . . .
>
> (*CP* 18)

The poetry audience occupies a privileged position in this undertaking: "Their steely determination / is one of the finest instruments / of modern times" (*YL* 89). Dorn is sharp enough to realize that the poet cannot preserve language on his own; he needs his audience to cooperate. Dorn demands in particular that his audience think critically about language. Again, to reevaluate the language is to reevaluate the thought behind it. In the 1965 poem "Song: Venceremos" Dorn elliptically quotes Olson's "Memory, Mind, and Will": " 'there are men with ideas / who effect[ / public policy via / politicians].' "[19] The poet must "force those men" (*CP* 152) to act on their ideas. In this sense the poet who stresses ideas can obliquely affect political decisions by directly affecting the language and thought behind them.

*Hello, La Jolla* and *Yellow Lola* probe not only the verbal but also the intellectual failings of contemporary America. Many poems shoot out a lightning left jab and then back off:

> Poetry is now mostly government product
> the work of our non-existent critics
> is unnecessary, the grades assigned
> to meat will do nicely . . .
>
> (*YL* 62)

After these lines we know we have been hit. Dorn's belief in "the shared mind" or "collective voice" (*I* 28) permits him to generalize about the state of the national consciousness just as

---

19. Charles Olson, *Archaeologist of Morning* (New York: Grossman, 1971), p. 210.

he does about the state of the language. He finds the "inch-a-minute public mind" (*HLJ* 71) fixated in patterns of thought and behavior that no longer promise any hope for cultural change. As his love of contention suggests, Dorn assumes change to be intrinsically valuable. But he proposes no specific program, and is not, in any literal sense, a revolutionary poet. In 1961, engaged in a heated debate over political poetry with LeRoi Jones, he wrote thus to Jones: "Revolutions are invariably shortsighted enough to determine usefulness, thus starting the assininity [*sic*] of set process all over again."[20] Dorn characteristically translates political arguments into metaphysical ones—change vs. "set process" or stasis.[21] *The North Atlantic Turbine*, Dorn's metaphor for the movement of trade in the Western Hemisphere, has an "unalterable and predictable action" (*CP* 187), while "Oxford" wrestles with "*permanently intended disablement*' / 'the idea that civilization is static" (*CP* 206). In "An Unremote Recombinant" even genetic progress grinds to a halt:

> Eventually,
> They're going to put you in a petri dish
> And therein they're going to grow you.
> Not all of you though. For instance
> They're not going to grow your head
> And they're not going to grow your body.
>                    (*HLJ* 83)

This poem inverts the expectation that "they're going to grow you," thus embodying the inversion of thought that Dorn wants to induce in his readers and culture.

20. Dorn to LeRoi Jones, 21 October 1961 (UCLA Library).

21. In contrasting Dorn's response to public situations with those of Lowell, Ginsberg, and Bly, Donald Wesling notes how Dorn tends to think on a global scale: "Dorn's analysis of the way things work . . . moves very often on the level of world-systems and commodities as well as the level of personal experience; to a greater extent he situates the psychological and individualist possibilities within a larger frame of reference." See "A Bibliography on Ed Dorn for America," *Parnassus* 5 (Spring/Summer 1977): 146.

*Slinger*'s mind-bending verbal antics show how much Dorn values mental agility as a means to combat intellectual stasis, particularly the stasis or predictability often imposed by ideological categories. *Hello, La Jolla* includes a poem "In Which We Are Paid the Dubious Political Compliment of Opposing Messages" (*HLJ* 53); *Yellow Lola* repeats that poem, with a considerably more bitter title—"A protest against still another empty-minded choice" (*YL* 97). When Slinger watches both "for the prosecutors of Individuality" and for its "advocates," he catches "all the known species of Cant" (*S* 162). Dorn talks of revolution in the broadest political sense, as not only a social but an epistemological turnaround:

I don't think that revolution except in rather particular places, namely South America or Southeast Asia, has any point. It has to be far more radical and far more subversive than that. I think the people just have to stop paying attention to that bullshit and turn their backs on it.

(*V* 116)

Dorn's own ideology resists easy summary because he proposes a political thinking that explodes simplified oppositions like left-right, Communist-Capitalist, liberal-conservative: "I have no love at all for the state or any kind of nation but, on the other hand, I listen to anti-state arguments that strike me as stupid also" (*V* 115). He shows as little sympathy for "the hippest member of the minority group" (*CP* 95), for socialism ("shit turned only half way round" [*CP* 208]), or for "Left Wing Urban Guerrillas" (*HLJ* 66) as he does for the more obvious targets like Nixon or the CIA. But one need not wave partisan flags to be an effective political poet. Dorn's successes are those of a nonpartisan skeptic, one who comments perceptively, convincingly, and relevantly on his culture's daily mechanisms.

*Hello, La Jolla* and *Yellow Lola* parody the either-or distinctions into which political poetry can too easily fall by setting up joke categories. One poem contrasts "those who want to go / & those who want to stay," on the tongue-in-cheek assumption that "humanity divides neatly / into two categories" (*YL* 88). Other poems distinguish "flies bred in dogshit" and "those bred / from the shit of horses" (*YL* 80—"just another Metaphysical question"), and "the synthetic / and the grown" (*HLJ* 25). To dismiss straightforwardly dualistic distinctions, however, is not to abandon discrimination altogether. Sometimes Dorn puts forward distinctions that initially resist understanding but that conceal a serious point. The difference, for example, between the "two main kinds of cruelty," "enthusiastic" and "unnecessary" (*HLJ* 32), seems mysterious at first, but Dorn's comment that "the period in which we live practises the latter" suggests a reference to Vietnam, a cruelty both "unnecessary" and, given how many resisted the draft, far from "enthusiastic." Other oppositions, simultaneously witty and serious, are less opaque: for instance, that between centralized and local government, "Central Arrogance and Local Mercilessness" (*HLJ* 45). By simultaneously asserting and undercutting the habit of discrimination Dorn can have his cake and eat it too—which he needs to do if he wants to undermine conventional moral and social categories while using poetry to judge the culture. Paradoxically, judgment involves accepting certain categories. But Dorn rejects any reader who avoids judgment, who is " 'lukewarm, and / neither hot nor cold' ": " 'I will spew thee / out of my mouth' " (*YL* 46).

The critical neglect that Dorn has suffered supplies a perverse measure of his success in undercutting familiar intellectual categories.[22] His recent work, in diction, syntax, tone, and

22. Donald Davie cites the two most recent examples of this neglect. Helen Vendler does not even mention Dorn in *Part of Nature, Part of Us: Modern American Poets* (Cambridge, Mass.: Harvard University Press, 1980); and in Daniel Hoffman's three essays on postwar American poetry in *The Harvard Guide to Contemporary American Writing* (Cambridge, Mass.: Harvard University Press, 1979), "Dorn . . . is named and that's all." See Davie, "Voices Modern and Postmodern," *The Sewanee Review* 89 (Winter 1981): 110–17.

subject matter, has very few parallels in contemporary poetry, so we lack ready (or at any rate familiar) frames for comparison. In contrast both to Dorn's earlier poetics of inclusion (his long, argumentative poems and the grab-bag *Slinger*) and to the contemporary taste for rambling interior narratives (Ashbery, Merrill), *Hello, La Jolla* and *Yellow Lola* represent a poetics of pruning or exclusion. The epigram is an art of calculated omission; J. V. Cunningham called one book *The Exclusions of a Rhyme*. Having got *Slinger* out of his system, Dorn particularly excludes from his recent work the need of much contemporary verse constantly to assert its own inventiveness: "Pure invention is just another idea" (*YL* 36). Block quotations form whole poems; a quick glance down *Hello, La Jolla*'s title page reveals "The Russian / Sanders / Broughton / Cobbett / Baron Macaulay / Burr / Quote" (*HLJ* 48, 55, 58, 63, 68, 84). A poetry of systematic quotation, as distinct from occasional allusion, is more interested in conveying ideas than in sounding original; Pound's history Cantos provide the model for most twentieth-century poetry of this type. One serious stylistic joke that Dorn pulls is to bury a poem's significant content in a footnote—the place we look, in an academic text, for sources or further information, the repository of inherited rather than invented wisdom. In other words, he opts for content over style, as "The Cobbett Quote" shows:

> *The learning is in the mind*
> *not in the* tongue: *learning*
> *consists of* ideas *and not of*
> *the* noise *that is made by*
> *the mouth.*
>
> (*HLJ* 63)

The stress that Dorn puts on content is a useful and necessary one in an age where much poetry is highly self-referential, concerned only with its own processes. Dorn assumes that poetry should refer to something beyond itself—specifically, to the conditions of the culture that produces it. He criticizes current poetry's "incapacitating ratio of subject to object" (*V* 119) and values journalism because it "precludes brooding over material" (*I* 104). Indeed *Hello, La Jolla* and *Yellow Lola* can usefully be discussed as an alternative form of journalism. Dorn calls the poems "dispatches" (*HLJ* vii). The literal news may be "mostly Hemoglobin" (*YL* 56), and it may be "generally pointless / to peddle the news in a poem" (*YL* 57). In fact, Dorn says, poetry should suffer "the least possible interference from information" (*HLJ* 24). But news need not consist merely of reportage. It can include commentary, the generalizations distilled from related facts. This raises the possibility "that the poem itself might or might not be news" (*YL* 57)—as it is in Ed Sanders's "The Party," to which Dorn alludes in *Yellow Lola* (*YL* 120).[23] In "Beware the Plural of Usual" (*HLJ* 24), which contrasts poetry and journalism, Dorn asserts that "the superiority of the poem's report / always consisted in the power / to see through the veil" of informational detail, where journalism stops, to what the information means.

Even though it precludes brooding, institutionalized journalism is not to be trusted: "I can't figure out why *anybody'd* / be surprised that Journalists / serve the see aye A" (*YL* 122). And neither is institutionalized poetry, "government product." Government claims to give people what they want; poetry as a government product self-referentially depicts its audience's definition of poetry—the blandest kind of social contract that art can undertake. A poetry that discusses its own process but is

---

23. Ed Sanders, et al., *The Party: A Chronological Perspective on a Confrontation at a Buddhist Seminary* (Woodstock, N.Y.: Poetry, Crime & Culture Press, 1977) is privately distributed; I do not know whether it is commercially distributed (it is not listed in *Books in Print*). Dorn owns a copy of the text, however. For more on the relationship between journalism and poetry, see Ed Sanders, *Investigative Poetry* (San Francisco: City Lights, 1976).

otherwise "essentially light" "is Brilliant & worthless" (*HLJ* 52). In looking at nothing but itself, this poetry becomes its own veil; Dorn would suggest, I think, that such work betrays poetry's "power / to see through the veil." We need not self-reflexiveness but self-evaluation, an "aesthetic to bring us back into a social world of intention" (*V* 36). *Hello, La Jolla* and *Yellow Lola* provide that aesthetic. Dorn sees piercingly, unrelentingly, and to our discomfort he names names: he has seen the enemy, and the enemy is us.

# Contributors

DONALD WESLING is Professor of English at the University of California, San Diego. His articles on English and American literature have appeared in *English Literary History*, *University of Toronto Quarterly*, *Mosaic*, *Prose Studies 1800–1900*, *boundary 2*, and elsewhere. He has published the following books: *Wordsworth and the Adequacy of Landscape* (London: Routledge, 1970); *The Chances of Rhyme: Device and Modernity* (Berkeley: University of California Press, 1980); coeditor of *John Muir, To Yosemite and Beyond: Writings from the Yosemite Years, 1863–1875* (Madison: University of Wisconsin Press, 1980). Previous work on Edward Dorn's poetry: "A Bibliography on Edward Dorn for America," *Parnassus* 5 (Spring-Summer 1977): 142–60.

ROBERT VON HALLBERG is Associate Professor of English and Humanities at the University of Chicago. He is the author of essays on contemporary poetry in *Contemporary Literature*, *boundary 2*, *English Literary History*, *Modern Philology*, and *Chicago Review*. He received an NEH fellowship for 1980–81 to write a book on American poetry and politics of the 1930s. Previous work on Edward Dorn's poetry, with much else of related interest, appears in his book *Charles Olson: The Scholar's Art* (Cambridge, Mass.: Harvard University Press, 1978).

PAUL DRESMAN is currently Visiting Lecturer at the University of California, San Diego. He has published short stories, poetry, and translations in numerous small magazines and in three chapbooks. He has edited an anthology of eight San Diego poets, *Ocean Hiway* (San Diego, Ca.: Wild Mustard Press, 1982). Previous work on Edward Dorn's poetry: *Between Here and Formerly: History in the Poetry of Edward Dorn* (doctoral dissertation, University of California, San Diego, 1980).

MICHAEL DAVIDSON is the Director of the Archive for New Poetry at the University of California, San Diego, where he is also Associate Professor of American Literature in the Literature Department. He has published four books of poetry and numerous articles on contemporary poetics. He is currently completing a critical study of the San Francisco Renaissance. Previous work on Edward Dorn's poetry: "Archaeologist of Morning: Charles Olson, Edward Dorn and Historical Method," *English Literary History* 47 (Fall 1980): 158–79.

WILLIAM J. LOCKWOOD is Associate Professor of English at the University of Michigan, Flint, and directs the poetry series there. He has published articles on Richard Hugo and Robert Bly in books of essays devoted to Western writers. An NEH research fellow for 1979–80, he is currently at work on a book titled *A Landscape of Contemporary New World Poets*. Previous work on Edward Dorn's poetry: "Ed Dorn's Mystique of the Real: His Poems for North America," *Contemporary Literature* 30 (Winter 1978): 56–79.

ALAN GOLDING is a Visiting Lecturer in the University of California, Los Angeles, Writing Program. His dissertation is titled *'Go Contrary, Go Sing': The Early Poetry and Poetics of Charles*

*Olson* (University of Chicago, 1980). His study of "Charles Olson's Metrical Thicket: Toward a Theory of Free-Verse Prosody" appeared in *Language and Style* 14 (Winter 1981): 64–78. He has also published articles on Poe, Olson, and Vincent Ferrini, and short reviews on contemporary poetry.

# Index of Works by Edward Dorn

# General Index

Abstractness, in Dorn's writing, 19–20, 79–80, 215–16
Airbag, Dorn's opinion on, 21–22
America, Dorn on the nature of, 15–16, 30, 83–86, 87–89, 101–2, 103, 112, 134, 149, 155, 205, 216–17, 228–29. *See also* Capitalism; Indian, the American
Attention, Dorn's poetics of, 22–25
Augustan sensibility, Dorn's, 15, 16, 19–20, 117, 215, 220. *See also* Byron, George Gordon (Lord)

Black Mountain: as college and as literary group, 7, 23, 45–47, 64, 113
Bureau of Indian Affairs, 3
Bureau of Indian Ethnology, 109–10
Byron, George Gordon (Lord),

Dorn's affinities with, 19, 117, 221–22

Capitalism, critique of in Dorn's writings, 41–44, 53–54, 60–62, 68–69, 71, 110, 116, 121, 122–23, 126, 184, 228–29. *See also* Robber barons; Shortage industry
Carroll, Lewis, 77
Castaneda, Carlos, 22–23, 24n
Castro, Don Amerigo, 185, 204
Clark, Tom, 30n
Closure, idea of, 148
Cosmology, 87–88, 95, 107–8, 113, 129, 140–41, 199–201, 206. *See also* Relativity, ideas of; Space, problematics of; Time, problematics of
Creeley, Robert, 23, 45, 46n
Cummings, E. E., 221

Designer: Wilsted & Taylor
Compositor: Wilsted & Taylor
Text: 10/12 Mergenthaler Sabon
Display: Mergenthaler Sabon
Printer: Thomson-Shore, Inc.
Binder: John H. Dekker & Sons